Contemporary Religious Movements:
A Wiley-Interscience Series

Edited by Irving I. Zaretsky

Changing Perspectives in the Scientific Study of Religion
Edited by Allan W. Eister

Trance, Healing, and Hallucination: Three Field Studies in Religious Experience
by Felicitas Goodman, Jeannette H. Henney and Esther J. Pressell

Hebrew Christianity: The Thirteenth Tribe
by B. Z. Sobel

On the Margin of the Visible: Sociology, the Esoteric, and the Occult
Edited by Edward A. Tiryakian

Hare Krishna and the Counterculture
by J. Stillson Judah

A. C. Bhaktivedanta Swāmi Prabhupāda

HARE KRISHNA AND THE COUNTERCULTURE

J. STILLSON JUDAH

A WILEY-INTERSCIENCE PUBLICATION

JOHN WILEY & SONS New York · London · Sydney · Toronto

Dedicated to the devotees who have found fulfillment of life in Krishna and to their parents to help them understand

Library of Congress Cataloging in Publication Data

Judah, J Stillson.
Hare Krishna and the counterculture.

(Contemporary religious movements)
"A Wiley-Interscience publication."
Bibliography: p.
1. Krishna (Cult)—United States. 2. Vaishnavism.
3. Youth—Religious Life. I. Title.

BL1220.J8 1974 294.5′5 74-8209
ISBN 0-471-45200-9

Printed in the United States of America

10 9 8 7 6 5 4 3 2 1

FOREWORD

J. Stillson Judah ends his study of the Hare Krishna Movement with a question: "The phoenix is born, but where will it fly?"

Although its roots are in fifteenth century Indian thought, the Movement as such is as recent as 1966, and like other religious groups of the past decade it has been sustained by the social and cultural patterns of an America in turbulence. Now, with the mood of the country shifting, with different emotional, psychological, and social attitudes developing, can it survive?

Judah thinks it might. Because of its substance and organization, the International Society for Krishna Consciousness may assume a permanent and stable place in our society. He suggests that by combining selected elements of the so-called counterculture with the ideals and goals of their natal religions—and then validating and internalizing these elements through the mechanism of their newfound religion—the devotees of Hare Krishna have created a subculture. Through the routinized experience of religious enthusiasm and discipline shared with like-mined individuals, participants in the group have been able to find a satisfying alternative life style, an ascetic and pious one that in their belief will lead them to loving fellowship with Krishna, the Supreme Consciousness, and to victory over all that is transient and materialistic. Consequently, by permitting its members to retain what they themselves feel are the positive experiences, beliefs, and practices of their natal or dropout milieus, while avoiding the limitations, loss of meaning, alienation, and insecurity common to those milieus, the Hare Krishna Movement may have succeeded in sacralizing one solution to the social patterns of the 1960s.

The Hare Krishna Movement has thus used religious life both to conserve some traditional cultural values inherent in the Judeo-Christian tradition and to become an instrument for social change through personal transformation. Through this combination, the Movement gains vitality and a hybrid vigor. And it is precisely this combination of elements that provides for devotees a bridge between their natal environments and their countercultural life choices. Participants in the Movement perceive of it as offering a strict moral code for personal and interpersonal behavior, similar to the message offered by many of the fundamentalist Christian groups currently proselytizing. It encourages the individual to transcend materialism and to search for lasting and real values.

The Movement suggests that one way of reaching this transcendence is through discipline, chanting, piety, and the shedding of ego and pride gratification. In pursuit of transcendence it discourages all use of pharmacological stimulants, and values altered states of consciousness only when reached through religious discipline and ritual. It offers community through its temple life and communion through shared rituals to individuals who previously felt anomie and disaffiliation from social collectivities. It encourages individuals to live in the now, to be concerned about appropriate conduct and thus exercise choice and the human prerogative of changing the consequences of one's past actions, karma, in the cycle of reincarnation. It allows for a concern with physical health and the environment through its dietary practices and belief system of man's place in nature.

Devotees attribute any generation gap that exists between them and their previous communities to their attempts to live the true values of their natal religions. In this sense, the ideals of their personal history and previous communities serve as a template and cement for present behavior.

The material for this study was collected by Judah through extensive field work in California and India and through library research into the documentary underpinnings for the belief system of the Movement. Although much research was conducted in the defunct Berkeley temple, the data accurately reflect what is happening in Hare Krishna temples around the country. This is partly because most of the members of the Berkeley temple spent time in other temples.

The study describes the philosophy and belief system of the Hare Krishna Movement and outlines its literary and philosophical antecedents in India; it describes the institutionalization process of the Movement in the United States relative to its branches in India and elsewhere; it outlines the daily life of the temple commune; and it explores the experiences of a number of countercultural youths who have been attracted to the Movement.

In the past several years, the Hare Krishna Movement has adapted from an age-stratified group appealing primarily to those under 30 to a generational group accommodating persons of all ages, individuals as well as families, full-time participants in temple life as well as those living outside the temple and participating in some of its rituals at certain times of the week. By offering schooling for young children, now it can accommodate more successfully the needs of families, whose children receive a multicultural religious and secular education. It has thus adapted from a total institution based on communal living to one more able to service members who cannot totally accept the daily discipline, dietary habits, living conditions, sartorial habits, and ascetism of communal life.

But even though believers may now live outside the temple, the Movement continues to lose some members. Some have simply become disillusioned with the Movement. Other reasons for dropping out may include an inability to share personal property in a communal context and to make a long-range commitment to the discipline. Some may have tried to usurp power and create doctrinal schisms; others, who entered the Movement as couples, may have been unable to tolerate the competing and primary role that religious life has assumed for their companion. Finally, there have been those who left the group to return to a more pious observance of their natal religion, with the explanation that Hare Krishna was for them a path back to their roots.

The Hare Krishna Movement, the Meher Baba Movement, the Guru Maharaj Ji's Divine Light Mission, and the Nichiren Shoshu of America, to name only a few of the groups originating in India, Japan, Korea, the Philippines, and elsewhere in Asia and Southeast Asia, are often thought of as basically identical religious groups. While many of these groups do share common features, they differ in the belief systems, practices, and functional alternatives they offer their members. Conversion to the Hare Krishna Movement as opposed to other movements is largely a question of the availability of the movement to an individual during a period of spiritual quest. This is one reason why some of the movements have taken to the street to proselytize and attempt to reach individuals in their workaday environments. Many become attracted to a group through contact with such proselytizers or through a network of personal friends familiar with a movement. Thus initial contact with a group frequently depends on little more than circumstance.

Of interest is the observation that while the metaphysical movements in the United States share to a great extent a population of "seekers"—individuals who during a given week may attend a Spiritualist church, a Theosophical Society meeting, a Science of Mind service, a Christian Science testimonial meeting, or who read Unity literature—there is relatively little sharing of membership among such groups as Hare Krishna, Meher Baba, and the Divine Light Mission. Although individuals transfer a great deal within various branches of any one group, the evidence does not suggest that there is seriatim affiliation with the different groups, or extensive intergroup migration.

Believers tend to identify their group as unique. Rennie Davis, a recent follower of Guru Maharaj Ji, said that the Divine Light Mission is "the most revolutionary movement that's ever come down the pike; it's a fundamental threat to every institution rooted in ego and pride" (*The New York Times Magazine,* December 9, 1973, p. 72). And yet the members' chosen criteria for the uniqueness of any one group may be equally well applied to features of other groups. The pattern however does seem to be that, after disaffiliation from a group, the former member pursues on his own, without similar institutional ties, those ideas he found appealing.

Although many of these groups may be in direct competition with each other for a basically limited population pool, the niche of religious enthusiasm is still sufficiently fertile in contemporary society to allow all of them to coexist. In the long run what will determine their longevity will be the securing of an economic base by becoming self-supporting, as the Hare Krishna Movement has set out to do by manufacturing and selling a variety of products; the retention of a hierarchical structure with loyalty to a central figure whose legitimate authority is vested in the succession of disciples; and the avoidance of schisms through a control of the rate and criteria for advancing individuals through the different stages of spiritual progression.

Achieving altered states of consciousness through religious rituals, communal living, and the implementation of Hindu-based philosophies—all go in and out of vogue in our society and are sought after in an almost calendrical and predictable cycle of personal and social disorientations. The prognosis for the Hare Krishna Movement in this country seems good because it may become a caretaker institution for such religious and secular practices.

The Series *Contemporary Religious Movements* was designed and worked on during several research periods when I was supported by grants from the following Foundations: Mabelle McLeod Lewis Memorial Fund, Smithsonian Institution post-Doctoral Fellowship Program, Wenner-Gren Foundation for Anthropological Research, The Lucius N. Littauer Foundation, National Endowment for the Humanities and the Russell Sage Program in Law and Social Science, Yale Law School. I gratefully acknowledge the support and encouragement I received from these Foundations.

IRVING I. ZARETSKY
Series Editor

New Haven, Connecticut
June 1974

TRANSCRIPTIONS AND ACKNOWLEDGMENTS

In transcribing words in both Sanskrit and vernacular languages, I have tried to give value to most of the different letters. I have often used the vernacular equivalents, when their usage seemed more popular among the devotees. I have made exception of the spellings of "Krishna," "Swāmi," "Goswāmi," "Brahmin," and *avatār,* which have received some anglicization. I have, however, followed whatever spellings were used in personal names, quotations, and in the titles of books. I have also made an exception in the text of the spelling of the *Caitanya Caritāmrita,* although the edition used for quotations has been anglicized. In capitalization I have distinguished between Yoga as the dualistic philosophy and the practice of *yoga* in various philosophies. A similar distinction has been made when the same word is used as a common noun and when the word represents a personification, as in the case of *māyā,* illusion, and Māyā, the female progenitor and personified power of Krishna. I have often used the word "*guru*" or spiritual master or teacher synonymously with the more specific titles Swāmi and Goswāmi, which represent specific statuses within an order.

I want to thank the many devotees of Krishna who have given so much of their time to help me understand better the meaning of Krishna Consciousness and their own personal transformations. I especially thank Jayananda dāsa Adhikāri and his wife; Lochan dāsa Adhikāri, Karandhar dāsa Adhikāri; Mani bandha dāsa Adhikāri; Garga Muni dāsa, Yaśodānandana dāsa Adhikāri, and his wife, Latikā; the spiritual master of ISKCON, A. C. Bhaktivedanta Swāmi Prabhupāda, for interviews granted to me, for which I am grateful. Tridandiswāmi Bhakti Prajnan Yati Mahārāj, Secretary of the Shree Gauḍīya Math, Madras, kindly supplied written material on the Gauḍīya Vaishṇavas and answered important questions during an interview in Madras. Swāmi B. H. Bon Mahārāj supplied important written and oral materials concerning the Gauḍīya philosophy and history. Mr. Gar Kellom, a student at the Graduate Theological Union, assisted me greatly in taping interviews that added much data for this work. Dr. Gregory Johnson made available interviews and materials collected by him concerning the movement in the 1960s in the Haight-Ashbury district as part of his Ph.D. dissertation. Professor Charles Y. Glock of the University of California, and Professors A. Durwood Foster and Charles McCoy of the Pacific School of Religion and the Graduate Theological Union; Irving I. Zaretsky, the editor of this series and presently a Russell Sage Fellow in Law and Social Science at Yale Law School; and Eric Valentine of John Wiley & Sons and Christine Valentine, manuscript editor, are thanked for their time spent in reading the manuscript and making helpful editorial suggestions. I am grateful to my secretary, Mrs. Dorothy Burns, for the important task of producing many drafts of the manuscript, and for helping in so many ways. Finally, I give thanks to my wife for her enduring patience with me during this time. For the contents, however, I must take full responsibility.

J. STILLSON JUDAH
Director of Libraries
and Professor of the History of Religions
Graduate Theological Union

Berkeley, California
December 1973

CONTENTS

Tables and Figures **xvii**

1 Introduction **1**

Method and Problems of Research, 2 Purpose of this Work, 10 Limiting Factors of the Hare Krishna Movement in America, 13 Hindu Philosophy in American Religious Thought, 14 Mission to the Counterculture, 16

2 Historical and Literary Antecedents **18**

Important Texts and Sects in the Development of Vaishṇavism, 19 Sources of Vaishṇavism to A.D. 1100, 26 Vaishṇavism from the Eleventh to the Fifteenth Century A.D., 31 Social and Religious Conditions in Bengal Before Chaitanya's Time, 33 Life of Chaitanya, 33 The Development of the Chaitanya Movement, 37 Later History of Chaitanya's Vaishṇavism, 39 The Gauḍīya Vaishṇavas, 40 The Beginning of the International Society for Krishna Consciousness, 40 The Hare Krishna Movement in India, 43

3 Krishna, the Cosmic and Personal Deity **46**

Vaishṇavism Versus Brahmin Orthodoxy, 46 Chaitanya's Theology in Outline, 47 Chaitanya's View as Mediating Synthesis of Hindu Philosophy, 51 Krishna, the Cosmic Deity and Ocean of Bliss, 51 Krishna's Expansions,

52 Krishna's *Avatārs,* 53 Krishna as Creator, 54 Future Life and Spiritual Worlds, 57 Krishna, the Cowherd Deity of Vṛindāvan, 60

4 Man and His Relation to Krishna **69**

Man's Nature, 69 Man's Fall and His Salvation, 71 Ethical System, 73

5 The Way to Krishna **79**

An Alternative Life Style in Communal Living, 80 Stability of the Hare Krishna Life Style, 80 Limitations in Membership, 83 The Alternative Hindu Culture of the Society, 84 *Bhakti-yoga,* 87 The Daily Schedule of Discipline, 92 The *Ārātrika* Ceremony (*Ārati*), 93 Hare Krishna Festivals, 96 The Organization of ISKCON, 97

6 Hare Krishna and the Counterculture **98**

The Changing Scene, 98 Classes of Hippiedom, 99 Interpretations of the Counterculture, 102 Two Stages of a Counterculture, 108 The Hare Krishna Devotee as Part of the Counterculture, 110 Age and Social Status, 111

7 Countercultural "Protestants" **112**

Protest Against a Surfeit of Possessions, 112 Protest Against the Vietnam War, 115 Protest Against All War, 116 Protest Against the United States Form of Government, 117 Protest Against the Established Methods of Education, 119 Protest Against the Established Codes of Sexual Morality, 124 Protest Against Authority, 125 Protest Through Drugs, 127

8 **The Protest Against American Forms of Religion** 138

Decline of Liberal Christianity in the 1960s, 138 Factors in the Decline of American Liberal Churches, 144 Organized Religion and the Counterculture, 147 Krishna Consciousness and Former Faiths, 149 The Meaning of Conversion to Krishna Consciousness, 154

9 **From the Counterculture to Conversion to Krishna** 159

Tension, 159 Type of Problem-Solving Perspective, 160 Seekership, 160 The Turning Point, 162 The Situational Factor, 163 Crisis in Personal Distress, 163 Instrumental Factors, 165 Finding Religious Experience and Community, 165 Finding a Viable Authority, 170 Reading the Literature about Krishna, 172 Finding a Personal God to Love, 173 Finding a Sacralized Countercultural Life Style, 174 Cult Affective Bonds, 178 Extra-Cult Affective Bonds, 178 Intensive Interaction, 180

10 **Birth of the Phoenix** 182

The Future of the Hare Krishna Movement, 182 Psychological Elements for Stability, 184 The Counterculture as a Cultural Climax, 186 The End of an Age? 187

References 199

Select Bibliography for Further Study of Vaishṇavism 207

Glossary of Important Names and Terms 215

Appendix: Kṛṣṇa, the Reservoir of Pleasure 265

Index 285

TABLES AND FIGURES

Table 1 Classes of Literature and Specific Parts on Which the Hare Krishna Movement Depends 21–23

Table 2 Showing Educational Dropout Point of Hare Krishna Devotees 120

Table 3 Average Grade Levels of Hare Krishna Devotees at the Time They Dropped Out of School 120

Table 4 Correlation between Spiritual Discipline Practice and the Use of Drugs 130

Table 5 The Religious Affiliation of Parents of Hare Krishna Devotees 147

Table 6 Ages at Which Hare Krishna Devotees Abandoned Their Parents' Religion 148

Table 7 Reasons Why Hare Krishna Devotees Abandoned Their Former Faith 151

Table 8 Reasons Why Devotees Were Attracted to the Hare Krishna Movement 153

Table 9 Circumstances of Devotee's First Encounter with Krishna Consciousness 162

Figure 1 Genealogy of the Deities as Expansions of Krishna 48

Figure 2 Lutherans in America 140

Figure 3 Episcopalians in America 141

Figure 4 Membership of the United Methodist Church Compared with the Southern Baptist Convention from 1960 to 1970 142

Figure 5 Membership Comparison of Six Churches from 1958 to 1970 143

Figure 6 Proportionate Membership Increase in Baptist Churches from 1940 to 1970 144

Figure 7 Growth in Number of Centers of ISKCON as Reported in *Back to Godhead* from August 1969 to February 1974 183

CHAPTER ONE

INTRODUCTION

This is the story of the Hare Krishna Movement, more formally known as the International Society for Krishna Consciousness, and of its American devotees. Its founder, A. C. Bhaktivedanta Swāmi Prabhupāda, brought its philosophy and religious practice to the United States from India in 1965. In India, this philosophy and religious practice represent a tradition dating from the time of Śrī Krishna Chaitanya, who lived during the latter part of the fifteenth and the early part of the sixteenth centuries A.D. His thought is notably represented there today by Vaishṇavas of the Gauḍīya Maths, who worship the deity, Vishṇu, in the form of Krishna as the highest personality of Godhead.

The material for this work was gathered through literary investigation of the Hare Krishna Movement and the counterculture, and also through questionnaires, extensive interviews, and personal participation. Questionnaires were completed by devotees at the former Berkeley temple and from the Los Angeles center. Undocumented materials appearing in this book are the tabulated results and conclusions derived from the sixty-three questionnaires and from interviews. I regard the data received from these sources as quite representative of the Hare Krishna Movement in the United States for the following reasons:

1. There was little variance in the answers to the same questions in the two temples.

2. The devotees interviewed had come originally from all over the United States and Canada. Only a little more than one-third had lived in California most of their lives.

3. The population of devotees at both temples showed considerable

flux. Of approximately 94 percent answering the question concerning other Hare Krishna temples in which they had lived, only 8.5 percent had not resided in any other temple than their present one; 52 percent had lived in one to two others; the remaining had lived in three to ten other temples.* One who had been a devotee for only three months had already lived in a total of six centers; another, in ten. This mobility is all the more remarkable when one realizes that 88 percent of respondents had been devotees for no more than two years.

I have approached this subject as an analyst rather than as a critic, a fact that owes much to my encounter with the Society. After first watching the devotees chanting and dancing on the streets of Berkeley, it was suggested by a colleague that I should treat the Movement in a paper I had been invited to present the following year. My interest mounted steadily as I became involved and the data increased. I participated in their devotions each week for more than two years, until the Berkeley temple was discontinued because the landlord sold the building they rented. During that period I interviewed many of the devotees in Berkeley and San Francisco. My assistant, Mr. Gar Kellom, spent many more hours taping interviews up and down the Pacific coast.

Method and Problems of Research. Four methods of research were used to obtain the necessary material for this book: the use of printed works, questionnaires, interviews, and personal participation. Each had its value and each its limitations.

Written materials disclosed the principles of the basic philosophy of Chaitanya, but they omitted the personal element of the people involved. I soon became curious to learn more about the devotees themselves and about the transformation that worship of Krishna had made in their lives. This involved studying their participation in the counterculture.

Questionnaires had their value for discovering basic background information concerning the devotees and common patterns of ideas and attitudes. I tried to learn everything about the devotees—their ages,

* This freedom of mobility is now being discouraged. Devotees are generally asked to stay in the temple to which they first attached themselves.

their education, even the vocations and financial status of their fathers. Latikā, one of the devotees and a former graduate student in sociology, aided in selecting the most pertinent questions, allowing multiple gradations of answers. Among other things, the statistics revealed the various levels of attitudes toward popular countercultural subjects, such as sex, money, authority, and the Vietnam war, and the devotees' extent of former involvement with various kinds of drugs. The questionnaires enabled us, then, to obtain a statistical profile of the average devotee. But close examination of other answers in the respective questionnaires also enabled us to discover possible reasons for unexpected variants in particular cases.

Although this method was important, it too had its shortcomings. The questionnaires pointed to trends and common denominators that had to be further investigated by interviews. Even the most carefully worded questionnaires may have ambiguities. In fact, the very specific question, whether in a questionnaire or an interview, can sometimes be unreliable. The desire to cooperate may lead the person interviewed to offer information he believes is wanted, rather than accurate information. For this reason the broad discussion question is valuable. In responding to such a question, the informant often discloses data on related subjects more reliably through free association.

In the beginning of the research, the single-mindedness of the devotees made the task of collecting the information difficult. They wanted to talk about Krishna rather than about themselves. Analysis for the sake of learning more about themselves was not wanted; their only reason for associating with outsiders has always been to spread Krishna Consciousness. Not even their parents have been an exception. So it did not take me long to realize that the main function of their splendid cooperation with me was twofold: first, to teach me more about Krishna, enabling me to become Krishna Conscious; second, to spread the knowledge of Krishna through the publication of my manuscript.

For data about themselves and their way to Krishna Consciousness every devotee was a suitable authority. For the factual information about the Movement or concerning some highly technical point, I was always referred to an expert. Two salient characteristics of the Movement are that I have rarely discovered a disagreement among devotees over any one fact or philosophical point, nor have I ever discovered anyone giving his own interpretation. The spiritual master is ultimately the only authority, ensuring a unity of meaning. The *sannyāsis,* those who have taken the highest initiation, journey from temple to temple in order to check on the maintenance of discipline and the correctness of belief.

Probably of equal importance in obtaining information was my participation in their *saṅkīrtans* (public chanting) at the Berkeley temple. This participation accomplished several things. First, I felt the contagious strength of their dancing and chanting to the rhythm of their *mantras.* I recalled what Thomas Merton had written about them: "Once we live in awareness of the cosmic dance and more in time with the Dancer, our life attains its true dimension. It is at once more serious and less serious than the life of one who does not sense this inner cosmic dynamism" (Bhaktivedanta, 1968b:19).

Second, I discovered the importance of this shared routinized experience that filled the devotees with feelings of transcendence—a reality beyond the physical. I began to realize how the discipline and experience of following their complete and severe regulations could validate for them the alternative life style they had been seeking. It gave them meaning when there had been no meaning.

Third, I was able to experience a feeling of community, that fellowship with others who were striving for similar goals. I soon profited greatly by being treated almost like one of the devotees, and thereby attained a good measure of trust and confidence from them. Because of such a relationship, they became candid and open with my associate and me. Thus we were probably able to converse with them on a more intimate level than might have been otherwise possible. No question was taboo. They willingly shared with us any information required. The relationship worked both ways.

Because of this close association with the devotees, I offered whatever help and advice I could give when these were sought. It is my hope that this book itself will repay our common effort together, and that it will enable others not only to become better acquainted with the philosophy and history of the Movement, but also to better understand the devotees themselves within the context of their transformation in cultural change.

Since I have not personally gathered similar data from other countercultural groups as a control, I have made use of models and research of various investigators in order to study the transformations in the devotees of Krishna.

Fourth, my participation helped me to understand more fully what Krishna Consciousness meant to the devotees. But this statement must be carefully qualified. That which involves the Movement's goal and way of achieving it is most simply defined as "the revival of the original consciousness, of the living being—the conscious awareness that one is eternally related to God or Krishna" (*The Krishna Consciousness Handbook,* 1971:3). Swāmi Bhaktivedanta had said that if I was to understand and write about the Hare Krishna Movement I should participate in the *saṅkīrtans* at the temple. To chant the "holy names of Krishna" and follow the four regulations are considered the minimum requirements for understanding. And yet for me, understanding seemed to demand more than that. I came to believe that it was impossible to have the same experience as the Hare Krishna devotee without responding to similar needs. Since most devotees belonged to an average age group that differed greatly from mine, we reacted dissimilarly to the same environmental conditions. We were bound to see the same thing from two differing points of view. Such factors as these often produce a generation gap between parents and their children.

Various investigators have shown that adolescence is universally a period of special stress, doubt, and alienation, and therefore not a unique characteristic of our present youth. Adolescent questioning of authority occurs when some newly discovered facts do not harmonize with beliefs formerly accepted and revered. This period may extend into the twenties, but rarely extends into the thirties (Pratt, 1920:115–116).

Furthermore, although the experience of conversion may occur at any age, it is the most common religious phenomenon of youth. A distinction exists between sudden conversion experiences and various religious ecstasies that may occur under the right conditions during one's later life. If the religious ecstasies of Krishna Consciousness occur to the young Hare Krishna devotee through strict discipline, as he believes, age still appears to be a factor in maintaining the discipline of the Movement in the United States.

Given the dissimilar needs of youth, I wondered whether I could have followed completely their severe discipline with any facility. Changing from a Western to Eastern way of living would in itself have created difficulties. What evidence exists indicates that older devotees experience a hindering generation gap. For example, a devotee in his forties who had shown various countercultural tendencies was asked what particular thing he should do to increase his Krishna Consciousness. He indicated that he did not do the required amount of chanting. He also continued to smoke tobacco. He said: "I find that I should do more *japa* (private chanting of the Hare Krishna *mantra*). The more I do, the more strength I feel, the more vigor I have and the more I understand things." He observed that few in his age bracket accepted Krishna Consciousness. He talked of his life prior to conversion, and of the transformation conversion had made in his life:

> Krishna Consciousness changed my life a thousand percent. I would say that if I didn't come to Krishna Consciousness six months ago, I probably would have been doomed to despair and probably would have taken my own life . . . I haven't taken a drink in six months. Sex was the biggest thing in my life . . . Now I've abstained from sex completely for six months, replaced both alcohol and sex craving with love for Krishna.

If it was evident that Krishna Consciousness had transformed his life, it still was not completely fulfilling. His age in contrast to the more youthful devotees had been an impediment. With evident alienation, he said:

> I still feel so fallen and miserable at times I think I don't belong here, that I'll never make it, that I should pack up and leave the temple here, not Krishna Consciousness. Somehow being older people we do not fit too well. The same is proven with other older people that came here.

Most of his older friends in the Movement were weekenders unable to follow the complete discipline. He suggested that there should be a division for older people, but then cautioned: "Don't get me wrong. It's not that we aren't accepted with the same love and respect offered any other devotees. . . . It's just that there is almost twice the difference in age."

This desire for a separate section would not lead to a schism in the Society, so long as the spiritual master were living. One of the cardinal principles for obtaining Krishna Consciousness is that the devotee cannot progress by himself. He must be accepted and initiated by the spiritual master, who is regarded as the *only* authorized guide in a long line of *gurus* descending from Chaitanya. In exchange for acceptance, the devotee must put himself totally under the guidance of the spiritual master. Even though there is compelling authority that holds the group together, differences in age seem at times to hinder the close fellowship, the feeling of belonging and support which aids the experience of Krishna Consciousness, as we shall see later.

Despite the disparity in our ages, I never felt rejected by the young devotees. But there were other differences as well—those that could be traced to our dissimilar backgrounds. Most of the devotees had some prior knowledge of Indian philosophy, usually obtained through their search for meaning through meditation or chanting. Although I had followed a course not entirely different from theirs many years earlier (Judah, 1967:8–9), I later involved myself in critical studies of Sanskrit and Indian philosophy. While I was frank with them about my academic training and position at the Graduate Theological Union, I never tried to impose my knowledge upon the devotees. To have done so would not only have risked an immediate argument, but would probably have caused their alienation from me. Therefore, I have always tried to accept their teaching through their eyes of faith, with the realization that it supports their devotional life and their subjective meaning of Krishna Consciousness. On their part, even though none knew Sanskrit except for memorized passages of texts and individual words interpreted by their spiritual master, none ever asked me for any information concerning Sanskrit or Krishna Consciousness. On the contrary, they always took the role of teacher, for which I was grateful. Their absolute certainty of the truth precluded any questions that I could answer.

Nevertheless, it must be recognized that my dissimilar background is a factor in my interpretation, which is admittedly only one of many possible. I hope for the devotees' charity and understanding, but expect that some will have viewpoints differing from mine.

All in all, my participation in the temple services had positive results. It helped my understanding in many ways. For example, I was able to learn in a way otherwise impossible the meaning of their literal acceptance of the "pastimes of Krishna," if not the events themselves. These pastimes are the miraculous events in the life of the deity when he had descended and lived for a time on earth. Although most scholars consider as mythological these descriptions of Krishna's life found in the sacred scriptures, the devotees of Krishna insist on their literal acceptance (see Chapter 9).

The systematic study and explanation of Krishna's "pastimes" alternate a couple of times daily with the devotees' dancing and chanting in the *saṅkīrtans.* As part of Krishna's worship, these "pastimes" become a medium for religious experience. When the devotees read about the events in their classes, or when they act out one of them as part of their worship, as sometimes occurs, they are repeating the events described in the life of Krishna. If we interpret this liturgical action according to Mircea Eliade, these are events occurring in "sacred time," which he defines as "primordial mythical time made present." This is a transcendent liturgical time that is inaccessible to a nonreligious man. Eliade views participation in such events during a religious service as their reactivation, and as one's mystical participation in being (Eliade, 1959:69, 71, 81, 106).

When a devotee enjoins one: "Chant 'Hare Krishna' and experience Goloka-Vṛindāvan!" he issues an invitation to participate in events that occurred in a primordial time in Vṛindāvan, in India, a village traditionally associated with events in Krishna's life. These same happenings, moreover, occur in Vṛindāvan or Goloka, its spiritual counterpart and Krishna's highest heaven. The latter is also sometimes applied to the temple or sacred space when chanting of Krishna's names occurs. These events then must be understood in reality as transcendental and occurring in eternal time. As such they represent an hierophany or an appearance of the sacred. Their true and full understanding comes only as the result of mystical experience attained by the devotee through the eyes of faith.

If to the outsider the "pastimes of Krishna" appear miraculous and illogical, the following question must be asked. Does not the awareness of a higher reality, which all religions declare to be a divine mystery, come most often through participation in the irrational, the paradox—and for the disbeliever, the absurd? For many Buddhists it may emerge through meditating on the paradoxes of the *Prajñāpāramitā* or the nonsensical *ko-ans;* for the Pentecostals it speaks through the incoherent babble of glossolalia; for the Roman Catholics, it involves the mystery of the transubstantiation of the bread and wine into the body and blood of Christ during the Mass. For the Moslem, it may occur during the pilgrimage to Mecca when he trots between the hills of Safa and Marwah imitating Hagar's search for water.

If one contrasts the experiences of Krishna Consciousness recorded about Chaitanya with those observed among the present-day devotees, they differ greatly. I have never seen a devotee in a state of religious trance, nor expressing religious sorrow as reported about Chaitanya. Nevertheless, I do believe that some devotees attain a condition of ecstasy through participation in dancing and chanting before the deities. Although one of the most used chants requests that the deity become visible to them, I have never heard such a claim. In fact the devotees would look askance at anyone professing such advancement, because humility is the mark of great devotion to Krishna. To brag of one's attainments would indicate lack of devotion.

Because my approach to the subject has been sympathetic, I treat the Movement objectively from the standpoint of the devotees' beliefs and their life situations without making a critical study of the beliefs themselves. In deference to the devotees I have included little critical discussion of such subjects as the Krishna traditions or beliefs, which they would consider inaccurate as well as objectionable. Instead, I cite and annotate such studies in the bibliography. Those who wish to consult them will find there the works of such men as Ramakrishna Bhandarkar, Sushil Kumar De, Bimanbehari Majumdar, and Hemachandra Raychaudhuri.

It is perhaps sufficient to note here that Swāmi Bhaktivedanta considers that the descent of Krishna and the recorded events of his life occurred 5000 years ago. Although they give varying dates for the composition of the *Bhāgavata Purāṇa,* the principal source of Krishna's biography according to the Gauḍīya Vaishṇavas, most scholars now ascribe its date to the Christian era—some as late as the tenth century. This gives rise to comparisons between the life of Jesus Christ and Krishna, inviting parallels between the stories of their nativities, for example.

Opinions also differ concerning the historicity of the events in Krishna's life. Many scholars at least feel that such a heroic person as Krishna perhaps lived, and was later deified and worshiped. I leave the final resolution of the critical and literary problems concerning Krishna to the reader. The answers are not the purpose of this work.

I have treated the Hare Krishna Movement as representing the philosophy and practices of the International Society for Krishna Consciousness without pejorative intent for two reasons. First, the present organization was founded by A. C. Bhaktivedanta Swāmi Prabhupāda. It is totally independent and operates separately from the parent organization, the Gauḍīya Maths in India. The latter were organized by Bhakti Siddhānta Sarasvatī Goswāmi, the spiritual master of Swāmi Bhaktivedanta. Second, the primary sources upon which the Movement relies were mostly written, translated, or interpreted by Swāmi Bhaktivedanta. Only two early primary sources representing works of his philosophical predecessors were available to link Bhaktivedanta's thought to theirs. One was Swāmi Bhakti Siddhānta's translation of the important fifth chapter of the *Shree Brahma-Saṁhitā with Commentary* by Jīva Goswāmi. The latter, Chaitanya's contemporary, was one of the most important formulators of his philosophy. The second was a translation of the *Śrī Śrī Caitanya Caritāmṛita* by Śrī Śrī Krishnadāsa Kavirāja Goswāmi. This work is regarded by the Gauḍīya Vaishṇavas and the Hare Krishna Movement as the most authentic seventeenth-century biography of Chaitanya. In addition, only portions of similar Sanskrit works or their English translations of the original interpreters have been available even in secondary sources. Important Bengali texts of the later centuries are likewise unavailable in translation. Nevertheless, I have compared Swāmi Bhaktivedanta's works with secondary sources of the Gauḍīya Vaishṇavas. I have also spoken with philosophers with whom I visited in India in the summer of 1973. As a result of these new sources of information I feel that Swāmi Bhaktivedanta essentially continues the philosophical tradition of his spiritual master and of Chaitanya in the tradition of the Gauḍīya Vaishṇavas. Slight adaptations in practices are noted later on. Included in the Appendix is *Kṛṣṇa, the Reservoir of Pleasure* by A. C. Bhaktivedanta Swāmi Prabhupāda, reprinted with the permission of the Bhaktivedanta Book Trust. It is a representative pamphlet of the spiritual master's philosophy which is sold by devotees on the streets.

Purpose of This Work. My experience and the data collected have led me to write this monograph not only to let the devotees tell their story, but also for three other reasons. First, I wanted to understand and to communicate something concerning Krishna Consciousness, and the discipline it requires. Although this is theoretically attainable in a moment's time, the goal seems generally to be reached through a long and strict discipline. This asceticism, the elements of which occupy the devotee's every waking moment, is described later in detail.

A second and perhaps the most important reason for this research was to reveal the devotees' search for meaning and the reason Krishna Consciousness is so important to them. Very early in the study I realized that conversion to Krishna represented not only a change in religious faith, but in culture and cultural values as well. Most of the devotees, who are young adults, had already departed from their parents' organized religions to become hippies. Hippiedom usually marked their intermediate phase before conversion to Krishna. This metamorphosis occurred in the counterculture's communal stage (see Chapter 6). In the lives of most devotees the transformation was in one sense radical. It represented a change from what some members of the adult establishment considered an immoral, disorganized hippiedom to an ascetic communal discipline. The latter engendered moral values acceptable in most cases to middle-class Americans, albeit not often followed to the same extent by them. It meant abandoning a hedonistic goal of sense gratification and the voluntaristic principle of doing one's own thing for a simple loving service to Krishna. In another sense it was the continuation of some of the devotees' accepted countercultural values now arranged in a more meaningful context. The extremities of the total transformation are important. I became interested in the dynamics. To understand the power of Krishna to change lives is to learn more about basic human needs and at least one way in which they can be resolved.

This study thus explores what happened to one segment of American youth in the 1960s during a period of cultural change. It investigates youth's protest against the establishment through the medium of faith. It tries to illumine the reasons for loss of meaning, the elements instrumental to its recovery, and the devotees' transformation from hippiedom. In Chapter 8 it considers why many young persons have left the traditional churches of their parents.

In addition to the statistical information, a large part of this book consists of the devotees' own stories. Some devotees may feel that I dwell unduly on analysis; my defense is that I hope to illuminate thereby how the teachings of Krishna Consciousness have been a vehicle for the protests of youth; how the chanting of the *mahāmantra* together with other devotees has given them meaning; how they have found a new world view and culture that meet their important needs. In fellowship with others who had followed similar countercultural paths, they now share the same experiences in a meaningful and alternative style of living. The Hare Krishna Movement has spoken to their condition of alienation from the established society and from themselves. It has helped unite their fragmented selves through a form of self-realization in a countercultural world created by their spiritual master.

Many studies of the counterculture have been written, but this is a specialized study. It applies only to those antiestablishment youths who have been attracted to the Hare Krishna Movement. Some of their protests may be identified with those that investigators of the counterculture have equated with elements of a different consciousness, the harbinger of a new culture.

In *The Greening of America,* Charles Reich has even speculated that the counterculture represents a third consciousness. Although this investigation adds no support to these particular categories of consciousness nor to the theories underlying them, it does reveal common elements (see Chapters 6 and 10). But while this research may concern the needs of all who comprised the amorphous and seemingly contradictory counterculture of the 1960s, it speaks chiefly for those who have found the fulfillment of those needs through Krishna. In a larger sense, however, Krishna becomes a symbol for one's regeneration of selfhood in an alternative way of life, which others have found among the Jesus People, or in Oriental religion other than the Hare Krishna Movement. If the counterculture has contained elements of a new consciousness that may survive to slowly change the dominant American culture, the Hare Krishna Movement in its own way represents part of that transformation.

A third purpose of this monograph was to outline the philosophy of the Hare Krishna Movement and then to point to relevant features of its beliefs that have coincided with countercultural views of its devotees. Mr. Kellom and I prefaced our tape-recorded interviews with a statement of purpose that informed respondents of our aims.

Limiting Factors of the Hare Krishna Movement in America. That the religion of Krishna will not be received by everyone is evident even to the Hare Krishna devotee. Many people are neither able to follow the discipline over a long period of time nor to live a communal life, although the latter is not a strict requirement. Married couples are requested to live outside the temples. One of the great strengths of the Hare Krishna Movement lies in its regulated living, which demands a certain type of common conformity. This very feature also limits the number of devotees. Few Americans over age thirty and living in the United States are apparently able to adapt to the rigorous discipline and to adopt the appearance of a Hindu Vaishṇava, which involves a shaved head, Indian clothing, and so forth.

Although it is theoretically possible for one to dedicate his work to Krishna and follow the minimum rules while living and working in the secular world, pressures toward strict conformity have made it difficult for some. It is especially difficult for older followers who have followed the principle of doing as they pleased in the counterculture.

As one who had not yet been initiated explained: "The devotees push . . . that one be 100 percent conformist. That's why I left society. I don't want to be a conformist." He was living and working in secular society outside the temple, and admitted that the ridicule he received from his "straight" neighbors when he shaved his head and began to wear Hindu clothing proved an even greater pressure to conform to Western styles. He soon began letting his hair grow back and returned to an American style of clothing.

He later touched upon another feature of regimental communal living, which may be a problem encountered by others. This was the loss of a feeling of individuality. Having once lived in the temple, he explained the merits and demerits of this style:

> Krishna Consciousness provides . . . a community they can feel part of. There they find a companionship and the faith they have needed . . . But I find too in our own case . . . everything is done on a communal basis, which negates any aspect of individuality. There seems to be no such thing within this community as individuality. My wife and I feel that there must be some personalism within it, just as there is personalism extended to Krishna. Krishna being the supreme personality, our personalities, though being just a mere speck

> of it, are still individual and they're not taken over and drowned by the greatness of the community as it is.

This tendency toward loss of individualism seems more likely among those living in the temple, because they follow the same discipline which compels them to read aloud and discuss together the same scriptures and dedicate every waking moment to the service of Krishna. Consequently it is soon noticeable to an outsider that they not only share the same ideas, but very often talk alike. Each tends to use the words and expressions of the spiritual master. This fact is less noticeable among those who are living outside the temple and thus have more contact with the secular world.

This similarity attests to the extreme reverence of the devotees for the words and expressions of their spiritual guide. It also compliments their humility. Melville T. Kennedy has noted that the word "Dās" (servant) used as the last name of so many Vaishṇavas helps to obliterate their individuality (Kennedy, 1925:54). As all are servants of Krishna, none is to regard himself as superior, but each is to follow the same path to Krishna that the spiritual master has clearly marked.

Hindu Philosophy in American Religious Thought. Generally speaking, the devotees of Krishna have been searching for meaning, a quest that has been undertaken by a growing number of other Americans who have not found satisfaction in the traditional organized churches and synagogues. The influx of numerous Hindu *gurus* and their ready acceptance by many Americans in recent years attests to their needs. Many Americans seem to feel that their traditional organized faiths cannot provide satisfactory answers to dilemmas posed by twentieth-century life. But it should be noted that Hindu philosophy made its first great impact on American thought in the nineteenth century, and became one basis for American transcendentalism. Emerson, Thoreau, Alcott, and others read such philosophical works as the *Upanishads* and the *Bhagavad-gītā,* which had appeared in translation. Alcott practiced *yoga.*

Through Emerson, Hindu thought also had an important influence on the philosophy of "metaphysical" sects (see Judah, 1967). These sects, which gave primary emphasis to mental healing, gave rise to the works of Emma Curtis Hopkins, Malinda Cramer, and others, who derived part of their philosophy from Hindu monistic thought. Their works played a large part in the development of New Thought and the ancillary Divine Science. The thoughts of Charles and Myrtle Fillmore, the founders of the Unity School of Christianity, showed a strong Indian influence, which came largely though their study of Theosophy and their indebtedness to Emerson. When Swāmi Vivekananda lectured in America in 1893 before founding the Vedānta Society, the Fillmores quoted him in their magazines and sold his books. At a much later date, Ernest Holmes, the founder of Religious Science, declared his indebtedness to India, which he attributed particularly to his studies of the Hindu mysticism of William Walker Atkinson, or Rama Charaka, as he called himself. Even Mary Baker Eddy, in the first edition of *Science and Health with Key to the Scriptures,* gave some acknowledgment to Hindu philosophy.

The force of the current occult explosion in America can also be traced back to nineteenth-century "metaphysical" movements, some of which gravitated toward occultism. Madame Helena Blavatsky and Colonel Henry Steel Olcott organized the Theosophical Society in 1875 and the Hindu and Buddhist influence was soon apparent. Its early teachings for the most part were ostensibly those of the great masters of the Far East, particularly India and Tibet. Present-day occult leaders continue to draw upon the resources of Theosophy.

Theosophical teachings after 1875 infiltrated the psychic philosophy of Spiritualism, which was first presented in America by the seer Andrew Jackson Davis beginning in 1847. Organized Spiritualism began in America in 1848 after the spirit rappings of the Fox sisters were publicized around the world. The two young sisters, Kate and Margaretta Fox of Hydesville, New York, in whose presence spirits ostensibly rapped out coded messages, attracted much attention. From 1850 on many other mediums appeared. Their philosophy initially reflected the views of Davis, who believed in a continual progression of the spirit without reincarnating (Judah 1967:50–58; 72–73; 93–96). Hindu philosophical influence then followed, and the doctrine of reincarnation became one of the principal reasons for splitting and proliferating the Spiritualist churches to this day. The form of Hinduism represented by the Hare Krishna Movement, however, is quite different from the other manifestations and generally serves a different group of people.

Mission to the Counterculture. Although the International Society for Krishna Consciousness should not be considered a hippie movement, there is a certain truth in what one of its devotees said:

> Prabhupād actually once said that our best customers are hippies. It's just that they are frustrated with material life. That's the prime qualification, that one is frustrated and confused in material life—not satisfied. He said if you're thinking you're happy in this material life, then you're a fool, and you're not well qualified for spiritual life.

Notable among the elements of the establishment that the devotees of Krishna have rejected are: (1) material success for themselves through competitive labor; (2) an education that promotes that end; (3) the accumulation of unneeded possessions for sense gratification; (4) authority, both civil and parental, that favors the status quo; (5) any war, such as the Vietnamese conflict, that is regarded as a product of imperialistic purposes with a selfish economic basis; and (6) the hypocrisy of many belonging to the establishment, especially regarding civil rights and racial relationships. In addition, some felt that they were trying to practice many of the ideals upon which their former religious faiths were founded, but which they felt were so little practiced by other churchgoers.

The devotees sought a transcendental, spiritual solution to their problems. They wanted to escape from the illusory world of *māyā,* which they equated with the world of the establishment with its emphasis upon sense gratification. While being in the world, they wanted nothing of it. Chanting would put them on a transcendental spiritual plane, they believed.

If there is any implicit tragedy in the situation, it is found only in the case of some of these countercultural youths who later come to feel differently about the establishment and the American way of life. If they were school dropouts, their opportunity for education and time for fulfillment may then have passed.

To be sure, hypocrisy, power seeking, and greed may be found among some of the devotees. In my opinion, however, as a group they are extremely dedicated. Because of their seriousness as ministers of their faith, they obviously deserve the same privileges as do ministers, priests, or rabbis of any faith. Therefore, I was willing to intercede with their draft boards on occasion, in trying to get deferments.

In concluding this introduction, let us note that the devotees of Krishna have formed a new subculture by making a selection of the elements of the counterculture. These they have internalized and validated as facets of their new religion. Krishna Consciousness becomes the symbol and epitome of their entire struggle, the rationale behind the formation of their social group as an alternative culture.

I suggest that the formula may be most simply expressed: alienation, insecurity, and loss of meaning through changing cultural values may be overcome through the shared, routinized experience of religious enthusiasm, and with adherence to a strict discipline in association with others of similar age holding similar cultural values. I suggest also that the devotees have validated and internalized the elements of their new culture and their alternative style of life through what they have experienced as Krishna Consciousness. Religion, which has usually been a force to conserve and maintain cultural values, is seen here as the validating instrument of cultural change. Those who have been able to continue the discipline given to them by their spiritual master are living and apparently enjoying the alternative life style they had been seeking.

With this brief perspective let us next turn to the historical and philosophical foundations for the Hare Krishna Movement.

CHAPTER TWO

HISTORICAL AND LITERARY ANTECEDENTS

This chapter presents a brief history of the Vaishṇava Movement. Special reference is given to the Movement begun by Chaitanya and presently represented most faithfully by the Gauḍīya Vaishṇavas of India and by the International Society for Krishna Consciousness.

A. C. Bhaktivedanta Swāmi Prabhupāda founded the New York temple of the International Society for Krishna Consciousness (ISKCON) in 1966, one year after his arrival in the United States. He has presented his views and practices as the *bhakti-yoga* or *yoga* of devotion initiated by Śrī Krishna Chaitanya Mahāprabhu (A.D. 1486–1533), who was born in Nadia (Navadvīp), India (Bhaktivedanta, 1968a:xxvii). According to him, the movement has continued without change through an unbroken line of spiritual masters. The Gauḍīya Vaishṇavas, who today claim heirship to this "disciplic succession" are, according to Edward Dimock, the strongest single religious force in the eastern part of the Indian subcontinent (Dimock, 1972:ix). Because of its great popularity in one locale, it is often referred to as Bengal Vaishṇavism, although it is not that region's only form of Vaishṇavism.

Krishna is popular in India; Hindus are continually reminded of him in many places and ways. He is the cowherd deity of Vṛindāvan, the scene of the pastimes, and is usually depicted as sporting in eternal loving dalliance with the *gopīs* or cowherdesses, among whom Rādhā is his favorite. His amorous pastimes with her and the other *gopīs* are pictured not only in temples, but also in the common places of everyday life, such as the interiors of airplanes or the walls of a YWCA tourist hostel. A common sight in New Delhi is a sidewalk artist surrounded by a crowd as he paints on the burning pavement a huge picture of Krishna holding Mount Govardhana over his head with a single finger.

Although we in America have become accustomed to the steady procession of Hindu *swāmis* who have offered their philosophies to us, we have generally identified their views with the monistic Vedānta, best exemplified by Śaṅkara (A.D. 788–820) and his followers. We have become familiar with their beliefs, such as reincarnation and the ultimate absorption of the self into an impersonal Reality or Brahman. Until now, however, we have not encountered the contrasting philosophy and devotional practices of this popular Hindu Vaishṇava movement. Swāmi B. H. Bon Mahārāj lectured at several universities in the 1930s, but his message concerning Krishna reached an academic audience quite unlike the target group of Swāmi Bhaktivedanta.

Even though the philosophy and devotional practices of the Hare Krishna Movement are later delineated in more detail, it is fitting to note here that Chaitanya and his immediate followers were not the originators of *bhakti-yoga*. If they contributed to the *bhedābheda* philosophy of difference in nondifference, if they represented the greatest development in the cult of Rādhā, Krishna's consort, and even if they emphasized the chanting of the names of Krishna publicly in their *saṅkīrtans,* they had numerous important predecessors. Moreover, even if Chaitanya's particular emphasis on Krishna is perhaps most evident among Vaishṇavas in India today, Krishna is not the only prominent deity. Many worship Śiva or some form of his energy (*śakti*) as their favorite deity. Even among Vaishṇavas, some worship other expansions or descents (*avatārs*), such as Rāma, as the supreme deity. The followers of Chaitanya, however, believe that Krishna is the supreme and original form. They consider Vishṇu, to be the same as Krishna, but he is Krishna's plenary expansion. Krishna is also the original primeval Vishṇu, and is "the source of all forms of incarnation" (Bhaktivedanta, 1972b:324, 590).

Important Texts and Sects in the Development of Vaishṇavism. This section is offered as a guide to the study of Vaishṇavism in the larger context of India's complicated religious history. It concerns the religious texts that have helped form Vaishṇavism as well as its preliminary sects. Table 1 enables the reader to see at a glance the whole array from the beginning to the Hare Krishna Movement. It emphasizes types that the Gauḍīya Vaishṇavas especially have utilized, and also those that the Hare Krishna Movement itself has stressed. One must assume, however, that even those works for which Swāmi Bhaktivedanta has not written commentaries are important to his own philosophy, since his philosophy is like the Gauḍīya school of thought.

Although Table 1 is designed specifically to show the Hare Krishna Movement's relationship to these texts and movements, it should not be considered a complete listing of all types of Hindu religious literature. Rather, it contains pertinent illustrative examples, most of which will be mentioned in the course of this book.

I have reluctantly added some dates, so that the texts may be observed historically. My reluctance stems from the fact that the dating of all early Hindu literature is subject to considerable controversy and must be considered tentative. For example, the four traditional *Vedas,* the compilations of hymns for various deities in the early Hindu pantheon, represent material that was transmitted orally in archaic Sanskrit for centuries. Originally only three existed. Although the *Ṛig Veda* is the oldest, the fourth and later *Atharva Veda,* while showing corruptions of some of the hymns, contains some material earlier than that of the *Ṛig Veda.* The *Brāhmaṇas* of the three older *Vedas* are sacrificial commentaries. They give instructions concerning the sacrifices at which the hymns were chanted, as well as a good deal of mythological literature that also shows a development of thought. The *Āraṇyakas,* the forest *Brāhmaṇas,* were originally composed as guides to meditation for Brahmins in their third stage of life. They again mark a transition between the sacrificial religion of the earlier *Vedas* and the more philosophical tradition of the *Upanishads.* Each of these also was still loosely attached to one of the *Vedas.* Since none of these compilations have manuscripts dating close to their time of origin, dating is risky, and one must depend largely on internal criticism such as changes in language, thought, and locale.

The later epic literature of the *Mahābhārata* and the *Rāmāyaṇa* offer still other problems. For example, the central story of the great war between the Pāṇḍavas and their cousins, the Kauravas, is gen-

Table 1 Classes of Literature and Specific Parts on Which the Hare Krishna Movement Depends[1]

Development of Vaishṇavism	VEDIC LITERATURE, ca. 2500 B.C. to 600 B.C.[2]
Slow development of foundation as a syncretistic theology	*Ṛig Veda* (Hymns to Vishṇu) Hymn to Purusha
	(*Brāhmaṇas*)[3] As a class are not very influential in Vaishṇavism
	Śatapatha Brāhmaṇa. Identifies Nārāyaṇa with Purusha
	(*Āraṇyakas*) Are not generally referred to by the Gauḍīyas
	Upanishads[4] (*Śvetasvatara Upanishad*) (*Kaṭha Upanishad*) (*Chandogya Upanishad*) *Iśa Upanishad.* As translated and interpreted by Swāmi Bhaktivedanta
Development of Bhāgavatism to 8th century[6]	EPIC PERIOD, ca. 500 or 600 B.C. to A.D. 200[5]
	(*Rāmāyaṇa*) Worship of Rāma as an *avatār* of Vishṇu
	(*Mahābhārata*) Worship of Vishṇnu and Nārāyaṇa
Krishna-Vāsudeva worship	*Bhagavad-gītā.* As translated and interpreted by Swāmi Bhaktivedanta.
Worship of Nārāyaṇa, and life of Krishna (aspect of power)	*Nārāyaṇīya* section
Life of Krishna with the *gopīs* (aspect of love)	(*Hari-vaṃśa*) Supplement
	(*Dharma-śāstras*) Law books: social and ethical philosophy
	SŪTRA PERIOD, ca. early Christian era
	(*Vedānta* or *Brahma Sūtras,* ca. early centuries of Christian era)

Table 1 (*continued*)

Development of the six orthodox schools: Pūrva-Mīmāṅśā, Vedānta, Nyāya, Vaiśeshika, Sāṅkhya, Yoga	SCHOLASTIC PERIOD, from early Christian era to 17th century when commentaries were written upon the *Sūtras* by philosophers including those of Chaitanya's school
	Purāṇas.[7] A number emphasize the eroticism of Krishna
	(*Padma Purāṇa*) Life of Krishna and his "pastimes" with the *gopīs*
	(*Vishṇu Purāṇa*)
Dated between the 5th and 8th centuries A.D.[10]	(*Pañcharātrā Literature*) Develops idea of *vyūhas* or Vishṇu's aspects for creation and emphasizes ceremonial worship of images
	Brahma Saṃhitā. Bhakti Siddhānta presented a commentary on this and on Jīva Goswāmi's commentary
Dated later than 8th century A.D.	(*Brahmavaivarta Purāṇa*). Introduces Rādhā as wife of Krishna[8]
	Bhāgavata Purāṇa. Principally the early life of Krishna and "pastimes" with the *gopīs*. Most important source for philosophy of the Hare Krishna Movement besides the *Bhagavad-gītā*. Not cited by any philosopher before 10th century[9]
	(*Tantras*). Influence doctrine of Krishna's *śakti,* or feminine energy
Beginnings of Vaishṇavism in the South not earlier than the 7th or 8th century A.D.[11]	*Works of the Alvars*
Beginning of Sectarian Vaishṇavism A.D. 1100 to 1500	Rāmānuja's works. (Śrī sect) Qualified non-dualism
	Madhva's works. (Brahma sect) Dualism
	Vishṇuswāmi's works. (Rudra sect) Pure non-dualism

	Nimbārka's works. (Haṁsa sect) Dualistic non-dualism
Other sources of Vaishṇavism, of Chaitanyaism	
12th century	Jayadeva's *Gīta-govinda.* Concerns the love of Rādhā and Krishna
14th and 15th centuries	Chaṇḍīdās' and Vidyāpati's love lyrics
16th century	Beginning of the Chaitanyaism of the Gauḍīya Vaishṇavas
	Philosophy of Jīva Goswāmi, Rūpa Goswāmi and Sanātana Goswāmi recorded by Swāmi Bhaktivedanta in his *Teachings of Lord Caitanya*
	Rūpa Goswāmi's *Bhakti-rasāmṛita-sindhu,* translated by Swāmi Bhaktivedanta as the *Nectar of Devotion* as standard work on *bhakti*
17th century	Krishnadāsa Kavirāja's *Caitanya Caritāmṛita* is the only early biography relied on by the Hare Krishna Movement
	GAUḌĪYA VAISHṆAVA MISSION established in 1886
19th century [12]	Bhaktivinode Thākur establishes the Gauḍīya Vaishṇava Mission claiming descent from Jīva Goswāmi
20th century	Works of Bhakti Siddhānta, Bhaktivedanta's spiritual master and of the Gauḍīya Vaishṇavas until his death.
	The International Society for Krishna Consciousness established by Swāmi Bhaktivedanta in New York, 1966
	Works of Bhaktivedanta

[1] Texts in parentheses refer to those that have not received particular emphasis by Swāmi Bhaktivedanta in his written works, although they may be included as forming part of the Vaishṇava tradition.

[2] Radhakrishnan, 1957:xv–xvii. Basic periods and dates are Radhakrishnan's with exceptions shown.

[3] Surendranath Dasgupta dates the end of Brāhmaṇa period not later than 500 B.C. (Dasgupta, 1949:14).

[4] Dasgupta dates earliest *Upanishads,* 700–600 B.C. (Dasgupta, 1949:28).

erally regarded as very old. Since the epics, unlike the *Vedic* scriptures, were not considered by the orthodox Brahmins as revealed literature (*śruti*), they were subject to change and interpolations by bards who recited them in the villages, or later by sectarian redactors. They show development in religious thought as well as growth of the popular religion of the masses. By sifting the material one may make judgments concerning the composition of the essential *Mahābhārata,* but internal evidence also reveals the work of later editors. Since the oldest extant manuscripts date only from the eighth or ninth centuries A.D., the problem is severe, at least for certain sections.

The *Purāṇas, Tantras,* and the *Pañcharātrā* literature and their associated movements are equally difficult to date with accuracy. While this literature mentions the Ekāntins, Sātvatas, Bhāgavatas, and Pañcharātrins, the exact status and beliefs of these groups are not always clearly differentiated. Like A. K. Majumdar, I find it difficult to distinguish the Ekāntins, the Bhāgavatas, and the Sātvatas, although these are mentioned in the *Nārāyaṇīya* section of the *Mahābhārata* (Majumdar, 1969:19). The same work speaks also of a king who worshiped according to the Sātvata rites and kept in his house great saints of the *Pañcharātrā* system. Adding to the confusion, Yamuna, who died in A.D. 1038, noted that the Sātvatas were erroneously considered as being only of low caste. Yamuna believed them

---

[5] Radhakrishnan, 1957:xv–xvii. Basic periods and dates are Radhakrishnan's with exceptions shown.

[6] De, 1961:2–3.

[7] Radhakrishnan omits the *Purāṇas* from consideration as philosophies, and places the *Tantra* system in the Epic Period (Radhakrishnan, 1957:99). I recognize that the devotion to the female energy of the deity (Śaktism) has its witness in the Mahābhārata. Still the *Tantras* as the principal texts of Śaktism, which have been cited by Jīva Goswāmi and other philosophers of the Chaitanya school, I regard as belonging to the early centuries following the Epic Period.

[8] De, 1961:11–13.

[9] Dasgupta, 1949:1.

[10] Jaiswal, 1967:22.

[11] Dasgupta, 1940:63–64.

[12] The intervening personalities and texts are omitted, since I have not been able to discover any particular contribution they have made to the philosophy of the Hare Krishna Movement.

to be the same as the more respected Bhāgavatas. The Sātvatas observe image worship, he said, and have adopted the *Pañcharātrā* texts. The latter he again defended as being based upon *Vedic* literature and declared that the Supreme God of the *Upanishads* was Vāsudeva, who as Nārāyaṇa was also the author of the *Pañcharātrā* literature (Dasgupta, 1940:14–17). Other schools of Hindu philosophy would strongly oppose each of his statements.

The Pañcharātrins had been reviled by some *Purāṇas* and praised by others. Yamuna's and later Rāmānuja's defense of them, and their favorable representation in the *Bhāgavata Purāṇa,* led to their wider recognition by the later Vaishṇavas.

That there was earlier distinction between the Pañcharātrins and the Bhāgavatas cannot be denied. The *Bhagavad-gītā* representing the Bhāgavata tradition does not include the doctrine of the *vyūhas,* which is contained in the *Pañcharātrā* literature. This belief is associated also with the *Nārāyaṇīya* section. Therein Nārāyaṇa, whom the Gauḍīya Vaishṇavas and the Hare Krishna Movement identify as an expansion of Krishna, was also Vāsudeva. In this version he was the only eternal principle who was immanent in the five material elements. From him emanated Saṅkarshaṇa or Śesha, who represents the *jīvas* or individual souls. From Saṅkarshaṇa comes Pradyumna, the mind, and from Pradyumna evolves Aniruddha, the *ahaṁkāra* or the ego. These represent also the process of the cosmic creation produced ultimately by Brahmā, who emerges from Aniruddha's "lotus-navel."

The *Harsha-caṛita* composed by Bāṇa in the seventh century likewise distinguished between the Pañcharātrins and the Bhāgavatas. Following P. C. Bagchi, Majumdar suggests that the Bhāgavatism at that time had already formed a syncretism of Vaishṇavite beliefs which incorporated the "Viṣṇu of Vedic Brahmanism, Nārāyaṇa of the Pañcarātrās, Kṛṣṇa-Vāsudeva of the Sātvata, Gopāla [that is, the Krishna of Vṛindāvan] of a pastoral people" (Majumdar, 1969:11, 28–29). With the later fusion of the two sects, the respect in which the Bhāgavata tradition had been held even by some kings helped rid the Pañcharātrā literature of the opprobrium it had received.

With the advent of the Alvar literature, one may truly speak of Vaishṇavism instead of Bhāgavatism. Immediately following begins the sectarian period of Vaishṇavism, which extends from Rāmānuja to the Hare Krishna Movement.

Sources of Vaishṇavism to A.D. 1100. Although *bhakti* or devotion to a personal deity is first fully expounded in the *Bhagavad-gītā,* which may have been composed as late as the second or third century B.C., the germ of it appears much earlier. In fact one may perhaps find the beginning of *bhakti* in some of the hymns of the *Ṛig Veda.* These are at least coeval with the Indo-European advance into India, which may have begun nearly 5000 years ago.

The later philosophical *Upanishads,* whose earliest works most scholars have placed in the sixth or seventh century B.C., are the principal sources for those seeking salvation by knowledge of the impersonal Brahman. And yet, even among these philosophical treatises there are some theistic ones. For example, in investigating the origins of *bhakti,* A. K. Majumdar calls attention to the *Śvetasvatara Upanishad* (VI, 18) in which one's salvation appears to depend upon surrender to a personal God. The *Kaṭha Upanishad* also anticipates the doctrine of grace that the Vaishṇavas later developed (Majumdar, 1965:1–2). Of course Swāmi Bhaktivedanta himself has translated and explained in the tradition of Chaitanya the theistic *Iśa Upanishad.*

While making Krishna (Vishṇu) the highest form of deity, Chaitanya and his followers have nevertheless included among his expansions many of the most popular gods of the Hindu pantheon. But in the past as well as at present various sects have held as supreme one or another of these other deities. Consequently, they share some of the same literary sources utilized by the philosophical school of Chaitanya.

The worship of Vishṇu himself is evident in various types of Hindu literature of all periods. In the *Ṛig Veda* Vishṇu plays a minor role in comparison with Indra and some of the other deities, since only 5 of 1028 hymns are dedicated to him. The principal source of early material forming the Vaishṇava tradition comes from the great epics, the *Mahābhārata* and the *Rāmāyaṇa.* Although the *Mahābhārata's* main story may reach far back into India's history, both this work and the *Rāmāyaṇa* were perhaps composed between 300 and 100 B.C., and certainly the final reactions came in the early centuries of the Christian Era. Following Pisani, Jaiswal notes that the *Mahābhārata* mentions various peoples such as the Romakas (Romans), Yavanas (Greeks), and Pahlavis (Parthians). Moti Chandra cites its mention of an ambassadorial mission to the Greek king, Antiochus. The earliest of several Greek kings to bear that name lived in the third century B.C.

Some scholars have concluded that the *Mahābhārata* was intended to rejuvenate the Brahmanical sacred order during the great social disorders occurring between 200 B.C. and the beginnings of the Christian era. During that time, foreign hordes invaded India in great numbers, and the introduction of new crafts allowed the lower castes to improve their economic position.

These troublesome times caused a weakening of the whole caste system. The *Vedic* rites had been forbidden to the low caste Śudras as well as to foreigners. But it was also a period when nonbrahmanical religious movements flourished. The Vāsudeva-Krishna movement became one of the most powerful, and the Brahmans were forced to recognize Vāsudeva-Krishna as an incarnation of Nārāyaṇa-Vishṇu. For these reformed religions, the epics and the later *Purāṇas* became the principal sources of authority (Jaiswal, 1967:8–13).

As part of the *Mahābhārata,* the *Bhagavad-gītā* becomes one of the most important literary sources for the Vaishṇavas and those of the Hare Krishna Movement. In this well-known and frequently translated religious text, Krishna acts as a charioteer to the hero, Arjuna, and gives his exposition of *bhakti* before the famous internecine battle of Kurukshetra.

Bhakti-yoga, or salvation by devotion to a personal deity, is one of three ways to liberation traditionally recognized in Indian philosophy: works, knowledge, and devotion. The *Bhagavad-gītā* concerns itself with all those. Salvation by works for their reward, which has characterized the Hindu sacrificial system, is given a new expression in the *Bhagavad-gītā.* One is enjoined to perform all actions for Krishna, with no thought of reward. The efficacy of the way of knowledge or *jñāna-yoga* is also recognized, although declared to be a more difficult path. The supreme way is by personal devotion to Krishna, the culmination of all *yogas* (Bhaktivedanta, 1972b:183–84, 358–59, 596, 600).

Epigraphic and literary evidence indicates that the worship of Krishna (Vishṇu) in some form already enjoyed some popularity in the third or fourth century B.C. Krishna Vāsudeva received converts from among the foreigners who had invaded India. There is a votive offering at Besnagar dating from the second century B.C. which Heliodorus, a Greek convert to Bhāgavatism, made to "Vāsudeva, god of gods." Megasthenes, a Greek ambassador sent from Seleucus Nicator to the court of Chandragupta in the fourth century B.C., referred to the worship of Krishna Vāsudeva, whom he equated with the Greek Herakles.

Looked at epigraphically, archaeologically, and literarily, one must view Vaishṇavism as a syncretistic development, whose various parts have often evolved as separate cults, each with its own supreme deity. Gradually, however, because of the Hindu genius to discover unity in diversity, Vaishṇavism grew more unified beginning in the twelfth century, although still leaving room for varying schools of philosophy. Many different *bhakti-yoga* * movements, which had at one time existed separately, were fused through a syncretistic evolution into Vaishṇavism which has only five distinct systems of philosophy. The apex of this development was Chaitanyaism, in which all the important deities were brought together into one system. Chaitanya made Krishna supreme; the other, once-supreme deities became his expansions or *avatārs* to perform various functions.

The genius of the immediate followers of Chaitanya, the six Goswāmis, is shown in their utilization of the vast array of historical texts. These again often represented various interpretations of sectarian views, which the Goswāmis drew upon and fitted into one system. As a result, Hindu scholasticism is complicated indeed. Let us now examine briefly this historical development.

The *Nārāyaṇīya* section of the *Mahābhārata* mentions the earlier discussed sects as worshiping Nārāyaṇa-Vishṇu Vāsudeva, the syncretistic deity which even today the Gauḍīya Vaishṇavas and the Hare Krishna devotees consider to be important expansions of Krishna. Nārāyaṇa is not mentioned in the *Vedas*. He appears for the first time in the *Śatapatha Brāhmaṇa* where he is pictured as performing the Pañcharātrā sacrifice so that he would be all in all things (Jaiswal, 1967:32–40). Therein he identified with Purusha, a primeval cosmic deity, who appears in the *Purusha-sūkta* of the *Ṛig Veda* as having sacrificed himself for the creation of the world and man (Dasgupta 1932:537). Such identification provided Nārāyaṇa status as a *Vedic* deity and gave him cosmic proportions.

Saṅkarshaṇa-Baladeva is both a component part of Krishna's *vyūhas* or emanations and his older brother, Baladeva. He first ap-

* The terms *bhakti* and *bhakti-yoga,* or the practice of devotion to a personal deity, which is Krishna here, are used interchangeably.

pears in the *Mahābhārata* as the son of Vāsudeva, Krishna's father, and Rohiṇī, one of his wives. Saṅkarshaṇa also had his own cult historically. His association with the juice of the Madana plant used as a sacrificial beverage indicates an association with a Dionysian role. In fact it is quite possible that he was the one whom Megasthenes identified with the Greek god, Dionysos. The *Vishṇu Purāṇa* also seems to support this. Prominent among his characteristics was his association with agriculture—he was called *musalin,* "one who wields a pestle," which was used for cleaning rice. Iconographically he is depicted holding both a pestle and a plough. Although pre-Christian inscriptions, images, and other archaeological evidence exist, evidence of his worship diminishes with time. Nevertheless, there were temples built to him (as Baladeva) in the South as late as the sixth century A.D. (Jaiswal 1967:53, 59).

The stories of the erotic adventures of the *gopīs* with Krishna are developed in the *Hari-vaṃśa,* a supplement to the *Mahābhārata,* and also in the *Purāṇas.* Rādhā, Krishna's consort, does not however, appear in the literature to any extent in the sensuous imagery until she appears in the *Brahmavaivarta Purāṇa* (De, 1961:7).

The literature of the Pañcharātrā sect is also one of the sources of Vaishṇavism. The traditional list of works numbers 108, but as many as 215 may have once existed. Few of these extant works have ever been translated. Because of the *tantric* elements found within so much of this literature, scholars have assigned the composition to a period between the fifth and eighth centuries A.D.

The *Ahirbudhnya Saṁhitā,* one of the earliest Pañcharātrā texts, recognizes the fivefold forms of the deity, which have become a part of the Vaishṇava theology. It also contains the doctrine of the *vyūhas,* which influenced the philosophy of sectarian Vaishṇavism in varying degrees.

The Pañcharātrins received the opprobrium of the more orthodox among the Brahmins because they extended the authority of the *Vedas* to include their literature, and also because they admitted to their sect both men and women of all castes (Jaiswal, 1967:22, 43, 45).

The *Purāṇas* supplied much material to the growing Vaishṇava tradition. The important *Vishṇu, Brāhmaṇda,* and *Vāyu Purāṇas,* which may be the earliest, could not have been in their present form before the fourth century A.D., since they include the genealogy of the Gupta kings. This of course does not mean that they could not contain earlier material. The same is true of the *Brāhma Purāṇa,* which Tadpatrikar has shown contains the oldest version of the story of Krishna.

The *Bhāgavata Purāṇa* elaborates on subjects found in the *Vishṇu Purāṇa,* and is therefore judged to be later, but scholars ascribe varying dates, ranging from the third to the tenth century A.D., to its composition (Jaiswal, 1967:16–17, 22, 45).

The *Bhāgavata Purāṇa* is by far the most important *purāṇic* source for the Gauḍīya Vaishṇavas and the Hare Krishna Movement. While the *Bhagavad-gītā* has enjoyed great popularity in English translation, this *Purāṇa* is relatively unknown in America, even though it was among the earliest Hindu religious works to reach the United States in the nineteenth century. Ralph Waldo Emerson remarked that it was a book to be read on one's knees. In India its words are "enshrined in the hearts of millions of men and women" (Rukmani, 1970:3, 6).

The setting of the *Bhagavad-gītā* precedes the famous battle when Krishna expounds his message and before his return to Dvārakā. The *Bhāgavata Purāṇa* provides in part a sequel, continuing with Krishna's association with his friends, the Pāṇḍavas. The most popular and influential part of this work for the Hare Krishna Movement is the tenth *canto,* which gives in detail the early life of Krishna during his descent to earth. In the eroticism of the *gopīs'* expression of love for Krishna is found one of literature's most impassioned symbols of souls searching, longing for, and finding the love of God.

The growth in popularity of Vaishṇavism can perhaps be measured by the increase of Vaishṇava inscriptions during the Gupta period, which began in the fourth century A.D. The epigraphs range from invocations to Vaishṇava deities, to grants made to various temples for their repair or maintenance. At the same time, images of Vaishṇava deities, which had begun to appear about the second century B.C., began to increase in complexity of iconographic forms, as though in rhythm with the developing philosophy. The blending of *tantric* and Śakta elements into Vaishṇavism, which had also begun in the Kushāna period, continued. These elements, emphasizing the female energy of the deity in personalized form, received veneration of devotees. Not until the late fifth century A.D., however, did Śrī Lakshmī appear as the power (*śakti*) of Vishṇu, through whom he acts to create and destroy the worlds.

It was also during the Gupta period that epigraphic evidence reveals the great cosmic proportions that Krishna had attained. The earliest of five Vaishṇava inscriptions (A.D. 404), after giving an invocation to Vishṇu, describes Vāsudeva (Krishna) as the abode of the whole universe, immeasurable, unborn, and all powerful.

The growth and development of Vaishṇavism under Gupta kings probably owes much to their tolerance, which was extended to other forms of Hinduism as well as to Buddhism. Coins of this period bearing symbols and emblems of a religious nature are evidence that a number of the Gupta monarchs patronized one or another of the Vaishṇava deities; some took the title *parama bhāgavata,* highest or chief *bhāgavata.*

By the sixth century A.D. Vaishṇavism had spread to Assam and Bengal. Bengal became one of its greatest strongholds; one finds there many sixth- to ninth-century sculptures depicting the various sports (*līlā*) of Krishna (Jaiswal, 1967:29–30, 108, 192, 195, 198).

In expanding into the Tamil Country of the South, Vaishṇavism was influenced by a group of *gurus* known as the Alvars, whom modern scholarship has placed in the period between the middle of the seventh and the middle of the ninth centuries A.D. The traditional date for the earliest Alvars is 4203 B.C. A collection of their extant works containing 4000 hymns known as the *Nal-ayir-divya-prabandham* was made by a disciple of Rāmānuja. These poetical works overflowed with their intense and devoted love for Vishṇu, and became the basis for the later doctrine of *prapatti* or pious surrender to the deity. Their doctrine that all beings should regard themselves as women in their love for God was later to be echoed in the philosophy and devotion of Chaitanya (Dasgupta, 1940:64, 68). Thus Śaṭhakopa, one of the Alvars, "conceived himself as a woman longing for her lover and entirely dependent on him" (Dasgupta, 1940:70). His feelings of anguish and longing over being separated from God are echoed in similar expressions by Chaitanya.

Vaishṇavism from the Twelfth to the Fifteenth Century A.D. In the twelfth century, Rāmānuja originated the Śrī Vaishṇava sect, the first of the important Vaishṇava groups that have continued to the present day. His philosophy, known as Viśishtādvaita Vedānta, is a qualified monism, in opposition to the *advaita* Vedānta, which is best characterized by the popular school of Śaṅkara. Rāmānuja viewed the soul as an individual part of God, which retained its individuality when liberated, rather than becoming merged into the Absolute, as the system of Śaṅkara would imply. The system also requires a complete surrender to God in his personal aspect, a doctrine that Rāmānuja derived chiefly from the Alvars.

The sect founded by Madhva in the thirteenth century was a philosophical dualism. It was the first to be based on Krishna's *līlā* at Vṛindāvan. As it depended heavily on the *Bhāgavata Purāṇa,* there was no place for Rādhā in his system. The next sect to develop, the Vishṇuswāmins, have almost disappeared today. Although their views were basically similar to those of Madhva, they extended their devotion to Rādhā as well as to Krishna.

In the thirteenth century, Nimbārka formed a new Vaishṇava sect. Its philosophy was *dvaitādvaita* or a dualistic monism; like the *bhedābheda* system of Chaitanya, it held that God was at the same time one with and yet separate from each soul. Nimbārka moved one step closer to Chaitanya's philosophy by conceiving of Rādhā as the consort of Krishna.

Except for the Vallabhāchāryas, which originated in the sixteenth century about the same time as the Chaitanya movement, there have been no other important Vaishṇava sects. The Vallabhāchāryas, which have almost completely absorbed the Vishṇuswāmin group, hold a view that combines features of Śaṅkara's monism with the veneration of Rādhā and Krishna, much like the Nimbārka sect (Kennedy, 1925:6–8).

Thus the first historically known instances of the cult of Rādhā are found in this 500 year period. The cult's greatest source of erotic imagery was the *Gīta-govinda* of Jāyadeva, which appeared in Bengal toward the end of the twelfth century A.D. It was this work that Chaitanya seemed to hold in highest reverence; recitation of its erotic poetry expressing the great love of Rādhā and Krishna often sent Chaitanya into an ecstatic trance. Most authorities agree that the poems of Chaṇḍīdās and Vidyāpati of the fourteenth and fifteenth centuries also had a great influence upon him.

This brings us to the period of Chaitanya. Let us set the scene for his entry.

Social and Religious Conditions in Bengal Before Chaitanya's Time. If it is true that life situations causing great insecurities for an individual tend to create the need for religious experience and religious enthusiasm, perhaps one may draw a parallel between the social conditions and religious needs of sixteenth-century Bengal and late twentieth-century America. In the centuries preceding Chaitanya, Bengal had been pillaged by foreigners of an alien culture and religion. Hindu suzerainty there passed to the Turks toward the close of the twelfth century, and "Hindus became aliens in their own homes" (Mukherji, 1970:1–3). As the Muslim invaders sought to supplant Hindu culture and religion with their own, the Brahmins tried to dominate the social order and to maintain the rigidities of the caste system and their religious leadership. The people therefore experienced bondage and heavy restrictions from both foreign and domestic sources.

Vaishṇavism became the most significant movement in Bengal. Though few in numbers, the Vaishṇavas gathered in small groups in one another's homes for religious devotions and readings from the *Bhāgavata*. Except for these groups, Hindu religion at the time of Chaitanya had deteriorated, and was characterized by esoteric cults of obsolescent *tantric* Buddhism and numerous cults of aboriginal origin, hardly above the animistic level. The *tantric* practices of the Vāmāchāri, "the left-hand" school of Śaktism, indicates by its name practices regarded as evil. It inculcated worship of the hypostatized female energy of the deity in rites including sexual licentiousness and orgies (see De, 1961:28; Kennedy, 1925:1–3).

Life of Chaitanya. Chaitanya Mahāprabhu was born in February, 1486 to the pious Vaishṇava family of Jagannāth Miśra and his wife, Sachī Devī. Although affectionately known in his youth as Nimai, his given name was Viśvambhara. As a boy he was full of mischief, but showed himself to be above average intelligence. He became proficient in his studies, while enjoying the social privileges of his Brahmin caste.

Chaitanya's father died when the boy was fourteen or fifteen years old. The boy soon assumed responsibility for his mother, became a householder, and married Lakshmī, the daughter of a Brahmin scholar. He started his own school, and attracted many pupils. At this time Chaitanya showed no inclination toward religious studies. According to his early biographers, he was recognized as a promising scholar, but appeared to be rather proud and arrogant. The death of his first wife by snakebite may have been the turning point in his life. Although his mother quickly arranged another marriage for her son, his union to Vishṇupriyā was short-lived.

During a pilgrimage to Gayā, made when he was twenty-one or twenty-two, he met the famous ascetic, Īśvara Purī, who became his *guru* and gave him a ten-syllable Krishna *mantra* to chant. Chaitanya returned completely changed—he was a *bhakta,* a devotee, entirely dedicated to Krishna. He no longer cared about his personal appearance nor about his work. Some considered him mad, so intense was his devotion for Krishna. Often he would go into a mystic trance; at times he raved and chanted Krishna's name continuously. Sometimes he would cry or faint, and his teaching suffered to such an extent that he had to discontinue the school. He next organized *saṅkīrtans,* often dancing and singing on the village streets, and he preached a message of universal love (Mukherjee, 1970:4–9; Kennedy, 1925:11–29; De, 1961:76–77). Sometimes he would take part in a Krishna *yātrā,* a type of dramatic presentation of one of Krishna's "pastimes" (*līlā*) at Vṛindāvan.*

Perhaps because of his intense religious passion, Chaitanya soon attracted devotees. His singing of the love of Rādhā and Krishna roused the emotions of others. As the volume of the chanting increased, the *kholes* (drums) and *kartālas* (finger cymbals) picked up the beat. With hands raised high above his head, he would lead the others in dancing, leaping up and down until falling exhausted in an ecstatic stupor. The *saṅkīrtans* were received with mixed emotions by the townspeople. Some sought to have the Muslim governor suppress them as a public nuisance. Chaitanya's response, however, was to organize such a large demonstration of chanting devotees that the magistrate

* This kind of acting takes place occasionally in the Hare Krishna temples during the *ārati* ceremony on Sundays, and also at festival times, such as during the Ratha-yātrā or Car Festival occurring in July each year in a number of cities.

had to recognize the religious nature of the activity and took part himself (Kennedy, 1925:23, 27).

To increase his movement, Chaitanya became initiated as a *saṅnyāsi* or holy man of the Bharati order, and received the name of Śrī Krishna Chaitanya. Having decided to leave his native town he left Bengal, and at the request of his mother he made his permanent home in Purī in Orissa (Mukherjee, 1970:16–20). There he was able to worship Krishna in the temple of Jagaṅnātha, whom the Gauḍīya Vaishṇavas worship as a form of Krishna. His first visit to Purī was brief, but eventful. His conversion there of a famous Vedāntist, Sarvabhauma, allowed him to gain full respect and support from the King of Orissa, and helped establish a strong future for Chaitanyaism there.

Shortly thereafter Chaitanya began a pilgrimage of almost two years to the south. During this time he is said to have performed miracles and made many conversions through his lectures and his contagious devotion. He visited many temples and had copies made of the *Brahma Saṁhitā* and the *Krishna-karṇāmṛita,* which he praised greatly. The former exists in preliminary form today; the latter was composed by Līlāśūka Bilvamaṅgala and is considered a Vishṇuswāmi work.

After his return to Purī, Chaitanya's Bengal disciples organized the first of their annual pilgrimages to visit and honor their spiritual master. The pilgrimage took place during the period of the Car Festival of Jagaṅnātha, which still draws many thousands to Purī every year. After passing several months in close fellowship and adoration of Chaitanya, they returned to Bengal.

Chaitanya spent the rest of his life in Purī, leaving it only twice. Accompanied by a few chosen disciples, he spent his time in devotion to Krishna, and never again saw his wife or his mother. His first plans to visit Vṛindāvan, the traditional home of Krishna's loving play, did not materialize. But he did manage to meet with and convert the men later known as Rūpa and Sanātana, who became acknowledged interpreters of his message. Chaitanya chose them to go to Vṛindāvan to make it the center for Vaishṇavism. After returning to Purī, the master again set out for Vṛindāvan the following year, traveling with one companion. Anything he saw on the way that reminded him of Krishna was sufficient to set him in a rapturous frenzy. On reaching the holy Jumna River, he rushed ecstatically into it and had to be rescued by his companion, who was soon joined by others. The sound of a flute called to mind Krishna's playing for the *gopīs,* and sent him into a trance. It is said that a band of Moslem Pathans came upon him and his companions right at this time. Thinking they had discovered a band of robbers who had drugged their victim, they were about to kill the devotees, when Chaitanya awakened and began to dance and chant the names of Krishna. A religious discussion marked the beginning of the Pathans' conversion.

Chaitanya disappeared in 1534 for reasons that remain a source of disagreement. Perhaps he drowned in the sea during a trance state, as has been suggested. In his *Caitanya Maṅgala,* Jayānanda attributes the disappearance to a wound in his foot by a stone, which caused fever and death (Kennedy, 1925:39, 46–51; De, 1961:84, 90–97). Hare Krishna devotees believe that he disappeared into the deities worshiped at the great Gopīnātha temple at Purī. Whatever the explanation, it is his life that was most important.

Chaitanya was a religious ascetic whose later life was entirely devoted to Krishna. His food and clothing were simple, and he disdained all comforts. Although the love of Rādhā for Krishna which he had expressed was couched in sexual imagery, Chaitanya preached a transcendental love that had no physical expression such as the Vāmāchāris exhibited. We know that he rigidly avoided contact with women, and demanded the same attitude from his disciples. One ardent devotee is said to have been banished forever from Chaitanya's presence because he had begged rice for his *guru* from an aged female devotee (Mukherjee, 1970:46–47; Kavirāja, 1959e:42–43).

If it was Chaitanya's charisma and contagious devotion that won so many to his faith during his lifetime, it was his close disciples Nityānanda and Advaitāchārya who at their master's command continued to win conversions in Bengal.

The *saṅkīrtan* or chanting and dancing developed by Chaitanya became at times a *nagara-saṅkīrtan,* or public chanting in the streets of the city. This was a way for the devotees to witness to their faith and devotion, even as Hare Krishna devotees in America do today. In addition, it was and is a way to acquaint others with the movement, and thus leads to conversions. This contribution of Chaitanya distinguishes his Vaishṇavism from other forms. The use of the *nagara-saṅkīrtan* in America, however, must be contrasted with the present practice in

India. The public *saṅkīrtan* is now used sparingly in India even by Hare Krishna devotees, and it is rarely seen among the Gauḍīya Vaishṇavas. Swāmi Bon Mahārāj disparaged the use of what he considered excessive emotion and therefore the frequent use of *saṅkīrtans.* When interviewed in 1973, Swāmi B. P. Yati Mahārāj, the Secretary of the Gauḍīya Math in Madras, seemed to have a similar view about saṅkīrtans, but for a different reason. He said that on one occasion Chaitanya refused to continue a *saṅkīrtan* at a friend's house because someone present was impure. The house was searched, the impure person was found, and after his removal the devotional exercise was begun anew. Nevertheless, biographical evidence indicates that in chanting publicly, the devotees in the United States are following a recommended practice of Chaitanya.

In giving up what they have considered excessive emotion, the Gauḍīya Vaishṇavas seem to be following a pattern that has been noted in the history of American religion, and that also reflects the differing needs of people and the evolution of a sect. For example, the religious enthusiasm of the early Methodist Church in America was far different from the lack of emotion in the denomination today. As the revivalism of the early American Methodists waned, the denomination ceased to satisfy all of its members. New groups, such as the Nazarine Church, were formed. These groups seem to then go through the same evolution in their turn.

The Development of the Chaitanya Movement. Although Chaitanya left the later development of the Movement and the formulation of his philosophy in written form to his disciples, one must recognize his own contribution to the philosophy. His chief ability was perhaps to convert and inspire capable men to carry out his wishes. His close disciple Advaitāchārya worked to propagate the faith, but because of his advanced age he was not as effective as the equally revered Nityānanda.

Nityānanda carried out to the letter Chaitanya's injunction to regard all people as spiritually equal, and admitted many low in caste to the Movement (Kennedy, 1925:61–63), thus causing rifts between himself and Advaitāchārya. Sushil Kumar De is not alone in alluding to these disagreements in his book, *The Early History of Vaishṇava Faith and Movement in Bengal.* In *Caitanya Bhāgavata,* Vṛindāvan Dāsa defends his friend and associate Nityānanda against his critics. His was the earliest Bengali account of the life of Chaitanya, written ostensibly at Nityānanda's request perhaps about fifteen years after Chaitanya's disappearance (De, 1961:46–50, 197). Since Nityānanda is regarded as part of the divine incarnation of Krishna by the Gauḍīya Vaishṇavas and the Hare Krishna Movement, Swāmi Bon Mahārāj also maintains that he did nothing that could be considered schismatic—as part of Chaitanya's divine descent, he could do no wrong. The devotees of the Hare Krishna Movement share this opinion.

Nityānanda made his home at Kardaha, somewhat to the north of Calcutta, where a number of devotees gathered and helped him in spreading the faith. Twelve of these who appear in the later literature of the Movement are reverenced as the twelve Gopāls.

Besides the work in Bengal that began in Chaitanya's lifetime, important treatises on Chaitanya's philosophy were written in Sanskrit at Vṛindāvan in the North. Though Chaitanya himself left a literary legacy of only eight verses, disciples known as the "six Goswāmis" of Vṛindāvan formulated and recorded his philosophy. Many of their concepts appear in Swāmi Bhaktivedanta's book, *Teachings of Lord Chaitanya.* The same author also translated and commented on Rūpa Goswāmi's important treatise on *bhakti,* the *Bhakti-rasāmṛita-sindhu.*

Through the efforts of the persevering Goswāmis, the traditional sites of Krishna's "pastimes" at Vṛindāvan and Mathurā were rediscovered and restored. In addition to Rūpa and Sanātana, whose names have been mentioned, Jīva Goswāmi, their nephew, became equally famous for his writings and work. Gopāl Bhaṭṭa, Raghunātha Dās, and Raghunātha Bhaṭṭa completed their number. Through the influence of these men the famous temples now to be seen at Vṛindāvan were built. Vṛindāvan became a center of learning for Chaitanyaism. Until the passing of the six Goswāmis, anything written elsewhere had to receive approval at Vṛindāvan before it could be accepted as authentic. This supremacy may have continued until the beginning of the eighteenth century (Kennedy, 1925:64–68).

Such was the work of the six Goswāmis in making Vṛindāvan a holy site for all devotees of Krishna that even today pilgrims journey from afar to visit it and pay homage to Krishna. Others come to die alone outside one of its temples, the name of Krishna on their lips.

Later History of Chaitanya's Vaishṇavism. Immediately after the death of Chaitanya, his Movement declined. The sound of the *saṅkīrtans* that had flooded the countryside was not heard on the banks of the Ganges for some time. During this period of decline, however, the lines of descent were established. Nityānanda and Advaitāchārya, were considered Goswāmis or *gurus,* and passed their titles and privileges on to their descendents. Thus two lines of Goswāmis have continued to this day in Bengal with further divisions. Three distinct groups presently claim descent from Nityānanda. According to Swāmi B. H. Bon Mahārāj, these separate lines of *āchāryas* are not to be considered as schisms in the Chaitanya Movement.

Other lines descending from Chaitanya's devotees also began and have continued in Bengal. In addition, there are Vaishṇava groups owing no allegiance to Chaitanya (Mukherjee, 1970:58; Kennedy, 1925:61–68; Ray, 1965:58–63).

Vīrabhadra, the son of Nityānanda, continued his father's work of admitting low caste and outcaste devotees to the Movement. Perhaps the most important of these were 2500 male and female mendicants, remnants of a decadent Buddhist order, the Nera-Neris, who were living as outcastes in the Hindu community.

The seventeenth century saw a period of renewal of the Chaitanya faith, due to the influence of three men: Śrīnivāsa Āchārya, Narottama Datta, and Śyāmānanda Dās. All three had studied under one of Chaitanya's disciples and at Vṛindāvan. Śrīnivāsa's conversion of Vīra Hamvīra, a wealthy *rāja,* carried with it the money and influence needed to aid the spread of the Movement. Narottama Datta, son and heir apparent of a wealthy *rāja* of Kheturi, left his life of luxury to become a Chaitanya ascetic of great influence. Kheturi became an important Vaishṇava center from which many of Narottama's disciples went forth to spread the faith. Śyāmānanda Dās was responsible for the new expansion of the Movement in Orissa. He had studied under Jīva Goswāmi at Vṛindāvan, but returned to Orissa to proclaim anew the *bhakti* of Chaitanya. His work was aided by the conversion of Rasikā Murāri, another wealthy *rāja* who used his wealth to help spread Chaitanya's message. During this period the poems and songs of Achyutānanda, Balarāma, Jagaṅnātha, Ananta, Yaśovanta, and Chaitanya popularized the work of these three men. The strong feelings of the people for Chaitanya there even today owe much to the work of these poets of Orissa, who are known as the six Dāsas.

The next two centuries again saw a decline in Vaishṇavism, until a gradual renewal began to be noticed in Bengal in the mid-nineteenth century. The popularity of the Brāhma Samāj, a Hindu reform movement, may have contributed to this reawakened interest during the third quarter of the nineteenth century. Keshup Chandra Sen introduced many features of Chaitanya's *bhakti* into its practices; the public *saṅkīrtans* with the use of the traditional drums and cymbals was revived, for example (Kennedy, 1925:69–78).

The Gauḍīya Vaishṇavas. This brings us to the Gauḍīya Vaishṇavas, to which Goswāmi Bhakti Siddhānta, the spiritual master of Swāmi Bhaktivedanta, belonged. The Gauḍīya Vaishṇava Mission, established by Bhaktivinode Thākur in 1886, had the formal name of Śrī Viśva Vaishṇav Rāj Sabhā. This association of Vaishṇavas is interested in propagating Chaitanya's philosophy and practices, and claims descent from its founder, Jīva Goswāmi, one of Chaitanya's "six Goswāmis." Bhaktivinode was a city magistrate in the city of Purī in Orissa and the superintendent of the Jagaṅnātha temple. His son, Śrī Śrīmad Bhakti Siddhānta Goswāmi, had been a professor of mathematics and astronomy before his renunciation. Thereafter, he continued his father's work of revitalizing Vaishṇavism and informing the English-speaking world of Chaitanya's message during the first half of this century. He founded the Gauḍīya Math Institute for teaching Krishna Consciousness in 1918, and during his life established sixty-four missions (Ray, 1965:64; International Society for Krishna Consciousness, 1970:2; *Back to Godhead,* 1967:28). One of his disciples was A. C. Bhaktivedanta Swāmi Prabhupāda, whose efforts have had such a marked influence on the American youth of the counterculture.

The Beginning of the International Society for Krishna Consciousness. A. C. Bhaktivedanta Swāmi Prabhupāda, or "Prabhupād," as he is affectionately called by his devotees, was born as Abhay Charan De in Calcutta in 1896. After being graduated from the University of Calcutta with majors in English, philosophy, and economics, he worked as manager of a chemical firm until his retirement in 1954. His present work, however, was foreshadowed as early as 1922, when he first met Bhakti Siddhānta. Bhakti Siddhānta became his spiritual master, and gave him the idea of spreading Chaitanya's message throughout the world. After Abhay Charan De's formal initiation took place at Allahabad in 1933, shortly before his spiritual master's death in 1936, Bhakti Siddhānta had ordered him to carry the teachings of Krishna Consciousness to the Western world. In 1947 the Gauḍīya Vaishṇava Society recognized De as Bhaktivedanta. In 1959 he took *sannyāsa,* the religious order marking one's total renunciation of life for devotion to God (Bhaktivedanta, 1968a:xiii). *Sannyāsa* entails permanent separation from wife and family.

After the death of Bhakti Siddhānta, controversy arose among his followers. "Unfortunately," Swāmi Bhaktivedanta said, when interviewed, "some of the ambitious disciples wanted to capture the whole thing itself, and in this way two parties were formed." This precipitated legal battles that are still in the courts, so that what was once a spiritual movement "has turned out to be a material thing on account of fighting for profit." Swāmi Bhaktivedanta claimed during our interview that his own authority through "disciplic succession" was derived from Bhakti Siddhānta's earlier request. At the time he felt he could not honor this because of family obligations. "Disciplic succession" involves initiation by a "bona fide spiritual master" and carries with it the duty of spreading to others the teaching one has received (Satsvarūpa dās Adhikāri, 1972:20).

Swāmi Bhaktivedanta continued: "I thought that Bhakti Siddhānta Sarasvatī Goswāmi wanted me to preach this cult—not only he, but before that Bhaktivinode Thākur wanted this cult to be preached all over, especially in the Western countries. I did not carry out his order. And my brothers—God brothers—are now engaged in litigation, and they are not pushing forward this movement. So after my retirement I began thinking of coming to the Western countries."

I also interviewed the Secretary of the Gauḍīya Math in Madras, B. P. Yati Mahārāj Tridandiswāmi, who alleged that Bhakti Siddhānta had selected Śrī Śrīmad Bhakti Vilas Tirtha Goswāmi Mahārāj as his successor before his death. He said that Tirtha Goswāmi Mahārāj had not felt worthy of immediately assuming the position of his spiritual master at the time of Bhakti Siddhānta's passing. Intense controversy then broke out among the three trustees concerning the leadership. Tirtha Goswāmi Mahārāj, however, is now recognized as president of the Gauḍīya Vaishṇavas by perhaps the majority of the organization, even though his position is still contested by others. Although Swāmi Bhaktivedanta is not without criticism from some of the Gauḍīya Vaishṇavas, as might be expected, he has also received plaudits for spreading the teaching of Chaitanya to the Western world. The continuing litigation has had no effect on the International Society for Krishna Consciousness, because of the latter's separateness from the Gauḍīya Vaishṇavas in India.

On his arrival in New York in 1965, Swāmi Bhaktivedanta began chanting the names of Krishna while sitting beneath a tree in Tompkins Park on the Lower East Side. He soon attracted followers, many of them hippies. Conversions took place. The first center of the International Society for Krishna Consciousness opened in New York in 1966. The beginning of a temple in San Francisco's Haight-Ashbury district followed in 1967. From then on the movement continued to spread. Young American devotees wearing loose and flowing Hindu apparel have become familiar sights on the streets of many of our large cities. Some chant their *mantras* and dance to the throbbing rhythmic beat of the *mṛidañga* drums and *kartālas*. Others sell literature about Krishna and talk incessantly about the benefits of chanting to anyone who will listen.

In just eight years since the founding of the New York temple, the Society had expanded to sixty-eight listed centers. Of these, twenty-eight are in the United States. Temples can also be found in Canada, Mexico, the West Indies, Japan, Hong Kong, India, Sweden, France, Germany, Holland, Switzerland, England, Scotland, New Zealand, and Australia (*Back to Godhead,* 58:2).

Although the total number of full-time devotees is not large, the Society is apparently having an influence far beyond its membership. There is a report that the English language edition of its *Back to Godhead* magazine is now selling about 300,000 copies of each issue, and is being translated and published in French, German, Japanese, Chinese, and Hindi. Its books and other publications are also finding a ready market. It has been reported that Swāmi Bhaktivedanta's translation and commentary of the *Bhagavad-gītā As It Is* sold about 50,000 copies in the first six months of publication.

The organization also has a flourishing business in the manufacture and sale of incense. With a large factory already in Los Angeles and another planned for Mexico, the enterprise is now expanding to include the production and sale of other products such as soaps, shampoos, and scented oils. Businesses like these employing many of the devotees give financial stability to the organization, and permit the continuation of alternative life styles for its devotees.

The Hare Krishna Movement in India. India has long received Christian missionaries from the West, and conversely, the United States is used to the visits of Hindu *swāmis* and *yogis*. It may appear unusual, however, that in recent years hundreds of American devotees of Krishna have been sent to India as missionaries to the Indians. There they have been trying to revive and spread the message of Krishna Consciousness among the Hindu population. They have established several temples in India, following their American pattern of utilizing buildings originally designed for other uses. American devotees may take their turns visiting India for what seems in most cases to be a rather brief tour of duty. Garga Muni, president of the ISKCON temple in Calcutta, explained that the climate and living conditions in India prove difficult for most of them. Few have stayed longer than a year.

Their success in making conversions among the Hindus has been limited. Garga Muni and others estimate that they have not converted more than twenty-five or thirty Hindus to their ranks. This may be traced to the great strength of family life in India, where sons live with their families and assume responsibility for their parents when they become old. Although India, like the United States, has experienced a countercultural movement among youth of the middle class, its expression has been different in that country. Even if outwardly the Indian youth of more affluent families have often aped countercultural American youth in clothing and hair styles, they have not formed a large hippie class. Drug abuse has not been a problem among Indian youth as among their American counterparts. While there has been noticeable antiestablishment feeling among some against authority and against the rigid social and sexual mores, the emphasis has not been placed on discovering an alternative style of living nor of searching for religious experience. At least two reasons account for this difference. First, the strength of family ties calls for obedience to the wishes of the parents. Second, the great motivation seen among Indian youth everywhere is to improve their economic position—to make money, to have the possessions and affluent type of life that the American counterculture has rejected. Well-to-do Indians form a very small class; the great majority of Indian youth are dissatisfied with their impoverishment.

In the light of these realities, one may wonder why the Hare Krishna Movement continues to exert efforts in India. While there, the devotees follow the discipline observed in America, but the public *saṅkīrtans* take place less often than they do here. The devotees feel that since they are following teachings and culture inherited from Chaitanya, their mission in India is to help preserve Hindu culture which they see as threatened by the growing secularism.

They have chosen as their major work the construction of a multimillion dollar temple towering 300 feet. The plans have already been made, and the property purchased at Māyāpur, modern name for the birthplace of Chaitanya near Calcutta. Meanwhile, the first of several three-story hostels is almost completed. Its first floor, which houses their interim temple, is large enough to accommodate more than a thousand devotees at their *saṅkīrtans.* Large septic tanks ensure sanitation; their deep well provides pure water. They have already developed a farm and dairy that will provide all their food. The corn stalks provide food for their cows. That which is not eaten is cut up and added to cow dung and water and allowed to ferment in large tanks to produce methane gas for their kitchens. Realization of these projects requires that some of the devotees' time in India be spent in raising large sums of money.

In both India and the United States, houses have generally been adapted to serve a religious purpose, although in Denver the devotees purchased a building that was formerly a church of the United Church of Christ. The large Los Angeles temple is also a former church building of the United Methodist Church. But in contrast to the United States, the devotees in India are undertaking a far more ambitious project, of which the proposed temple at Māyāpur is one example. India has long been famous for its many thousands of temples. The greatness of past and present religions are measured by the beauty, size, and endurability of these temples, some of which were constructed through the donations of industrial tycoons or wealthy *rājas*. The International Society of Krishna Consciousness has therefore found it culturally appropriate to represent the new organization by building a temple at the birthplace of Chaitanya, a temple that will overshadow in size and magnificence those constructed in recent years by the Gauḍīya Vaishṇavas. It will add new splendor to the tradition of Chaitanya, and when completed will annually draw thousands of pilgrims to visit, stay a while, and worship there. Besides this work, other promising goals are very evident.

Although the Hare Krishna Movement is not growing rapidly in India, it is developing industries that will ensure its sustainment. At Māyāpur the devotees paint beautiful ceramic images of Krishna that illustrate events in Krishna's life. The fashioning of *khole* drums from the local clay is another growing business, as is the manufacture of wearing apparel for Hare Krishna devotees everywhere, which may possibly develop into a major source of clothing for Hindus as well.

Although it is said that Chaitanya's desire was to have the message of Krishna spread throughout the world, a desire shared by Bhakti Siddhānta, not one of the foreign converts is allowed even to enter one of the major Vaishṇava temples. Whether the temples are controlled by Gauḍīya Vaisṇavas or by others, none but native born Hindus may enter them. This applies even to the famous Jagannātha temple at Purī, the temple so closely associated with the life of Chaitanya, which was supervised formerly by Bhaktivinode Thākur, father of Bhakti Siddhānta. This prohibition is not an anomoly, however; Chaitanya himself sanctioned such a practice. While he made no distinction spiritually between Brahmin and outcaste, Chaitanya apparently did observe the social distinctions that birth implied. Kennedy calls attention to Kavirāja's biography of Chaitanya wherein Haridās, although one of Chaitanya's favorite disciples, was not permitted in the temples at Purī. His former association with Islam made him a social outcaste (Kennedy, 1925:118).

CHAPTER THREE

KRISHNA, THE COSMIC AND PERSONAL DEITY

This chapter outlines the principal beliefs of the Hare Krishna Movement, as formulated by the followers of Chaitanya and as brought to the West by Swāmi Bhaktivedanta. The Movement represents a philosophy and an interpretation of Vaishṇavism believed by millions of people in India, but almost unknown in the West except for the devotees.

Vaishṇavism Versus Brahmin Orthodoxy. Vaishṇava philosophy and devotion in general represent important differences from the older Brahmanism in India. Conservative Brahmin orthodoxy believes that the *Vedas,* which have the authority of revealed literature, ended with the *Upanishads.* The individual treatises often closed with the word *vedānta,* meaning "end of the *Vedas.*" Like the Pañchārātrins, Madhva, Chaitanya, and other Vaishṇavas, Bhaktivedanta extended the authority of the word "Vedic" beyond the *Upanishads* so as to apply to the *Purāṇas,* the *Mahābhārata,* and the original *Rāmāyaṇa* (Bhaktivedanta, 1968a:227). The influential Vaishṇava philosopher, Madhva, taught that the ultimate aim of all revealed and traditional texts was to testify to the superexcellence of Vishṇu as the supreme Lord (Dasgupta, 1949:78). How natural then for the Gauḍīya Vaishṇavas, who believe that Krishna is the Supreme Personality of Godhead, to accept as equally revealed the words of Krishna in the *Gītā,* or of Chaitanya, his *avatār.* In interpreting the *Bhagavad-gītā,* Bhaktivedanta has taught that the *Vedas* themselves are all emanations

Errata

for Hare Krishna and the Counterculture

by J. Stillson Judah

'ermission to reprint the following material is gratefully acknowledged:

'igure 2. p. 48: from Dean M. Kelley, "Lutherans in America," *Why Conservative Churches are Growing,* Harper & Row, 1972, p. 3. Adapted from Edwin Scott Gaustad, *Historical Atlas of Religion in America,* Harper & Row, 1962.

'igure 3. p. 140: from Dean M. Kelley, "Episcopalians in America," *Why Conservative Churches Are Growing,* Harper & Row, 1972, p. 4. Adapted from Edwin Scott Gaustad, *Historical Atlas of Religion in America,* Harper & Row, 1962.

'igure 4. p. 142: from Dean M. Kelley, "Membership Comparison: 1960–1970," *Why Conservative Churches Are Growing,* Harper & Row, 1972, p. 22. Adapted from Edwin Scott Gaustad, *Historical Atlas of Religion in America,* Harper & Row, 1962.

'igure 5. p. 143: from Dean M. Kelley, "Membership Comparison: 1958-1970," *Why Conservative Churches Are Growing,* Harper & Row, 1972, p. 23. Adapted from Edwin Scott Gaustad, *Historical Atlas of Religion in America,* Harper & Row, 1962.

'igure 6. p. 144: from Dean M. Kelley, "Baptist Branches," *Why Conservative Churches Are Growing,* Harper & Row, 1972, p. 30. Adapted from Edwin Scott Gaustad, *Historical Atlas of Religion in America,* Harper & Row, 1962.

'rontispiece and Appendix. from Bhaktivedanta book trust, *KRSNA, The Reservoir of Pleasure,* 1972.

.s indicated throughout the text, there are a number of quotations from A. C. Bhaktivedanta Swāmi, *The Bhagavad As It Is.* These are reprinted with the permission of Bhaktivedanta book trust and Macmillan.

from the breathing of Krishna. He also considers Vyāsa as an *avatār* of Krishna, and the author of the *Bhāgavata Purāṇa.* This work he affirms to be a commentary on the *Vedānta Sūtras* and the summation of all the *Vedas* (Bhaktivedanta, 1972b:24, 179, 713).

Although conservative Brahmin orthodoxy is unable to accept these later literary accretions as having the same validity as the *Vedas,* they have had to make concessions to popular demands. The popularity of the *Bhagavad-gītā* is such that important Hindu philosophers, including the impersonalist Śaṅkara, felt the need to comment on it and fit it into their interpretations. Brahmin orthodoxy has attempted to unify all religious elements as far as possible into the larger system, and so Śaṅkara accepted the validity of Krishna for the unliberated, even though he relegated him to a lesser reality than the qualityless Brahman. Thus it became possible for a Brahmin *advaitin,* who believed in the ultimate reality of the impersonal Brahman, to give devotion to Vishṇu, Krishna, or to other deities, or to the personified energies of one of these deities.

One feature of Chaitanya's Vaishṇavism that more orthodox schools would not accept was its inclusion of the *Bhāgavata Purāṇa* as a revealed text. Jīva Goswāmi also accepted revelation or authority (*śabda*) as the only truly authentic independent source of knowledge (Chakravarti, 1969:3–4). Narrowing the ways of knowing to one valid source increases the tendency toward a literal approach to the scriptures, and emphasizes the absolute authority of the spiritual master when revelation is extended to include as much as Chaitanyaism does. Although the more orthodox schools have varying interpretations of the *Vedas,* unlike the Bengal school they do not consider any of the *Puraṇas* nor the epics as of equal revelation or as the commentaries of the *Vedas* (Chakravarti, 1969:8–9). But the devotee of Krishna accepts unconditionally his paradoxical tenets of faith without needing recourse to logic.

Chaitanya's Philosophy in Outline. The philosophy of Chaitanya and his followers is known as *achintya bhedābheda* or the incomprehensible philosophy of unity in difference. It combines into one system elements of dualism and monism. Even though Chaitanya was not the originator of this system, his application of it to Vaishṇava thought

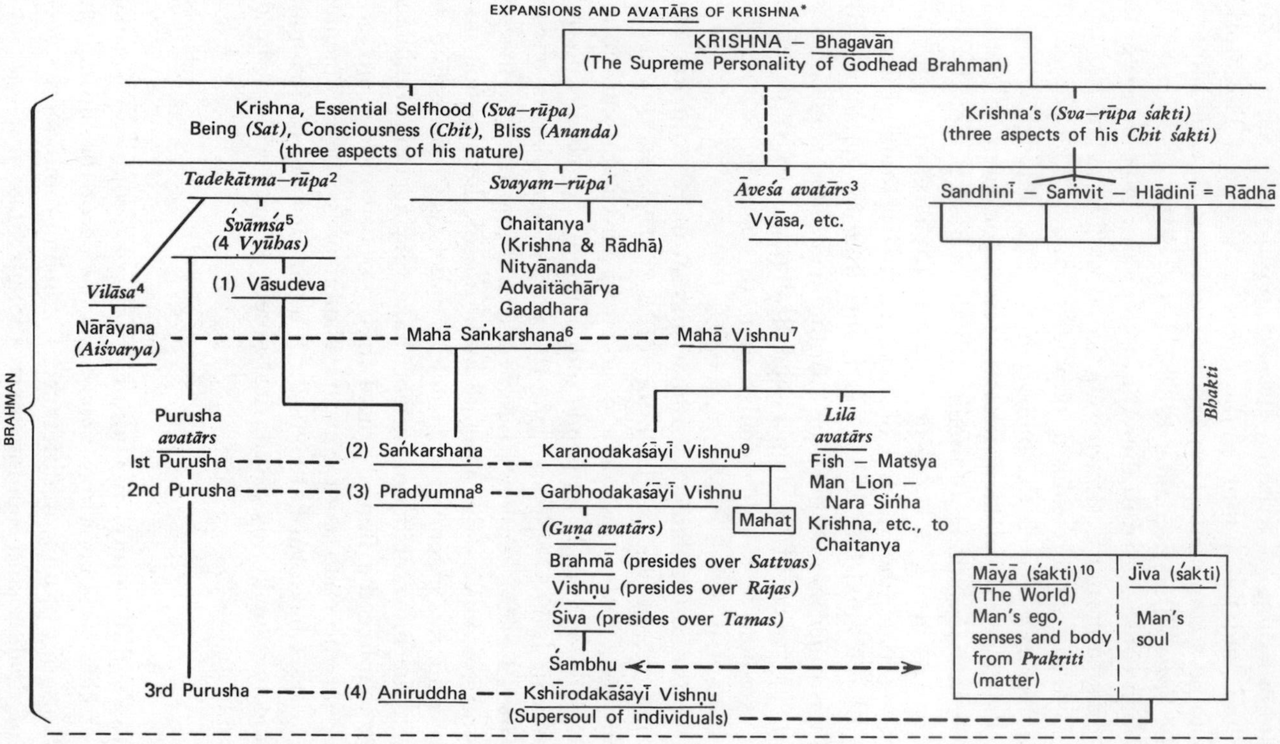

Figure 1. Geneology of the deities as expansions of Krishna.

marks perhaps its most significant development. Before we consider this philosophy in more detail, its main features must be introduced. Otherwise it is all too easy to lose one's way in the morass of categories with their divisions and subdivisions, which seem so often to delight Hindu philosophical minds. Even though only a brief outline of the principal features is attempted, the reader who is unfamiliar with Vaishṇavism may find the extreme complications of this type of Hindu philosophy confusing. The outline is drawn not only from the works of Bhaktivedanta, but also from the works of his spiritual master, Bhakti Siddhānta, other Gauḍīya scholars, and Hindu authorities on Chaitanyaism. To aid the reader to see the outline at a glance, Figure 1 gives a "geneological tree" of the relationships among the various deities and Krishna. The scholar's indulgence is requested for the oversimplification that unfortunately causes some distortion in the chart.

Krishna, the Supreme Personality of Godhead, is characterized by the Gauḍīya Vaishṇavas as existing in a number of different ways besides that of his original nature. Some *Upanishads* speak of an attributeless, differenceless reality, or Absolute, which they call Brahman. The followers of Chaitanya say, however, that this is only one aspect of Reality. The Ultimate Reality is Brahman with qualities. It is highly personalized as Krishna. Brahman is spirit in which individual living entities form a part without losing their identity. Bhaktivedanta teaches further that Brahman is the effulgence or halo of Krishna, the Brahmajyoti, which includes everything that exists. It is the complete whole, and is called material nature when the effulgence is covered by *māyā*, illusion or sense gratification (Bhaktivedanta, 1972b:12, 248, 261).

---

* Material for outline: BHAKTI Siddhānta, 1932:43–69; Chakravarti, 1969:70–75, 92–98, 128–168; De, 1961:240, 241–244.

[1] Krishna's self-existent nature.

[2] Form identical in essence but different in appearance.

[3] Entities inspired by Krishna, e.g., Vyāsa, traditional author of *Purāṇas.*

[4] Expansion of Krishna equal in power.

[5] Expansion of Krishna inferior in power.

[6] Extended personality of Nārāyaṇa.

[7] Mahā Vishṇ plenary part of Mahā Saṅkarshaṇa. Is totality of souls and matter in undifferentiated state; also is Advaitāchārya, a disciple of Chaitanya and part of this *avatār* of Keishna in later "pastime" (*līlā*).

[8] *Paramātman* as inner controller of selves in totality.

[9] Karaṇodakāśāyī Vishṇu, creator of Mahat.

[10] Māyā *śakti* as perverse aspect of *chit śakti.*

This personalization of Brahman as Krishna or his rays is characterized as having innumerable powers or energies (*śakti*). These are one with their possessor, Krishna, as well as being separate from him; they are both identical with him and yet different; they have varying degrees of personalization as well as different functions. The analogy of the sun and its rays has often been used to describe their relationship to Krishna. The sun's rays belong to the sun, originate from it, and are part of it. Still, as they go forth they are also entirely separate from it, and their action upon the earth has no effect upon the sun. This transcendent aspect of Krishna is known as the supreme spirit (*parā-brahman*), the Infinite Self, Lord Vishṇu or his own original nature (*sva-rūpa*). Its attendant internal power is his highest energy (*parā-śakti*) or the energy of his original nature (*sva-rūpa-śakti*).

Krishna (or Vishṇu) has the power to create living entities in which he then resides as the Supersoul. This he does through his marginal potency or energy (*jīva-śakti*). He creates the material universes through his external or inferior potency or energy (*māyā-śakti*).

He has also the power to expand himself into innumerable forms, which may be temporary or permanent. In these he often exists under various other names, according to their respective functions or the manner in which he expresses his power. Part of this power is the ability to descend to earth as an *avatār* when needed at a particular time in history. Finally, he has a type of descent in the form of an image, in order to receive the worship of his devotees. In his original form he is Bhagavān or Krishna, the cowherd deity of Vṛindāvan, according to the Gauḍīya Vaishṇavas and the Hare Krishna Movement.

Krishna therefore exists as a cosmic deity of infinite greatness as well as smallness; has expanded into other forms of deities bearing different names; has various *śaktis* or potencies. He is also a very personal deity who loves and seeks to be loved by his devotees. Through his scripturally recorded life and "pastimes" (*līlā*), his devotees may know him quite intimately. He is the supreme controller of all that exists, and nothing exists without him as its foundation. While including everything within himself, he completely transcends all creation, is forever separate from it and is unaffected by it in any way. And yet as a personal deity he is attendant to the slightest desire of each of his devotees, and when they dance and chant together the Hare Krishna *mantra,* Krishna is said to be dancing with them on the tongue of each.

Chaitanya's View as Mediating Synthesis of Hindu Philosophy. The Vaishṇavism of Chaitanya uniquely incorporates into one philosophical system the ideas of many varying and often contradictory views. In its own way it is able to use seemingly divergent literary sources ranging from the *Upanishads* to the *Purāṇas* and even the *Tantras.* Krishna's ability to take various forms allows him to be identified with many widely known deities and *avatārs* of the Hindu pantheon, such as Nārāyaṇa, Rāma, Brahmā, Vishṇu, and Śiva, as well as many more locally worshiped deities, such as Jagannātha, the "Lord of the World," at the famous temple in Purī. Thus Krishna becomes creator, preserver, and destroyer of all the material universes.

Because this Vaishṇava philosophy has aspects of both dualism and monism, it is able to reconcile ideas of the dualistic Sāṅkhya and Yoga systems with the nondualistic Vedānta. And because of the comprehensiveness of its system, like the *Bhagavad-gītā* it is able to give some validity to the varying schemes of salvation of these philosophies. It can point to them as steps along the way to the final liberation, which it believes all must eventually rediscover: the original consciousness of one's loving fellowship with Krishna in one of his spiritual worlds. One may obtain this by following the path of *bhakti-yoga.*

Krishna, the Cosmic Deity and Ocean of Bliss. Krishna's nature, according to this view, includes, therefore, the negative Brahman of Śaṅkara's nondualistic philosophy; the *paramātman,* the highest or transcendental self of the Yoga school; and the concept of a personal deity, who has majesty, beauty, wisdom, and power. This is Krishna, or Bhagavān.

As an expression of his majesty, he is Nārāyaṇa, "Lord of lords and God of gods." As the fulfillment of beauty which overpowers his majesty, Krishna, with Rādhā representing his ecstatic energy, is God of gods according to the Gauḍīya Vaishṇavas.

Krishna has three paramount attributes: *sat, chit,* and *ānanda.* Realization of the impersonal aspects of Brahman is the realization of his *sat* (being) nature. The cognition of his knowledge or *chit* characteristic is the *paramātman* realization, such as in Yoga. Finally, since Krishna is the ocean of *rasa,* the "ecstatic principle" or "relish," the true discovery of Krishna is the realization of bliss (*ānanda*), which in complete form includes the other two characteristics. Although a very small portion of this ecstatic principle is in man, man's subjection to the illusory *māyā,* Krishna's lower energy, perverts it to sensual pleasure.

Analogous to the three above inherent attributes of his original nature are three superior or internal energies or potencies: *sandhinī, saṁvit,* and *hlādinī.* These are attributes of his "spiritual power" (*chit-śakti*). *Sandhinī* signifies his power to produce all existence associated with the action of his ecstatic principle; *saṁvit* is the potency governing all spiritual relations and affections; and *hlādinī,* the most important of all, is his power to enjoy and to cause others to enjoy delights. It is this last energy, the basis for the other two, which is personalized as Rādhā, his consort. The description of Brahman as bliss and relish in the scriptures is interpreted to signify the unity in duality of Ultimate Reality, the unity of the energy and the possessor of the energy, which are personalized as Rādhā and Krishna finding completion in one another.

Krishna's own bliss becomes even more relishable for him when it is reflected in his devotees and associates, who are his spiritual parts. Then it is transformed into their intense love for him, which is *prema* or *bhakti* (Chakravarti, 1969:41, 48–49; Bhaktivedanta, 1972b:12–13; Bon Mahārāj, 1973:20–21).

Krishna's Expansions. Although the Vaishṇava literature tells of the many expansions and descents of Krishna, the Hare Krishna Movement venerates Krishna most highly as the cowherd deity who tends the cows and plays erotically with Rādhā and the other cowherdesses. In this sportive capacity as one who gives pleasure to the senses, he is often called Govinda.

Krishna's essential selfhood, his highest nature (*sva-rūpa*), has three major devisions: his personal form (*svayam-rūpa*), representing his self-existent nature; his hypostatic manifestation (*tadekātma-rūpa*), which is a form identical in essence but differing in appearances; and his *āveśa* form, in which he possesses or inspires a living entity (Chakravarti, 1969:141). His inspiration of Vyāsa to compose sacred texts is an example of Krishna as an *āveśa avatār.*

His personal form (*svayam-rūpa*) is again subject to various categories of divisions, according to the type of expansion. For example, he expanded himself into multiple forms when he danced the *rāsa* dance with the cowherdesses, so that he was actually dancing with each who took part. He also appeared in 16,108 forms to marry that many wives.

His *tadekātma-rūpa* form, or hypostatic manifestation, the second major division, also has two further divisions and subdivisions. If the expansion is equal in power with Krishna's self-existent nature (*svayam-rūpa*), it is called a *vilāsa*. Nārāyaṇa, representing Krishna's expansion as majestic power, is an example. If the expansion is less in power, it is called a *svāṃśā* manifestation (Chakravarti, 1969:141–142). Representative of this are the expansions into the original four-armed forms, the four *vyūhas* or manifestations as Vāsudeva, Saṅkarshaṇa, Pradyumna, and Aniruddha. Although these forms play an important part in the creative process in the earlier Pañcharātrā literature, the emphasis in the Gauḍīya philosophy is on the Purusha *avatārs*. From the *vyūhas* there are again twenty-four different manifestations with various names. These are all alike except that they have different arrangements of their symbols in their hands,—the mace, the disc, the lotus flower, and the conch shell. Bhaktivedanta has clarified this multiplicity of forms somewhat by pointing to the Supreme Original Personality of Godhead as Krishna ("the son of Nanda"), as he is in Vṛindāvan (Bhaktivedanta, 1968a:66, 70).

Krishna's *Avatārs*. Included also in the hypostatic manifestation are Krishna's descents or *avatārs*. There are first the three Purusha descents, representing three forms of Vishṇu who is himself a plenary expansion of Krishna: Kāraṇodakāśāyī Vishṇu, Garbhodakāśāyī Vishṇu, and Kshīrodakāśāyī Vishṇu. These have importance in the process of creation. Second, as the *guṇa* descents, Krishna expanded himself as Brahmā, the creator, Vishṇu, the preserver, and Śiva, the destroyer of the material manifestation at the end of a cycle. His *manvantara* descents, which are so many as to be uncountable, and his *yuga* and *āveśa* descents need not concern us here.*

There is also a list of twenty-five ** different descents called the *līlā*

* These terms are defined in the Glossary.
** Some authorities list twenty-four *avatārs* (Chakravarti, 1969:151).

(sport or pastime) *avatārs*. They include the boar, fish, man-lion, tortoise, dwarf, Balarāma, Krishna, Buddha, and a number of others until the twenty-fifth. This was the Kalki descent, the last to come during this cycle of creation. According to the Gauḍīya Vaishṇavas, this was Chaitanya (Chakravarti, 1969:178; Bhaktivedanta, 1968a:63–72, 75–78). Among the purposes for Krishna's descent were to make firm the belief in One Supreme Personality of Godhead and to further the cause of devotional service among all people.

At the time of Chaitanya, Krishna was said to have manifested himself through five different persons for as many different reasons, while still remaining one. The Gauḍīya Vaishṇavas and the Hare Krishna Movement teach that these were Chaitanya and his four associates: Nityānanda Prabhu, Advaitāchārya, Gadādhara, and Śrīvāsa. Of these Chaitanya was the descent of Krishna; Nityānanda and Advaitāchārya were his expansions. Gadādhara was a representation of Krishna's internal energy as a pure devotee; Śrīvāsa was his marginal energy as a confidential devotee. Chaitanya, however, was lord of all.

The Hare Krishna Movement regards Chaitanya as the embodiment of both Krishna and Rādhā. It is said that Krishna wanted to experience how Rādhā, his pleasure potency, gave him such pleasure. Therefore, he tried during the descent to live the part of Rādhā. Actually Rādhā and Krishna are one, but separated for Krishna's enjoyment. In order to understand himself through Rādhā, he united with her as Chaitanya (Bhaktivedanta, 1968a:157–161, 8–9).

Swāmi Bhaktivedanta says that even with all these expansions of the original Krishna of Vṛindāvan, there is really no difference in reality between the self of Krishna and the expansions. Varying manifestations execute unique activities. Therefore, even his original form of Vṛindāvan differs from the form that appeared on the battlefield of Kurukshetra, because of the inconceivable energy of his own Yogamāyā (Bhaktivedanta, 1965:855). This is the energy of his internal nature, which covers him so that only surrendered souls or devotees can ever see him (Bhaktivedanta, 1965:844; 1972b:515).

Krishna as Creator. The world is created out of Krishna's inferior energy. Since this potency is part of him, it can be said that the world is also contained within his wholeness. But because the energy is also different from him, according to the concept of *bhedābheda,* he also transcends the material creation and is unaffected by it.

Since the world actually represents a transformation of Krishna's ("Brahman's") energy, the Bengal school calls its doctrine *avikṛita-pariṇāmavāda,* or transformation without change (in Brahman). This distinguishes it from the *pariṇāmavāda* of earlier Vaishṇavite thought according to which Brahman itself has substantial modification during creation. Of course, according to the monistic view of Śaṅkara, the *vivartavāda* or doctrine of illusion, the world is only an unreal appearance (Chakravarti, 1969:46; Kavirāja, 1969d:503).

Krishna acts in creation by means of three Purushas, which link the thought of the Chaitanya school with the *Vedic* philosophy. We had noted earlier Nārāyaṇa's association with Purusha of the Purusha-*sūkta* or Purusha hymn (*Ṛig Veda* X, 90). The same identification for Krishna should cause no difficulty, if we remember that Nārāyaṇa is also believed to be a manifestation of Krishna. In the Vaishṇava philosophy, Purushottama or the highest Purusha which Swāmi Bhaktivedanta interprets as the Supreme Person, is identified with Krishna. Purusha or "the enjoyer," as the spiritual master defines the word, is Vishnu, the Supersoul in each living entity (Bhaktivedanta, 1972b:514, 648).

The three Purushas are identified with three forms of Mahā-Vishṇu, or Vishṇu regarded as including his three manifestations. Vishṇu here, according to Bhakti Siddhānta Sarasvatī Goswāmi, is the plenary portion of Mahā-Saṅkarshaṇa. The latter is a form of Balarāma, and is also identified with Nityānanda. Mahā-Vishṇu is also Advaitāchārya, according to the *Caitanya Caritāmṛita* (Bhakti Siddhānta, 1932:44; Kavirāja, 1959a:85).

Kāraṇodakāśāyī Vishṇu, the first Purusha, is the cause of all causes, and lies in the cosmic causal ocean beyond the highest spiritual world. In his person he holds all the universes. He is the creator of Mahat, the universal intelligence, that is, the principle of intelligence, the eleven senses, the five elements, and so forth. He becomes the cause of the universe when he casts his glance toward Māyā, Krishna's inferior energy.

From the pores on the body of Mahā-Vishṇu many universes emanate. With each breath he exhales, they are produced through

Brahmā, the predominating deity of each universe. As he inhales, each universe and its creator, Brahmā, disappears within him.

Garbodakāśāyī Vishṇu, the second Purusha, lies in a middle ocean. From his navel a lotus springs, and through the agency of Brahmā, who emerges from the flower, the world is created. This same Purusha also sustains and destroys he world, in his capacity as the *guṇa* descents, Vishṇu and Śiva.

Kshīrodakāśāyī Vishṇu, the third Purusha descent who lies in the ocean of milk, is the Supersoul of the individual beings (Bhaktivedanta, 1972a:75; 1972b:519; Bhakti Siddhānta, 1932:150; Kavirāja, 1959a:69; 1959d:506; Chakravarti, 1969:150).

Krishna never has direct contact with his material energy. According to Bhakti Siddhānta, the glance at Māyā made by Vishṇu, as the plenary portion of Mahā-Saṅkarshaṇa, is far removed from the deluding energy. Even here Vishṇu acts through his spiritual potency, Romā, who carries the function of his glance. Romā, consort of Vishṇu, is the regulatrix of all beings.

At creation, a halo appears. This halo is Śambhu (Śiva), the masculine symbol of Vishṇu and the "twilight reflection of Krishna's effulgence." The symbol functions as the masculine progenitor of the world. The conceiving potency is Māyā, "symbol of mundane feminine productivity." Through the intercourse of these two the faculty of perverted cognition is produced. This is a mere "reflection of the seed of the procreative desire of the Supreme Lord." Bhakti Siddhānta explains further that Māyā's generative organ is again only a shadow of Romā, Vishṇu's divine energy. Thus mankind in his conditioned state is a perversion of the spiritual energy of Krishna. Bhakti Siddhānta says, however, that when the *jīvas,* the spiritual parts of the Oversoul, come to realize themselves to be eternal servants of Krishna, they will have no relationship to the mundane world. They will then have liberation (Bhakti Siddhānta, 1932:44–51).

The world is only a temporary manifestation of Krishna's lower energy; Nature, though eternal reality, is covered temporarily by *māyā*. Therefore, all phenomena of which we may become aware, including our bodies, are called *māyā*. Because they are also Krishna's energy, his *prakṛiti,* however, they are also real and thus reflect a bit of himself, even though perverted. Swāmi Bhaktivedanta says that Nature is like a shadow of reality in the platonic sense of Book VII of Plato's *Republic* (Bhaktivedanta, 1967:7–8; 1968b:169).

Future Life and Spiritual Worlds. The world and its conditioned entities last for four billion, three hundred million years, after which all creation, including hundreds of thousands of universes, the living entities, and even all of the Brahmās, the creators, are inhaled back into the body of Vishṇu. There they remain during the night of Brahmā for many millions of years, until the Brahmā of each universe is reborn with Vishṇu's next breath. Then the living souls are again manifested. Those, however, who had previously become Krishna Conscious would have been transferred to Goloka-Vṛindāvan, where they live eternally blissful and happy. This spiritual world is described as a place where desire trees grow that give any type of food requested, and where all desires are granted. There one finds beautiful palaces in which to reside, and *surabhi* cows or "cows of plenty" that give all the milk one can drink. There too Krishna lives in all his beauty, tends his cows as he plays his flute, and participates in the *rāsa* dance, while hundreds of thousands of goddesses of fortune serve him. Although Krishna always remains in this wholly spiritual realm, through his material energy he still pervades the entire material world.

Goloka-Vṛindāvan is part of the Vaikuṇtha spiritual planetary system, consisting of many spiritual planets over which millions of Krishna's four-armed plenary expansions govern. It is a manifestation of Krishna's internal and higher energy, just as the material worlds are the products of his lower exterior energy. As a system it is beyond all material planets of which the very highest is Brahmaloka, the abode of the creator, Brahmā. If one does not attain Vaikuṇtha, he will not be able to escape the sufferings of material existence—birth, disease, old age, and death—no matter on what material planet he is reborn (Bhaktivedanta, 1968b:35, 193–194; 1972b:431–433; 1972d:42, 85; Kavirāja, 1959a:66).

Those who are not Krishna Conscious may be subject to continual reincarnation. Where a person is reborn and even in what form and condition is dependent upon his *karma,* the deeds he has previously performed. Because of his particular material desires he may be reborn as a demigod, a man, or a beast. Until one has Krishna Consciousness he is under the influence of the three modes of material nature which give him a material consciousness. This continually causes him to reincarnate.

Where one spends his next life is also conditioned by his worship. Swāmi Bhaktivedanta says that one who worships the sun god, goes to the sun; one worshipping Indra attains his particular planet. Every planet is governed by a particular demigod. This, however, is not final liberation. The demigods, like the living entities, are all parts of the body of Krishna; they are as perishable as are the results of worshiping them. This belief specifies that the demigods themselves are only living entities as we are. They too will vanish at the end of the material world. Therefore, one is enjoined to seek beyond the temporary material gratifications that the demigods can give (Bhaktivedanta, 1968b:35–36, 1972b:396, 647, 234). This entails a life of serving Krishna entirely for his pleasure.

The love sport of Krishna with Rādhā surpasses even conjugal love; the friendliness of Sakhīs (female friends) alone may reach it. This love-*līlā* grows through Rādhā's loving friends. This means that none but the female friends of Rādhā can know and realize this love.

Kavirāja tells of the inexplicableness of the female friends who attend Rādhā, for they do not seem to desire any loving association with Krishna. They wish only to help Rādhā in such association. By such help they attain a greater joy than their own association with Krishna could give them.

Rādhā is compared to a vine of love, and the female friends are its leaves, sprouts, and flowers. By pouring the nectar of love on the root of the creeper, the sprouts and leaves receive nourishment and pleasure much greater than if the nectar were scattered on themselves. The consummation of Rādhā's love with Krishna means the consummation for all, since they are all of the same nature as Rādhā. Therefore, even though they have no desire for the loving association with Krishna, Rādhā causes this association to happen, because "she is in them as they are in her."

At other times, however, she sends Krishna to them, and then she herself receives greater joy than from her own association with him. Thus the *Caitanya Caritāmṛita* says that this is the love for which devotees of Krishna aspire. This love, however, we are again reminded, only resembles sexual love, but really transcends it. It is not for self-gratification, but only for Krishna's satisfaction (Kavirāja, 1959b:169–171). Although men and women may aspire to such a high condition in relationship to Krishna, they cannot attain to the reality of Rādhā.

In the development of Krishna Consciousness there are five different stages of growth or tastes. These correspond to various kinds of devotional feelings with which one responds to the deity. The first stage is designated as *śānta,* which means "peaceful." At this stage one can fix his mind steadfastly upon Krishna with faith and with no material desires. The second stage is *dāsya,* signifying that one regards himself as an eternal servant of Krishna. If one feels like treating Krishna on an equal level with love and respect as a friend, this is the *sakhya* state. Or maybe he develops the fondness of a parent for him. This would be *vātsalya,* expressing the fourth degree of advancement. In this stage, "instead of the Lord being worshipped, the living entity as a parent of the Supreme Person becomes the object of worship for the Supreme Person." He has the feeling of being the "maintainer of the Supreme Personality of Godhead." Finally, the *mādhurya* status is the conjugal relationship of a lover. All higher stages contain the qualities of those preceding them (Bhaktivedanta, 1968a:32–38).

These stages can be reached by following sixty-four carefully set rules—this is the regular process or *vaidhī.* Or they can be reached spontaneously (*rāgānugā*), perhaps as an outgrowth of the first process. A person who follows the discipline carefully over a period of time may develop a passionate desire for mystic union with the deity. In this way, he finally transcends the rules of the regular process. It has been said that this is the type represented by the cowherdesses in the spiritual world of Vṛindāvan.

This Vaishṇava view declares that the essential nature of mankind partakes of the *hlādinī* energy of Krishna, which is the feminine counterpart of Krishna's *ānanda* (bliss) quality. In its highest form this is personalized as Rādhā, and as a part of her energy some may experience part of the ecstacy of her love for Krishna. Further, this love (*prema*), which is the nature of man's spiritual expression in his pristine state and to which he must return, has been perverted by materiality. Its lower expression is mankind's lust (*kāma*), the physical manifestation on earth.

Swāmi Bhakti Siddhānta teaches that we can approach Krishna with our "confidential service" in any one of his five ways, which is not the case in his other forms. Moreover, Krishna "would always wish His devotees to accept Him as the Consort, if they have the capacity" (Bhakti Siddhānta, 1967:73–74).

When the Gauḍīya Vaishṇava philosopher, Swāmi B. H. Bon Mahārāj, was interviewed at Vṛindāvan, India, he expressed the opinion that all will not have the same possibilities. The permanent relationship between anyone and Krishna is an eternal one. Therefore, a man's highest relationship to Krishna as a *mañjarī,* in his highest heaven world, is not for everyone. Let us examine the concept in context. Krishna is absolute beauty and Rādhā is really Krishna's projection of himself in beauty, since there can be only one absolute. That beauty serves Krishna's demands for a maximum of love. When Krishna sees his own projection, a wave of bliss flows in his heart. Rādhā does not see this beauty in his face, "but the beauty of bliss flowing in his heart as an effect of his seeing his own beauty in the beauty of Rādhā." She reciprocates by being happy upon seeing the happiness of Krishna. One who sees the bliss in Rādhā's heart is called a *sakhī* (friend), according to the Gauḍīya Vaishṇavas. These friends of Rādhā can see the real form of bliss flowing in Rādhā's heart as a reflection of Rādhā's seeing the bliss flowing in Krishna's heart. One who sees the bliss flowing in the heart of a friend of Rādhā is called a *mañjarī* in the Gauḍīya school. This only applies to those attaining the conjugal stage. The other, lower relationships are supreme for those souls to which they apply.

Therefore, it would seem that the highest relationship is between Rādhā and Krishna, in which Rādhā is Krishna's projection. Next is the projection of Rādhā into eight friends of Rādhā and a number of mistresses. The friends of Rādhā in turn project themselves into *mañjarīs,* the highest possibility for individual souls, which is a blissful state in loving conjugal relationship with Krishna in the heavenly world of Goloka-Vṛindāvan.

Krishna, the Cowherd Deity of Vṛindāvan. The most important source the Gauḍīya Vaishṇavas and the Hare Krishna Movement have used for the biography of Krishna has been the tenth canto of the *Bhāgavata Purāṇa.* They consider its events to have occurred approximately 5000 years ago.

The pastimes or events in Krishna's life in his original form are of greatest importance to the young "Vaishṇavas" of the Hare Krishna Movement. They are tenets of living faith. Moreover, his loving affairs with the cowherdesses, Bhaktivedanta says, "are exactly like the loving affairs between young girls and boys within this material world." According to him, the attraction we have contains the same sex feeling that is in Krishna, but more minutely and pervertedly because of our conditioned state. Therefore, while these pleasures appear materialistic, just listening to them causes us to lose our lust as we become more spiritual (Bhaktivedanta, 1970c:xxi).

Since these pastimes are also to be considered as both eternal and transcendental, even a person little advanced in absolute knowledge may be able to think of these and receive full benefit. Swāmi Bhaktivedanta says that this is because there is no difference between the pastimes and the actual form of Krishna; his name and form are identical. Likewise those who are absorbed in devotional service in full Krishna Consciousness are not to be considered as being in the material world (Bhaktivedanta, 1970c:20–21). Chanting the names of Krishna puts one on the spiritual plane.

Therefore, these recorded events in the life of Krishna, miraculous though they be, are more than mere occurrences in history. They are eternal, because Krishna includes within himself all that is or ever was. This transcendental and eternal nature is revealed quite clearly in one recorded event. It is told that on one occasion when Krishna was a young boy he had reportedly been eating some clay. On looking into his mouth, his mother saw the entire space of the world with its mountains and rivers, as well as the other planets and stars. She saw herself also, as she was some time before, taking the baby Krishna on her lap to nurse him (Bhaktivedanta, 1970c:61–62).

Krishna's advent on earth at Vṛindāvan, Swāmi Bhaktivedanta says, was due to the strife occurring among demoniac kings. The creator deity, Brahmā, at the request of Bhūmi, the predominating deity of the earth, laid his case before Vishṇu. The latter lay in the ocean of milk on the planet called Śvetadvīpa. In this form, as Kshīrodakāśāyī Vishṇu, he is the source of all incarnations in this universe. As a result of this plea, Krishna was to appear as the son of Vāsudeva along with the incarnated forms of demigods and their wives who were to assist him. At this time Vāsudeva, the son of King Surāsena of the district of Mathurā, had just married Devakī, and was being driven by her brother, Kaṁsa, to her father-in-law's home. All was quite pleasant until a voice was heard from the heavens informing Kaṁsa that the eighth child of his sister would kill him some day. Kaṁsa, the most evil of the Bhoja dynasty of kings, was only prevented from killing his sister immediately because of Vāsudeva's promise to turn over to him any sons that his sister might bear. After occupying the kingdom of Surāsena and other neighboring realms, Kaṁsa became the most powerful king of that part of India. One by one, he killed Devakī's first six children as they were born.

At the time Vishṇu arranged that his plenary expansion, Ananta Śeshanāga, should be conceived by Devakī. In his original form he is a giant cobra who holds all the planets on the hoods of his millions of heads. Through the power of Yogamāyā, the embryo that Devakī carried was transferred to the womb of Vāsudeva's other wife, Rohiṇī. The latter and many others fled from the wrath of Kaṁsa, and she was residing at the home of King Nanda and Queen Yaśodā in Vṛindāvan. The child she would bear would be Balarāma, the brother of Krishna.

Krishna, the eighth child of Devakī, entered in his original form first within the heart of Vāsudeva and was then transferred to Devakī from his mind to hers. Although Krishna appeared with all his plenary expansions in the body of Devakī, it is understood that he was in no way subject to materiality. His body transcended all matter.

Both Devakī and Vāsudeva had been imprisoned by Kaṁsa at his home. After Krishna's forthcoming birth was announced to Devakī by demigods, Krishna was born to her during the night in the form of the four-armed Vishṇu. Recognizing him as Vishṇu or Krishna, and being afraid that he would be too easily recognized by Kaṁsa, Vāsudeva prayed that he assume his two-armed form. Vishṇu replied by first requesting that he be taken immediately to Gokula (Vṛindāvan) to replace the daughter that was being born to Yaśodā. Having so spoken he took the form of a normal human baby. At that very moment, Yogamāyā, the internal potency of Krishna, was born to Yaśodā. Through her influence Vāsudeva was able to carry Krishna away and make the substitution undetected. Even Yaśodā, asleep after the labor of childbirth, did not remember whether her child was a boy or girl. On hearing the cries of the newborn baby, Kaṁsa intended to dash her against a stone despite the pleas of Devakī. The child slipped from his hands, however, and ascended to the sky where she assumed her eight-armed form as Durgā, the younger sister of Vishṇu. From above she rebuked him and announced that one who would kill him had already been born somewhere else (Bhaktivedanta, 1970c:1–12, 22–33). From this time on, Krishna grew up with his brother in Vṛindāvan.

In Vṛindāvan, when the cowherds and the cowherdesses learned that Nanda, the father of Krishna, was celebrating the birth of Krishna, they were exceedingly joyful. They came bringing presents and offered them to the savior, the infant Krishna, just as gifts were offered to another child born in a manger.

Kaṁsa was relentless in his attempts to find and kill Krishna. At the advice of his counselors, Kaṁsa at first decided to slay all children born in the time and place of Krishna's birth. After the birth ceremony, Nanda went up to Mathurā to pay his tax to Kaṁsa's government. Vāsudeva came to see him concerning Balarāma and Krishna. He was worried about Krishna because of Kaṁsa's search for him.

On one occasion while Krishna was still an infant, Kaṁsa sent a witch named Pūtanā to find and kill him. She entered without permission the county of Gokula, where she visited Yaśodā. Because of her beauty all thought that she was the goddess of fortune paying her respects to Krishna. On finding Krishna, she offered him her breast, which was smeared with poison. Thereupon Krishna took it into his mouth and immediately killed her by sucking out the very life from her body.

On another occasion Krishna, at the instigation of Kaṁsa, was seized by the demon Tṛiṇāvarta, who by taking the form of a whirlwind carried Krishna high into the sky. Krishna, although still a very small boy, assumed such a weight that the demon crashed to the ground and was killed. Krishna was later found by cowherdesses happily playing on the demon's body (Bhaktivedanta, 1970c:43–45, 53–54).

As the boys grew older, they became extremely mischievous. One of their tricks was to steal butter and yogurt and distribute them to the monkeys. On one occasion Krishna stole the clothes of the young cowherdesses (*gopīs*) when they were swimming in the Jumna River.

It is related that Krishna was also responsible for killing or subduing many more demons, among them the Aghāsura demon, who was in the shape of a serpent, and Kāliya, a great water snake who was polluting the Jumna River with his poison.

Vaishṇavas also recall his pastime concerning Govardhana Hill, where he and Balarāma tended their cows accompanied by the other cowherds. The occasion began when Krishna criticized the cowherds for preparing a sacrifice to the demigod Indra, to thank him for bringing needed rain clouds. Krishna said that as Vaiśyas tending cows, they had no need to make such a sacrifice—performing their duties as Vaiśyas should be sufficient to satisfy the demigods. Therefore, they should perform a sacrifice for Govardhana Hill instead. To let them know that the hill and Krishna were identical, Krishna then assumed a transcendental form and proclaimed that he was Govardhana Hill. When the sacrifice was performed, Indra in great anger sent a devastating rainstorm. When the people and cows were beginning to suffer from the effects, Krishna picked up Govardhana Hill, just as a child might pluck a mushroom. He held it over the cows and inhabitants of Vṛindāvan like an umbrella, balancing it on the little finger of his left hand. It is related that Indra then realized that he had been puffed up with his own importance and that Krishna was really his master. It had been hard for him to believe that Krishna was actually living in Vṛindāvan among the cowherds. Thus he came down to seek out Krishna, in order to confess his mistake and to apologize (Bhaktivedanta, 1968c:166–182). At this time Krishna was seven years old; it was one year before the famous *rāsa* dance began.

The *rāsa* dance with the *gopīs,* it is said, takes place on the "platform" or plane of Yogamāyā representing Krishna's interior potency, rather than *māyā,* his lower external energy. Swāmi Bhaktivedanta says that the dancing of "ordinary young boys and girls" would be *māyā*. The distinction between these two potencies is parallel to that between lust and love. Following the thought of the *Caitanya Caritāmṛita,* he says that lust means sense gratification for one's self, while love is sense gratification, but only for the sake of Krishna. Accordingly, these two, lust and love, exhibit the distinction that exists between material and spiritual activities, or that between material consciousness and Krishna Consciousness.

Since all the cowherdesses who loved Krishna and wanted him as their husband appeared to be married, the feeling they had was that of a paramour's love, which is called *parakīya-rasa.* However, as the supreme enjoyer, Krishna is already in reality in one sense their husband. Everyone belongs to Krishna. The cowherdesses in Goloka-Vṛindāvan, the heaven world, share this sentiment of *parakīya-rasa,* which represents the highest relationship one may have with Krishna. Since the material world is the perverted reflection of the spiritual world, it is said that there is no possibility of enjoying such a relationship when conditioned by matter.

When the full moon rose just one year following the Govardhana event, Krishna was desirous of dancing with the cowherdesses. He began playing his flute, which completely enchanted them, and they became lustful to give Krishna his sensual satisfaction. Regardless of what they were doing at the moment, they left their homes to see Krishna. Even though admonished by their guardians, they still rushed forth. This shows, as Bhaktivedanta instructs us, that when one is attracted to Krishna and has Krishna Consciousness, worldly duties are no longer a concern.

When the cowherdesses had all assembled they were surprised by the politeness of Krishna's manner. While complimenting them on their appearance, he rebuked them for going out without protection and for leaving their families. While he had appreciated their love for him as the Supreme Personality of Godhead, he told them that faithfulness to their husbands was the best religious principle. Bhaktivedanta says that he spoke with no sarcasm, but stressed the importance of feminine chastity. But when the cowherdesses' love for Krishna developed, the case was different. They were not ordinary women in the conditional state. In essence they were the same as he. They were the expansions of his pleasure potency. Nevertheless, they were saddened because of his chastisement. They begged that he might accept them not as his wives, but as his maidservants to satisfy his transcendental desires. They emphasized that Krishna was actually the only male, the only enjoyer. "Everyone is meant to be enjoyed by you," they said. Having heard their pleas, Krishna relented. He embraced and kissed them as they wished. All enjoyed these pastimes, which were without any trace of mundane sensuality.

Later he began to dance with them. In order to appear to dance with each one alone, he expanded himself into as many forms as there were cowherdesses. He clapped his hands to the rhythm of their singing. The more they danced the more attracted to him they became. Some cowherdesses touched his cheek with theirs, and Krishna offered them betel nuts he had already chewed, which they exchanged with him to their great pleasure by kissing. So enthralled were they with the love for Krishna, the husband of the goddess of fortune, that they completely forgot their own husbands. As he embraced them, they forgot everything. They became filled with spiritual energy. With hair and garments scattered, they completely forgot themselves. Since they had earlier prayed to the goddess Kātyāyanī to have Krishna as their husband, he now enjoyed them "exactly as a husband."

After these dances, the cowherdesses who were attracted to Krishna wanted to be with him at all times. Since they could not associate with him during the day, they had strong feelings of separation. Chaitanya encouraged these feelings among his followers as a transcendental pleasure.

Swāmi Bhaktivedanta warns, however, that this dance must not be misunderstood. Among the points he makes are the following. Krishna could not have been lustful in a material sense, since he was only eight years old at the time. Second, Krishna, as the supreme authority, need not adhere to the rules of the material world. Like the raising of the Govardhana Hill, the dance should therefore be regarded as an extraordinary activity that cannot be imitated by an ordinary person. Rather, since people in general have duties to perform, they should follow the instructions that Krishna gave in the *Bhagavad-gītā*. Swāmi Bhaktivedanta points to the danger of imitating Krishna, because Krishna neither suffers nor enjoys the effects of his action. He transcends all activities and all religions or irreligious principles. Third, only a great sage or devotee completely cleansed of his material conditioning by Krishna Consciousness can act freely without being materially contaminated. Only then can one transcend the laws of pleasure and pain according to the three modes of material nature. Fourth, in answer to the moralist's query concerning why Krishna should perform the *rāsa* dance, Swāmi Bhaktivedanta replies that it is a special mercy to those who have fallen into this conditioned state. It offers to those who are attracted by sexual pleasures in the material world a chance to "enjoy the same life with Krishna," and to escape from material conditioning. By listening to these transcendental pastimes with the cowherdesses, they will be liberated from the contamination of the material world (Bhaktivedanta, 1970c:188–207; 214–223). It is said that the people of Vṛindāvan, by remembering all his pastimes, enjoyed a transcendental bliss.

The sage, Nārada, desiring to bring affairs to a fulfillment disclosed

Krishna's identity and dwelling place to Kaṁsa. The latter, after again sending various demons to destroy Krishna and Balarāma to no avail, invited both boys to Mathurā to engage in a wrestling match. There he intended to kill them, if not before. When the messenger arrived at Vṛindāvan, Krishna and Balarāma were then in the "spring of their youth" and were at the time supervising the milking of the cows. The next morning they set out for Mathurā together with all the cowherds. Upon their arrival all gathered to see them. The women were immediately attracted to them; they embraced Krishna and Balarāma mentally and became ecstatic.

While passing along the street, Krishna and Balarāma met a washerman who was a servant of Kaṁsa. When Krishna promised him good fortune if he would give him some clothing, the washerman refused. He angrily rebuked Krishna for requesting clothing meant for the king, and warned him against doing so again. At this, Krishna killed the man by severing his head with a blow from his upper hand. He and Balarāma then dressed themselves as they desired, and offered the rest of the clothes to the cowherd boys. However, Krishna offered salvation in a body like Nārāyaṇa Vishṇu's in the spiritual world of Vaikuṇtha to a tailor whom they met and who prepared suitable clothing for Krishna and his brother.

When the two boys entered the wrestling ring the next day, they fought and killed all the leading wrestlers, and the others fled. Krishna then turned on Kaṁsa and killed him. Like all enemies who fight with Krishna, however, he received immediate salvation. Because he had been thinking of Krishna continually for many years, we are told that he attained a form like Vishṇu's and was also sent to the high heaven world of Vaikuṇtha.

Krishna and Balarāma then freed their parents, Vāsudeva and Devakī, whom Kaṁsa had imprisoned. Falling at their feet, Krishna and Balarāma offered prayers to them. Since Krishna's parents knew his divine status and were standing reverently, by use of his higher energy Krishna made it possible for them to treat him and his brother as children. Krishna then humbled himself to Vāsudeva and Devakī, saying that each person owes an unpayable debt to his parents for giving them the benefits of human existence, since it is only through human life that one may find liberation. Therefore, one who does not try to give his parents satisfaction by his actions is to be punished and made to eat his own flesh after death. Vāsudeva and Devakī could not answer Krishna; they merely embraced their two sons in great affection (Bhaktivedanta, 1970c:231–282). Thus, honoring one's parents is an important virtue in the Hare Krishna Movement, even as it is in the Judeo-Christian tradition.

When Krishna grew to young manhood he married Rukminī in the *rakshasa* style—by kidnapping her. He then escaped to the fort called Dvārakā, which he had built for the protection of the Yādavas, who had made him their king. According to the *Caitanya Caritāmṛita,* Rukminī is the supreme goddess of fortune, Mahā-Lakshmī, who is one of the many expansions of Rādhā through her internal potency (Bhaktivedanta, 1970c:349–350).

Even though his pastimes are considered transcendental, it is declared that Krishna lived for 125 years in this Vṛindāvan incarnation. As a youth, it is said that he never appears more than twenty to twenty-five years old (Bhaktivedanta, 1970d:100; 1970c:xii; 1972b:223; 1972c:738). Krishna finally disappeared from the world, however, after he was shot with an arrow by a hunter. Swāmi Bhaktivedanta reminds us that his body was only the "material conception" of his form, his *virāṭa-rūpa,* the same as was seen at the battle of Kurukshetra. Therefore, he left the "so-called material body in the material world." Krishna, however, is regarded as including everything by means of his energy or potency, and is at the same time both one and different from matter. He is not an ordinary mortal (Bhaktivedanta, 1972c:738).

CHAPTER FOUR

MAN AND HIS RELATION TO KRISHNA

Man's Nature. Man's true nature is spirit. While part of Krishna, he is in a conditioned state with a material body. Since both spirit and matter are rooted in Krishna's nature, however, they are not to be considered as unreal, but as covered over by illusory *māyā*. Man has five component parts: the Supersoul, the individual soul, the material body, Time, and activities. Four of these are eternally related to Krishna.

The Supersoul, the *paramātman,* exists in each living entity as Vishṇu. According to Swāmi Bhaktivedanta, the practice of *yoga* is meant to discover this localized aspect of Vishṇu within one's heart (Bhaktivedanta, 1968b:157–158). It is in the capacity of the Supersoul that Krishna acts as the inner controller of man's actions. Although Krishna is the controller, as Vishṇu he allows man certain freedoms. If man wants to gratify his senses, he is free to do so, but he must pay the consequent penalty. In fact it is said that Krishna "created this material world for the conditioned souls to learn how to perform *Yajñas* (sacrifices) for the satisfaction of Vishṇu" (Bhaktivedanta, 1968b:94).

The individual soul (*jīva*) and the source of man's consciousness is both one with and yet distinct from the Supersoul. Man's soul is qualitatively one with Krishna as part of his marginal energy (*jīva-śakti*), but quantitatively is atomic in size. It is called his marginal energy because it is intermediate between his internal and external potencies, his higher and lower energies.

Third, there is the material body. The soul is the proprietor of its own body, but Krishna is the proprietor of all. The conditioned soul, although transcendental, is trapped in material existence. Its natural body is subject to the three modes of nature according to its *karma.* Man's false ego, his intelligence, the five senses, and the mind are all representations of the material conceptions. Taken together they are all part of man's material body, which is a nonpermanent entity composed of *prakṛiti* (Bhaktivedanta, 1972b:622–623, 625–626, 628; Bhakti Siddhānta, 1967:99–100).

The living entity, or soul, is composed of superior *prakṛiti.* There is also inferior *prakṛiti,* which is Krishna's lower material nature. Although this manifestation is temporary, it is not false, according to the Vaishṇava teaching. Material nature is energy that is separated from Krishna, while the living entities are unseparated energy, and are eternally related. Another difference between the higher and lower *prakṛiti* is that the former has consciousness similar to Krishna's but never as expanded. Man's consciousness is perverted because of his material conditioning, whereas Krishna even during a descent is unaffected by matter. Because of our conditioned consciousness we identify ourselves with our material bodies. We believe that we are enjoyers and are lords of the material world, when it is Krishna who is enjoyer and creator. We are the created and the enjoyed.

The road to liberation from this conditioned state is *bhakti,* which is said to purify our activities because devotion to Krishna is transcendental to material conditioning. Swāmi Bhaktivedanta considers this the first step. (Bhaktivedanta, 1972b:8–11).

Matter is divided into three modes or *guṇas:* goodness (*sattva*), passions (*rājas*), and ignorance (*tamas*). These form various combinations under the control of eternal Time, the fourth element of man. These modes of matter cause activities (*karma*), his fifth component part, to come into being. Although these productions comprising conditional man are only temporary, they are not false. All of man's component parts, with the exception of his *karma,* are eternally related to Krishna. Because he has this partly material nature in his present state, he is conditioned by these three material modes. The mode of goodness, being the purest, frees one from sinful reactions. It gives man a sense of happiness and allows him to develop knowledge. This very achievement, however, keeps him bound and prevents his liberation.

The mode of passions develops in him a desire for material enjoyment, such as a wife, children, and a home, as well as honor in society or in the nation; it gets him to work hard to achieve his goal.

Consequently, he again becomes bound by becoming too closely associated with the fruits of his work.

The mode of ignorance leads to degradation and madness. Swāmi Bhaktivedanta says that this is best exemplified by people working hard to accumulate money with little care for the eternal spirit.

The mode of goodness leads to rebirth on a higher planet; the mode of passions brings one back to reengage in more activities for their rewards; but the mode of ignorance allows the possibility of rebirth as an animal (Bhaktivedanta, 1968b:265–268).

Man in this conditioned life enjoys or suffers from the fruits of his actions, but is in bondage. Although the Supersoul employing a type of prevenient grace is continually giving him directions on how to act, the living entity being controlled by his *karma* forgets what to do. Having determined to act in one way he becomes entangled by the fruits of his action and becomes frustrated. In this way he goes from life to life until a time arrives when he is in the mode of goodness and decides to end his bondage through *bhakti* (Bhaktivedanta, 1968b:26–28).

Man's Fall and His Salvation. The title of the Hare Krishna Movement's periodical, *Back to Godhead,* reflects the view that man's present conditioned state is not his original one. Some time, somewhere we have all fallen from grace, and must therefore try to return to that Golden Age, back to Godhead. Swāmi Bhaktivedanta teaches that none can trace the living entity's entanglement in material energy. It is said to have existed even before the creation of the worlds, after which it simply manifested itself in its conditioned state. It is understood that there are other living entities who are like us, but who have never been so involved and are still living in the heavenly worlds of Krishna.

The reason for the fall of man is clear to the Vaishṇavas. To increase his own spiritual bliss through their loving devotion, Krishna expanded himself originally into many living persons (*jīvas*). As parts of him, they too participated in that happiness. But these entities were also given a partial degree of independence, which they misused. Therein lies the problem. Free will must be exercised with knowledge; because of his limited power, man became influenced by ignorance. The original love for Krishna became lust, and thus Krishna manifested the material creation in order that man might satisfy his lustful propensities. In this state man has forgotten his real nature. Consequently, he must be born and live in the material world. His actions are recorded, however, and he is subject to rewards and punishments both here and hereafter. Depending on his actions, he may be reborn on a higher planet due to his good deeds (Bhaktivedanta, 1968a:52–53; 1972b:204, 288, 488).

When I asked Swāmi Bhaktivedanta about man's fall from Krishna's spiritual worlds, he said: "Man has forgotten that he is the eternal servitor of Krishna. He wants to lord it over matter. He thinks that he is the controller." Because fallen man is the product of Krishna's marginal energy, a combination of spirit and matter, he has a propensity toward either good or evil. He wants to surrender to Krishna, but he also desires to be independent and to find sense gratification (Bhaktivedanta, 1968a:161).

Although this belief is analogous in some respects to the Christian doctrine of Original Sin, there are some differences. Believers of either faith are taught that people are born with the propensity to sin, and are already tainted by sin. But in orthodox Christianity this is seen as the heritage of Adam's fall. In the Vaishṇava faith, it was caused by man's lust and his own propensity to forget his eternal relationship as servitor of Krishna. These were mistakes each man made before creation. Chakravarti reminds us that ignorance (*avidyā*), as the origin of sin in Chaitanya's scheme, may be contrasted with Christianity's concept of sin as willful rebellion against God. He notes that Bengal Vaishṇavism does not put the same emphasis on sin and guilt as does Christianity, because man does not have a completely free choice of action.

Because man has forgotten his true relationship to Krishna, his only escape to liberation lies in accepting Krishna's grace, which is continually offered through his bona fide pure devotee. Man's task is to remove the obstacles so he may receive that grace (Chakravarti, 1969:386–388). Its acceptance results in Krishna Consciousness. This is liberation. At that time one will reach the state of which the *Bhāgavata Purāṇa* (5:5:2–3) speaks. No longer will one associate with people who are only interested in material life. One will accept from the world only the modicum necessary for minimum physical needs. One will have no selfish interests in wives, children, or money, but will be kind, calm, and free from anger.

The devotees of the Hare Krishna Movement enjoin everyone to remove the obstacles from their return to their original state of Krishna Consciousness by surrendering themselves to a bona fide spiritual master like Swāmi Bhaktivedanta, who is to be regarded as Krishna's representative on earth. They are taught that he will give them the proper guidance to lead them back to Krishna, if they follow the discipline. In essence they are to devote all their efforts, thoughts, and love to Krishna for his pleasure alone. As eternal servitors of Krishna, they will regain their original love for him as they attain Krishna Consciousness.

Ethical System. The ethical principles of the Hare Krishna Movement emphasize and reinforce its philosophical system. The search is for liberation from a world filled with misery. The injunction is to do that which will lead one to eternal happiness as a servitor of Krishna.

Because the soul has fallen into a material state, it is conditioned not only by the Supersoul, but also by its own *karma* and by the three modes of nature. Even though the Supersoul continually gives directions concerning one's actions, material conditioning causes man to often act in a sinful way, and "sometimes even against his will" (Bhaktivedanta, 1968b:128–130).

Cast down from the spiritual world as he is, man now has certain duties to perform. These duties are determined by the Hindu social system. The *Bhagavad-gītā* teaches that Krishna originated the four divisions of human society: the Brahmins, "the intelligent class belonging to the material mode of goodness"; the Kshatriyas, the administrative class born into the mode of passion; the Vaiśyas, the merchants, who are mixed between the modes of passion and ignorance; and the Śudras, the laboring class, who are in the "ignorant mode of material Nature." Krishna created these divisions to allow men to work according to their particular material modes. Bhaktivedanta declares, however, that a person who is in Krishna Consciousness is above all four classes (Bhaktivedanta, 1968b:120–121).

The social order requires the performance of specific duties, but the doer is enjoined to have no attachment to the reward or result. Duty performed in a disinterested manner leads one to liberation. One is not to be affected by either good or evil, since he will recognize that in the material world such dualities occur. Instead he should fix himself in the transcendental mode of Krishna Consciousness, which is unaffected by good and evil (Bhaktivedanta, 1968b:83).

Although there has been dissension among the followers of Chaitanya over the recognition of each caste's birthrights, the position of Chaitanya seems fairly clear, as indicated in Kavirāja's *Caitanya Caritāmṛita.* This is the position supported by Swāmi Bhaktivedanta. When the scholar Sarvabhauma asked Chaitanya why Īśvara Purī, his *guru,* had allowed a Śudra to be his disciple, he answered: "The Lord God, oh Sarvabhauma, is entirely without prejudice. And his mercy does not observe the injunctions of the *Vedas.* It knows no distinction of caste or creed." And again Chaitanya said: "Even Śudras if they have faith in Lord God are the best class of saints; and those that have no such faith are indeed Śudras whatever caste they might belong" (Kavirāja, 1959b:233, 142).

Bhaktivedanta too observes that Krishna recognizes even a low caste person who is a devotee above a learned Brahmin who is not one. A Brahmin who is not a devotee of Krishna is to be regarded as the lowest of the low. According to Swāmi Bhaktivedanta, a civilized society should follow the rules laid down for its particular divisions so as to have a peaceful administration of the social life. For spiritual advancement, however, all should abide by the four traditional Hindu stages or *āśramas* marking the four periods of their lives: student, householder, "retired," and renounced life (Bhaktivedanta, 1968a:43–44, 246). As noted earlier, however, Chaitanya seems to have upheld the social rules that each person should follow according to his caste as determined by his birth.

The attainment of Krishna Consciousness involves far more than following the social demands of the caste system, however. To escape bad reactions to one's sinful deeds one must practice the regulative principles of religion, act piously, and accept devotional service. To attain Krishna Consciousness there are in addition a number of moral rules or virtues that are to be practiced without any selfish motive, since sinful acts are grounded in selfishness (Bhaktivedanta, 1972b:68, 404, 511).

The *Bhagavad-gītā* and the *Caitanya Caritāmṛita* list virtues to be practiced as well as vices to be avoided. The virtues include charity, self-control, nonviolence, truthfulness, cleanliness, tolerance, humility, mercy, kindness, friendliness, gentleness, modesty, and compassion.

The vices to be avoided are faultfinding, greed, lust, vanity, conceit, arrogance, anger, covetousness, envy, pride, and passion for honor. Because of the importance of devotion there are also particular religious virtues, such as the cultivation of spiritual knowledge, purification of one's existence, performance of sacrifice, study of the *Vedas,* austerity and simplicity, and tranquillity and renunciation (Bhaktivedanta, 1972b:722, 728; 1968b:255; Kavirāja, 1959d:533).

The ethical goal in the Hare Krishna Movement consists basically in two things: one's attainment of Krishna Consciousness, and its dissemination among other people of the world. But there is a polarity in the meaning of "concern for others" that is often misunderstood in our Western culture. Since the attainment of Krishna Consciousness means greater love and service to Krishna, it would seem quite natural that this love should be extended to all, since their inner selves form part of him. This is so, and indeed scriptural references confirm this view. It must be understood within the total context of its philosophy, however.

In the *Caitanya Caritāmṛita,* Chaitanya spoke to Rāmānanda concerning those who have a deep love for Rādhā-Krishna. "The lovers of the Lord see His image everywhere—in all objects, inanimate and animate. And though they look at them, yet they always see the image of their dearly beloved one everywhere in objects both animate and inanimate." Quoting the *Bhāgavata Purāṇa,* he continued: "The greatest of saints is he who sees the presence of God in all creatures, and who also sees all creatures as existent in God and as revealed in his bosom" (Kavirāja, 1959b:178). From the same source, Chaitanya quoted Krishna's words to Arjuna: "Not they alone, Oh Arjuna, that are devoted to me are my devotees. For my best devotees are those who are devoted to my devotees also." (Kavirāja, 1959b:243).

Certainly these texts indicate that the devotee should love and serve all people, and especially Krishna's devotees. They do, but not in the way many Americans might expect. In these last few years social activism has come to the fore, especially for the more liberal Christian denominations. Following this current mode, one might expect these texts to cause the Hare Krishna devotee to work for the amelioration of all social conditions wherever possible. But the vital concern of Swāmi Bhaktivedanta is to help the *real* and *inner selves* of all people to attain Krishna Consciousness and permanent liberation, rather than to administer to the "temporary situations" of their physical bodies. He believes that only a person who is in Krishna Consciousness is truly engaged in welfare work for all people. Knowing that "Krishna is the Fountainhead of everything," and then acting accordingly, is to act for all. Humanity's suffering is due to its "forgetfulness of Krishna as the Supreme Enjoyer, the Supreme Proprietor, and the Supreme Friend." To revive this consciousness within the entire human society is therefore the highest social work. Furthermore, physical welfare work is not helpful, since it gives only temporary relief (Bhaktivedanta, 1968b:145–146).

This general attitude of the Hare Krishna devotees concerning material attachments marks again a fundamental difference between Eastern and Western attitudes. The Hare Krishna concept has its origin in Hindu philosophy. The *Upanishads* declare *ahaṁ brahmāsmi,* "I am Brahman." Both Śaṅkara and Bhaktivedanta would interpret this as a reference to the *ātman,* the real self, as distinguished from the *ahamkāra,* the empirical or "false ego," something which is as much a product of illusion as is the material body. Thus Bhaktivedanta says that when the sense of "I am" is applied to the false body, it is a false ego, and this implies that we need be attached only to the real self.

Nevertheless, Bhaktivedanta does recognize some attachments. He says (Bhaktivedanta, 1968b:257–258):

> As for detachment from children, wife, and house, it is not meant that one should have no feeling for these. They are natural objects of affection. But when they are not favorable to spiritual progress, then we should not be attached to them. The best process for making the home nice is to live in Krishna Consciousness.

He then adds:

> But if it is not congenial, not favorable for spiritual advancement, then family life should be abandoned. In all cases, one should be detached from the happiness and distress of family life, because the world can never be fully happy or fully miserable.

Again we must recognize the difference in thought. In liberal Christianity the emphasis has recently been upon a more secular concern.

God is to be found in the ghettos and elsewhere in the world. In Vaishṇava thought, the world is real but like a shadow of true reality. Its real nature is covered by the quality of illusion, which of course is still Krishna's inferior energy. One does not, therefore, concern himself so much with physical conditions, whatever they may be, but rather with the conditioned souls of mankind and their liberation from the illusory but temporary material condition.

This view differs considerably from that of the Judeo-Christian tradition, which is based on the Biblical conception of unity between soul and body, and the reality of matter that is not subject to illusion. Therefore the concern of the devotee is ideally for the Krishna Consciousness of his parents and friends rather than for other relationships. Moreover, since Krishna Consciousness is really the only concern of the truly dedicated Hare Krishna devotee, that which does not further this goal for himself or for others must be avoided. Unfortunately, this position has not been understood by the parents of devotees. If some alienation has not occurred between the devotee and his parents up to the time of his entering the Society full time, it often occurs shortly thereafter.

Another contrast between the two traditions is seen in their concept of love. In the Vaishṇava philosophy love is first directed to Krishna. Only through the primary relation between the devotee and Krishna can one be said to really love another. The love of one person for another is ideally one of nonattachment to the physical aspects, since these are illusory and subject to both pleasure and pain. The love that exists for Krishna transcends material categories and relationships, and is the only ideal love recognized between persons. The concern is for the real spiritual self, rather than for the illusory ego or the body. One sees this even in attachment expressed in the ideal of Krishna Consciousness. One who has become fully Krishna conscious will only seem to be on the sensual plane; he will have neither attachment nor detachment. He will be completely introspective, and as Swāmi Bhaktivedanta says: "The introspective man is always indifferent to materialistic happiness and distress. He goes on with his self-realization activities undisturbed by material reactions" (Bhaktivedanta, 1968b:85–86). Therefore, since Krishna Consciousness and its dissemination are the sole goals of a pure devotee, there is no real place for an association with parents, friends, or other people, except in the context of these objectives.*

The Judeo-Christian tradition, however, entails the amelioration of physical distress. Christianity enjoins the believer to be his brother's keeper in a real physical sense. The story of the Good Samaritan is an example of the ethical injunction to have concern for the *physical* well-being of all persons, whether enemies or friends. Liberal Christianity has perhaps emphasized this horizontal aspect of Christianity at the expense of the vertical or transcendental dimension.

With the growth of science many have felt that the place of God in the universe has been diminished. Science, it was thought, was better equipped than religion to explain creation; the psychiatrist's couch was more suited to resolving one's alienations than turning to religious faith. The results of a century of biblical criticism have also helped limit the validity of the message of Jesus for many Christians. Christianity has "come of age" with the growth of a secular gospel. And somewhere along the way its vertical and transcendental dimensions have been lost by many people.

Evidence shows that times of changing cultural values reveal a need of many to rediscover a reality beyond the realm of logical validation of an established culture. A source of new meaning, a religious foundation is needed. For many young persons today, liberal Judaism and Christianity have not provided this fulfillment. For the devotees of Krishna, Swāmi Bhaktivedanta has.

James Bissett Pratt wrote: "Religion is not so much theology as life; it is to be lived rather than reasoned about" (Pratt, 1920:7). We have looked briefly at the beliefs of the Hare Krishna Movement, but if Pratt is right, the lives of the Society's devotees are more important.

* One should note that a monastic life entails separation from family and friends, whether Hindu or Christian.

CHAPTER FIVE

THE WAY TO KRISHNA

Chanting and dancing Hare Krishna devotees have become familiar sights on the streets of many of our metropolitan cities. These devotees are witnessing to their faith and trying to spread the message of Krishna Consciousness, but the unfamiliarity of this type of religious ritual to the American people has caused varied reactions in many cities. In an article in the Denver *Post,* Don Nakayama reported the plight of the devotees there (October 21, 1973). The Denver police had often arrested devotees on charges of loitering or unlawful assembly, although in each case the charges were dropped. In 1972 the Society filed suit against the city for passing an ordinance prohibiting their activities at the International Airport. It is unfortunate that in a country known for its religious freedom such actions can still occur, largely through ignorance. Other Denverites have nevertheless shown their approval by giving the temple stereo equipment, automobiles, a refrigerator, a washing machine, and other gifts.

The mayors of New York and San Francisco have commended the Movement for its work with youth, who comprise about 85 percent of its membership. These cities and many others have recognized the transformations in thousands of youths who might otherwise be drug addicts and adding further to the increasing crime rates in our cities. Each year the San Francisco Police Department has given its cooperation in blocking traffic on the city streets where the Movement parades its huge image-bearing carts during its famous Ratha-yātrā Festival. Mayor Warren Widener of Berkeley has also expressed his approval of the Hare Krishna Movement for having given a purpose in life to so many alienated youth.

An Alternative Life Style in Communal Living. The Hare Krishna devotees are persevering. They continue in the face of opposition, just as members of other religions have done under similar conditions. Feeling that they have found a purpose and meaning they had been seeking when they left their homes, families, and traditional organized religions, they have separated themselves from the culture of the establishment. They have also separated themselves from the drug scene of the counterculture, in which most of them had been involved. The majority of the devotees live together at the temple where they form their own alternative society. The little evidence we have points to disavowal of the establishment even among those serving Krishna in secular positions. They now follow a spiritual master who has given them a discipline and teaching that they follow without question. This could not contrast more sharply with the "hang loose" ethic of "doing one's own thing" that had characterized the former countercultural philosophy of many.

When asked what type of person makes the best devotee, one devotee replied:

> The Movement has appealed mainly to youngsters who have led the hectic . . . hippie type of life, divorcing themselves from their families, living through the knocks of life, living on their own under all . . . adverse conditions until they find Krishna Consciousness. It not only provides them with a wonderful faith, but it is also providing them with a community that they can feel a part of, that is divorced from the society within which they lived.

This corroborates the evidence to be later introduced; they have found a close fellowship in an alternative style of living that is markedly different from the one we associate with the American way of life.

Stability of the Hare Krishna Life Style. Although the counterculture has produced many types of communal living, evidence, including some from Hare Krishna devotees who had lived in communes before, seems to indicate that there is greater stability in the Hare Krishna temples than in other communes. Six reasons can be given. First, there is a unity of purpose, in this case Krishna Consciousness, which is interpreted by a strong charismatic authority like Swāmi Bhaktivedanta. One devotee who had been a member of an unsuccessful commune said:

> Prior to coming to Krishna Consciousness, my wife and I were searching . . . studying all different forms of religion, trying this and that as if in a supermarket. Finding nothing, frustrated, and in despair, we left the country, gave up our jobs, our home, everything we had. We went to British Honduras . . . there were fifteen of us altogether. We formed a commune. We were going to try to search for God in our own ways, but couldn't do it. It was evident after a couple of weeks. Everybody was doing his own thing—into sense gratification. Once in a while we'd try meditating on the impersonal aspect of the supreme which got us simply nowhere. A few tried *yoga* . . . all in all nothing was accomplished. I was into drugs, heavy into alcohol, and after a few weeks everybody started leaving, until after four months the only ones left in the jungle was my family and I. It dawned on me that I needed a spiritual master, because I wasn't going to make it on my own . . . So we gave up our land and everything we owned . . . I had just enough to make it here to this temple . . . and it changed my life so much.

Second, there is a common discipline. This is a discipline that requires those living in the temples to concentrate on Krishna with all their thoughts and actions during their waking hours; its importance can be seen in the preceding quotation. The process is designed to strengthen faith in Krishna and in an entire way of living. Devotees are continually increasing their faith by reading about Krishna and discussing him with others in the temple, by reciting the *mahāmantra* to themselves, by listening to taped lectures of their spiritual master, by witnessing to their faith on the streets in their *kīrtans,* and by preaching his message to all who will listen.*

Third, there is a similarity in age and background. All devotees interviewed have shown some sympathy with countercultural ideas; they are all antiestablishment to varying measures. Although there are exceptions, similarity in ages has often been a factor in closer fellowship.

* Since the longevity of the Roman Catholic orders owes much to their strict discipline, one may wonder what effect the recent relaxation in the rules among some of them will have in time.

Only from older devotees who have sometimes not been able to conform completely to the rigid life have I heard any criticism of the discipline. Differences in the greater physical endurance and adaptability of youth have also been apparent. One of the older devotees who spoke to the problem said:

> It's not the age gap so much, as far as thinking goes, but it's being accepted wholeheartedly and also being expected to live some of the vigorous ways. For example, the bones don't always cooperate to squat on the floor *yoga* fashion for more than a few minutes, or else I might not be able to get up. But all in all there are other things we took to nicely. We sleep on the floor. We don't have fancy furniture at all. We just have a kitchen table and we have our own altar at home.

The same devotee, who lives with his wife and family outside the temple, but who participates in the devotional services, also complained about the food.

> I just finished having a very expensive bout with the doctor, not knowing what happened to my digestive system until it was shown that the heavy spices and the coarseness of the food just about sanded down my whole intestines. It not only hit me; it affected my wife's digestive system at times. I've talked with older devotees and they say the same thing—that the food does not need so much spice. If we can't take part of the remnants of the Lord's offering, I think we're losing. We're being deprived of part of the glories of Krishna Consciousness. Though we offer our own food at home, it's not quite the same nor as blissful as the association with the devotees which I continually strive to maintain.

The younger devotees also seem to have less compunction about public dancing and chanting when dressed in Hindu fashion than do the older ones. The same older devotee said:

> I think a whole new dimension of Krishna Consciousness should be formed without taking to the process of wearing robes or shaving heads . . . this can work; you don't have to look extraordinary . . . because the way we're mocked and laughed at, unless a person is really fixed up spiritually, he's not going to be able to swallow all that. I can't swallow it too

> well. I've gone on *saṅkīrtan* on Hollywood Boulevard, and all the laughs and snickers we get—it hit me wrong.

Fourth, there is a common ritual that offers the possibility of religious experience, as we shall later see. Together with the rest of the discipline, this ritual validates and internalizes their philosophy, culture, and way of life.

Fifth, its business enterprises offer the Movement a financial stability that further ensures its continuation.

Sixth, the Movement offers under one discipline, authority, and purpose a variety of alternative life styles. One may live in the outside world and carry on a business, profession, or trade for Krishna. Or he may devote his full time to the religious life associated with just the temple, while having the secure feeling that Krishna will take care of him. The latter alternative is especially attractive to those who have found fault with the establishment's principle of the competitive life.

Limitations in Membership. Although the Hare Krishna Movement contains these important elements for its stability and survival, it does not appeal to everyone to the same extent. The devotees themselves receive the message of Krishna Consciousness in various ways. And even though Krishna Consciousness is extended to all people alike regardless of background, education, creed, or color, the devotees follow definite rules concerning who is accepted to live in the temple.

First, only those who are seriously interested in developing Krishna Consciousness are welcomed. This excludes those who have no intention of following the minimum rules of the discipline, such as those who seek only to find shelter and food.

Second, the devotees give counsel to hippies, or others, who are on drugs. They invite them to chant the *mahāmantra* and follow the regulative rules as a way to drug release. They will not allow them to live in the temple while continuing the use of narcotics, however. I remember the example of an obviously stoned hippie who visited the Berkeley temple. He was too loaded to do anything but sit in the corner during the service. Although invited to return and to chant, he was not permitted to stay the night, and I finally drove him to a drug care hostel in Oakland. The autobiographical and statistical information later introduced confirms that chanting and following the regulative rules have given release from drugs in many cases.

Third, although former homosexuals may be found among the membership of the Society, their life style is strictly forbidden. This includes transvestites. The case of "Winifred" is an example. When I first met him he told me his story. It had included the use of drugs, being busted, a brief incarceration at Santa Rita Prison, and trying to get along in society dressed as a woman. Dissatisfied, frustrated, and failing in a suicide attempt, he had sought entry into the Hare Krishna temple as a woman. He was refused, since female and male devotees' sleeping quarters are kept strictly separate, but was advised to return to a male role. After a short period the change was made. The last time I saw him, he had a shaven head and was wearing Vaishṇava male attire. For a time he succeeded in making the change and finding his place in the Society.*

The Alternative Hindu Culture of the Society. These devotees have protested against the American mode of the establishment in definite ways. Having rejected it, they have found the answers they had been seeking in a form of Hindu religion and culture. The change has been radical, and their spiritual master has been their interpreter.

Most of them wear Hindu style clothing. Although some married devotees who have secular positions do not follow this practice, I have yet to see an exception among the youthful followers of Krishna living in the temples. The unmarried men wear flowing saffron colored cloths (*dhoties*), which distinguish them from the yellow-robed married devotees. The women follow similar patterns of dress by wearing *sāris.*

The men generally shave their heads except for a slender tuft of hair (*śikhā*), which denotes that they have surrendered themselves to the spiritual master. Each day upon arising they ornament themselves with *tilaka,* a wet mixture of clay that they paint on their faces and on eleven other places of their bodies. This is done for "sanctification and protection." These markings denote that they are Vaishṇavas and that their

* He has since left the Movement, and phoned to ask whether I knew of some other religious commune in which he might fit. He gave two reasons for leaving the Movement. It did not allow him to live as a woman, and he grew tired of continually taking orders. He felt he was becoming an automaton with little expression of his own will.

bodies are temples of Vishṇu, their Supreme Lord (The International Society for Krishna Consciousness, 1970:40, 15). Conformity is important, if not an absolute requirement.

After following the discipline carefully for six months or longer, the new convert becomes eligible for initiation when the spiritual master comes to the area. Devotees living in temples that he does not have time to visit will travel to the closest place where he is staying. When Swāmi Bhaktivedanta accepts a devotee, he gives him a Sanskrit name, and accepts the responsibility of guiding him to Krishna Consciousness. The student on his part is expected to take the spiritual master's orders as his own "life and soul," and to honor him as he would God, since he is to be considered as God's representative (International Society for Krishna Consciousness, 1970:10).

After one or two years spent in the first and celibate student stage (*brahmachārī*), the devotee is allowed to marry and become a householder (*gṛihastha*). Marriage has only two purposes in the Society: to raise Krishna Conscious children, and to help one another to deepen Krishna Consciousness. A married man generally moves out of the temple with his wife to occupy a separate dwelling. Marriage is by arrangement rather than by courtship. It is also for life, since there is no recognized divorce unless one considers de facto the Order of Saṅnyāsa that some male devotees take. This requires them to separate themselves forever from their wives, who of course may not marry anyone else. Although theoretically a married minister may voluntarily take the Order of Saṅnyāsa when his sons are old enough to take care of his wife, there is currently a growing number of young female devotees whose husbands have become *saṅnyāsis*. In every case of which I know the Society has assumed the role of protector and has continued to provide for them.

The Society has its own marriage ceremony, which is a sacrament of the faith. Instead of primarily denoting a relationship between husband and wife, it signifies the surrender of both parties to Krishna. It teaches that one can only really love another if he or she loves Krishna first, by no matter what name one designates the deity. But since Krishna must be regarded as the Supreme Personality of Godhead, a good part of the ceremony consists in chanting, dancing, and giving devotion to Krishna. All present are invited to participate. The wedding part of the ceremony follows closely the Hindu ceremony, and takes place as in a *Vedic* rite around a sacred fire that the priest builds and lights.

Those who live away from the temple are expected to maintain at least the minimum regulative rules. What one does for a living is not of great importance. Devotees of Krishna work to grant the fruits of their labor to Krishna, rather than for their own gain. Those working in secular positions are expected to give a minimum of 50 percent of their salaries to the Society. Those who labor in one of the ISKCON business enterprises are granted enough money to take care of themselves; the remainder goes to the Society. One is not expected to accumulate possessions, but to live frugally whether in his own home or in the temple.

Devotees accept the Hindu caste system as interpreted by their spiritual master. They follow the Hindu practice of venerating the cow and all its products, and abstaining from using leather from slaughtered cows. They accept unquestioningly the teachings of the Hindu scriptures as interpreted by their spiritual master, and follow the Hindu pattern of the four stages of life.

The third stage, which Swāmi Bhaktivedanta translates as "retired," is the *vānaprastha.* The spiritual master includes this category but does not recommend it for those seeking Krishna Consciousness, a search that requires action. Traditionally it was an anchorite stage that entailed moving into the forest to meditate. Its special texts for guidance were the *Āraṇyakas.*

The position of women in the Society may not appeal to Americans interested in women's liberation. Swāmi Bhaktivedanta says that all women other than one's wife are to be considered as one's mother, and yet he regards them as prone to degradation, of little intelligence, and untrustworthy. They should not be given as much freedom as men, but should be treated like children; they should be protected all during their lives, by their fathers when young, later by their husbands, and in their old age, by their sons (Bhaktivedanta, 1972b:200, 24). This view is largely consonant with the traditional one found in the ancient Indian law books. Females may not become presidents of any temple, nor occupy positions of authority. They may do the cooking, help with the devotional services and maintenance of the temple, and prepare flower offerings for Krishna. Regardless of their social positions, the souls of female devotees are to be considered of equal value with their male counterparts—incarnation as a male or female depends on one's *karma.*

Their status has apparently not bothered the female devotees; one of them said:

> Well, spiritually we have an equal position . . . We're subordinate now in Kali Yuga, but it doesn't mean we're inferior necessarily. Actually we are . . . I can see that women tend to flip out a lot more than men. They are more emotional. Women's lib tries to gloss over all of the very obvious differences . . . and it's nonsense . . . On the whole we are less intelligent, our attention is not so good . . . So we take our orders from the men and it's nice. They're very nice. It's no problem. You're protected and you're given instruction, and you don't have to make the decisions; it's really pleasant . . . The boys really have propensities for administration . . . that we just don't have. So it must be my female body, but I'm very pleased not to have to make very many decisions anymore.

Thus the devotees have to a great extent adopted the Hindu culture and practices of the Gauḍīya Vaishṇavas. The few notable exceptions include disregard of certain rules concerning pollution, for example, pollution of a woman following childbirth, or of a family following a death in it. They also permit female devotees to live in their temples and to be *pūjaris,* that is, to officiate at the devotional services in the temple, practices the Gauḍīya Vaishṇavas forbid. American devotees are more liberal in their inclusion of outsiders in their *saṅkīrtans* than are their Hindu counterparts. And as we have seen, their Hindu counterparts limit their public use to a much greater degree.

Bhakti-yoga. Let us now turn our attention to the discipline of the Hare Krishna Movement and the rules governing it. This is exemplified by the Movement's interpretation of *bhakti-yoga. Bhakti-yoga* for the Hare Krishna devotee means surrendering one's self to Krishna and recovering one's original relationship to him, which is Krishna Consciousness. It is obtained by following the discipline the spiritual master gives to each member. It promises a release from unhappiness and misery in the present life and the ecstatic experiences gained by chanting with other devotees. It is believed that its attainment results in the end of reincarnation after death and an eternal loving fellowship with Krishna in his heaven world.

Bhakti embraces everything leading to Krishna Consciousness. All Hare Krishna devotees are required to follow four regulative principles as a basic minimum. First, there are restrictions against gambling, the meaning of which is extended to include any frivolous sports and games. Also included here is the directive against having any conversation not associated with the teachings of Krishna Consciousness or with the fulfillment of one's duties. Second, the use of all forms of intoxicants, including alcohol, drugs, tobacco, coffee, and tea, is prohibited. Third, the Society has a dietary rule forbidding the partaking of any meat, fish, or eggs. Fourth is the injunction against illicit sex. This last rule is especially interesting, since lust played an important part in the Vaishṇava view of man's fall from Krishna's grace into the material world of sense gratification. Therefore, "illicit" sex includes any sexual act not performed for the procreation of children to be raised in Krishna Consciousness. The use of contraceptives and other methods for preventing conception Swāmi Bhaktivedanta considers as an abomination (International Society for Krishna Consciousness, 1970:13–14; Bhaktivedanta, 1972:725).

In addition to the four regulative principles, the devotee is asked to perform *japa,* the private chanting of the Hare Krishna *mahāmantra* for sixteen rounds daily on his 108 prayer beads. Although certain times during the day are especially devoted to this telling of the beads, the true devotee chants quietly at every idle moment. A lull of a few seconds in conversation is sufficient for a devotee quickly to chant the *mahamantra* one time. He moves from bead to bead with each single recitation; his hand holding the beads is hidden in a small bag that is attached by a strap around his neck. The hidden hand and the quiet manner of reciting the *mahāmantra* accord with the rule that one should perform *japa* in as unobtrusive manner as possible. The 108 beads of the necklace represent the *gopīs,* the milkmaids or cowherdesses with whom Krishna sports; one larger bead denotes Krishna. On reaching the large bead, the devotee does not pass it, but continues by telling the small beads in reverse.

Every devotee should partake only of *prasādam,* a meatless diet of food that has first been offered to Krishna. If the devotee is a householder living outside the temple, he is permitted to have his own altar for presenting his food ceremonially to Krishna. The *prasādam* is part of the offering made to Krishna four times daily during the *ārātrika* ceremony, which is usually referred to in the vernacular as *ārati* (pronounced "artee").

The food varies with the time of offering. For the morning ceremony, the devotees bring fruits and milk; at noon there may be rice, *dahl* (a lentil soup), *chapatis* (a type of thin flat wheat tortillas), vegetables, milk, sweet rice, and other vegetable foods. In late afternoon and at night the devotees offer vegetables, milk, and various sweetmeats (International Society for Krishna Consciousness, 1970:15–16). All the recipes are Indian and often quite spicy. One may enjoy at the free public Sunday feasts such dishes as curried potatoes, chick-peas in *ghee* (melted clarified butter), *burfly* (coconut and powdered milk), *dahl, chutney,* and *halvah* made of cereal grains, topped off with *laddu,* a pastry made of flour and cardamom. After the Sunday afternoon *ārati* ceremony, the devotees and their guests move from the temple housing the deities to an adjoining room. Since there are no chairs and tables, they sit together barefooted or in stocking feet on the floor, while they are served liberal quantities and varieties of *prasādam.* Generally no utensils for eating are supplied except cups and plates; solids are usually eaten by using one's fingers

At the Sunday feast the following grace is often given before all partake of the holy remnants of Krishna's meal:

> This material body is a lump of ignorance and the senses are a network of paths of death. Of all the senses the tongue is the most voracious and uncontrollable. But Krishna has sent us this very nice *prasādam* to help us conquer the tongue. So let us take this nice *prasādam* to our full satisfaction, glorifying his lordship, Rādhā and Krishna, and in love call upon Lord Chaitanya and Nityānanda to help us."

Since it is taught that this food offered first to Krishna acquires spiritual properties, to partake of it is a spiritually purifying act, equal to chanting the "holy names of Krishna" or to listening to his pastimes. The preparation of the food in the kitchen is also a devotional act that is performed according to exacting rules. In importance it equals the *ārati* ceremony, and the kitchen becomes as sacred as the altar. The action simulates that which the milkmaids perform for Krishna in his heaven world. The spiritual master reminds the devotees that the milkmaids can get all the food they want to offer from the desire trees, but to show their love for Krishna they nevertheless prepare it carefully themselves.

While cooking the food the first rule is to think of Krishna continually. Only clean clothes should be worn, and one's hands should be thoroughly cleansed when entering the kitchen. Only fresh foods may be used. Nothing that has touched a contaminated area, such as the sink, may be used unless immediately cleaned. Canned foods and leftovers are forbidden, as is the use of garlic, onions, and mushrooms (International Society for Krishna Consciousness, 1971:19–20). The specially trained and initiated devotees who prepare these delicacies for Krishna are not permitted to taste or even smell them—Krishna must be the first to enjoy these foods. It is said that in India those who prepare meals for Krishna in the temples wear masks over their noses and mouths.

When the food has been cooked, all dishes and pans used should be cleaned immediately, the floor should be mopped, and the walls and cupboards are often cleaned. Then the plates of food are prepared and are covered with a clean cloth before being later presented to Krishna. The entire process is to be conducted with no more conversation than necessary to perform the duties.

During the eating of *prasādam,* conversation is also limited. It is explained that when Chaitanya and his devotees partook of this sacred food, the only words spoken were "Krishna" or "Hare." Since guests would not understand this practice, it is now permissable to speak to them, but the conversation should only be about Krishna Consciousness.

Besides *prasādam,* the devotees must prepare daily garlands of flowers for presentation to Krishna. The female devotees whose work this is usually perform the task during the various lesson periods, and thus perform worshipful work for Krishna while listening to philosophical discussions about him or his pastimes. After they have been presented to Krishna, the garlands may be given to devotees to wear as a purification from disease or the contamination of matter.

Krishna should occupy all of a devotee's senses as much as possible. When he counts his beads while reciting the *mahāmantra,* he is remembering Krishna through his sense of touch. When he listens to the reading of Krishna's pastimes, the taped lectures of Swāmi Bhaktivedanta, the chanting of the other devotees, or an explanation of the philosophy regarding Krishna, he becomes aware of Krishna through the sense of hearing. Eating *prasādam,* he remembers Krishna through the sense of taste. When he gazes in loving devotion at the deities in the temple as he chants with others, he remembers Krishna through his sight. Finally, when he smells the incense burning in the temple, or the flowers that are offered to Krishna, he remembers him through the sense of smell.

There are yet other regulations that are considered necessary preliminary guides.

The devotee must accept a bona fide spiritual master and be initiated by him. The spiritual master, who is to be obeyed with faith and devotion, gives instruction in the performance of the devotional service.

The devotee must be ready to relinquish anything material for the satisfaction of Krishna. He must be ready to give up something that he strongly desires, while accepting something he does not like. He should concern himself with the material world only when absolutely necessary.

The fast days of Ekādāśī, which fall on the eleventh day after the full moon and the eleventh day after the new moon, must be observed. Only vegetables and milk in moderate amounts may be taken, but no grains, cereals, or beans.

The devotee should worship various sacred trees such as the banyan.

These injunctions are necessary for the beginning of devotional service. If they are followed, it is said that the devotee will be able to progress quickly in Krishna Consciousness. Progress also depends on willingness to give up the company of anyone who is not a devotee. Teaching should not be offered to anyone unwilling to participate in devotional service. The reading of books is to be limited. Neglect of one's duties is frowned upon, as is lamenting any loss or rejoicing in gain (International Society for Krishna Consciousness, 1970:26–27).

The devotional service to Krishna is also covered by special rules—devotees should participate in the congregational chanting and take *prasādam* after first offering it to Krishna, for example. They should accept *charaṇāmṛita* as an act of devotion. This is water used in bathing the deities. It is also important for them to listen to the reading of the *Bhāgavata Purāṇa* and to understand it.

In addition to these rules requiring positive actions, there are offenses to be avoided. One is not to "blaspheme the devotees" who are dedicated to spread the name of Krishna, nor to consider the names of any other deities to be equal to Vishṇu (Krishna). A devotee should not disobey the spiritual master's commands, nor blaspheme the *Vedic* literature. Although chanting is believed to free one from the reactions to one's sins, to continue acting sinfully believing that chanting will neutralize this action is a transgression. The devotee who has complete faith in the chanting must also avoid maintaining material attachments. Although anyone may participate in chanting, care must be taken not to reveal indiscriminately "the transcendental glories of the Lord," since very sinful people will not appreciate them (International Society for Krishna Consciousness, 1970:28–30).

By following the discipline, the devotees say that *prema* or love for Krishna develops. This recovery of the original love one had for Krishna results from devotion. It develops from the transcendental stages of emotion to ecstasy, and finally to extreme intense attachment. Rūpa Goswāmi noted four developmental stages (Bhaktivedanta, 1968a:25, 31). One becomes free of all material desires, and eventually free of the desire for spiritual enjoyment itself. This includes desire for union with Krishna.

The Daily Schedule of Discipline. The exact time of rising and retiring in any particular temple may vary slightly, as can the materials read or discussed during the lesson periods at any one time. But the general routine is by and large the same in all temples. Every part is not an absolute requirement, but each devotee is expected to be as dutiful as possible.

The schedule begins now at 3:00 A.M. The devotees rise, take showers, and apply their *tilaka.* At four o'clock the deities are awakened and offerings are made. To greet the awakened deities, the first *ārati* takes place from 4:30 to 5:00 A.M. *Japa* meditation is then conducted privately until six o'clock. A class on one of the sacred scriptures is held from six to seven o'clock, followed by another half-hour of *japa.* From then until 8:30 A.M. special duties, such as preparation of *prasādam* and tidying of the temple, are performed, after which the devotees have their first meal of *prasādam.* The meal is followed by another brief period of chanting. The devotees are now ready to take to the streets to sell their literature, perform their public chanting, or at times to put on brief dramatic skits demonstrating some of Krishna's pastimes. Because it is felt that people can be reached better by devotees going from door to door, selling their books and issues of *Back to Godhead,* and giving brief sermonettes on the teachings of Krishna, less time is currently devoted to public chanting than was once the case. This practice was found successful by the Jehovah's Witnesses in propagating their own ideas and selling their literature.

At 12:30 P.M. the devotees may return for *prasādam,* bringing with them any who might wish to know more about Krishna. Between one and five o'clock in the afternoon most go out to repeat their efforts of the morning. Those remaining in the temple at four o'clock may participate in an afternoon *ārati* after the deities have been awakened from an afternoon siesta. Those returning to the temple at five o'clock again take showers, making themselves ready for the evening classes and devotions. They may also have a light snack and time to study the scriptures before evening devotions. *Ārati* lasts from 7:00 to 7:30 P.M. A half-hour class follows, and then another period for study or for *japa.* This lasts until another *saṅkīrtan* begins at nine o'clock. Afterwards they may drink milk, eat a little fruit, and prepare themselves for bedding down on the floor by 9:30 P.M.

The *Ārātrika* Ceremony (*Ārati*). The principal ceremonies of each day are performed in the temple. They begin with the *pūjari,* who is in charge of making the sacred offerings, doing obeisance to the deities. While ringing a tiny tinkling bell, he recites prayers and kneels beside the closed shrine. Then the curtains surrounding the shrine are opened, and as the devotees enter the temple, each prostrates himself before the deities and recites two set prayers. Food that has been covered with a cloth is now brought into the temple and presented to the deities at the shrine.

The images of the deities may vary. Those of Rādhā and Krishna, or the Jagannātha figures are almost equally popular. The latter are those worshiped in Purī in Orissa at the temple where Chaitanya spent most of his life. There Jagaṅnātha, the Lord of the World, reigns as the *archā* descent of Vishṇu or Krishna. He is always shown with

Krishna's brother, Balarāma (Balabhadra), and Subhadrā, his sister. All temples also have one or more pictures of Chaitanya, Swāmi Bhaktivedanta, and the *pañchatattva,* that is, Chaitanya and the four other parts of his *avatār:* Advaitāchārya, Nityānanda, Gadādhara, and Śrīvāsa.

The devotees do not regard the images as idols. It is taught that Krishna incarnates into the figure representing him, whether it be of wood, stone, or metal, as long as it has been made according to the authorized descriptions. This is his *archā* incarnation. Krishna is really in spiritual form (International Society for Krishna Consciousness, 1970:15–17).

In the *ārati* ceremony, the first offering is incense to please the senses of the deities. Burning camphor and *ghee* are next to be offered to them, and then to the devotees as purificatory agents. The *pūjari* next places water in a conch shell for the deities to wash their hands and mouths after partaking of the *prasādam.* They are next offered a flower to please their senses, and finally are fanned to keep them cool. In some temples the *pūjari* waves a yak's tail before them in order to keep away insects. Toward the close of the ceremony a conch shell is blown three times to signal the close of this phase of the *ārati,* which then ends when one of the devotees recites "obeisance and respects" accompanied by responses from the other devotees. They are offered first to Bhaktivedanta and various earlier Vaishṇava masters, then to Rādhā and Krishna and often to the places sacred to them, next to the sacred *tulasī* plant, and finally to the assembled devotees.

While the *pūjari* is conducting his preliminary service to Krishna, the devotees begin their first chant, which is always:

> namā om viṣṇu-pādāya kṛṣṇa-preṣṭhāya bhūtale
> śrīmate bhaktivedānta-svāmin iti nāmine.

The spiritual master's translation of this chant is: "I offer my respectful obeisances unto His Divine Grace, A. C. Bhaktivedanta Swāmi, who is very dear to Lord Kṛṣṇa, having taken shelter at His lotus feet" (*International Society for Kṛṣṇa Consciousness,* 1970:65).

Thus one commences his approach to Krishna through the spiritual master. The devotees accept the latter's words as being exactly the same truth that his own *guru* spoke, and so on back to Krishna. To surrender to him in obedience means also to surrender to Krishna. One is enjoined to put absolute faith in him for guidance to Krishna. Indeed the devotees appear to give him the love and adoration that is expected to be given to Krishna.

After this first invocation to the spiritual master, the chants may vary according to the will of the leader, who first chants alone one of the many *mantras* that may comprise a devotional service. Each time he completes a *mantra,* the devotees join in its repetition, chanting with the same cadence and melody as the leader. A chant of a particular *mantra* may be continued two or three times or for a much longer period, depending on the desire of the leader.

Usually several different *mantras* are sung before the second key invocation. This is to Chaitanya and the four others who comprised the full incarnation, as well as to all his devotees.

> Bhaja Śrī Kṛṣṇa Caitanya
> Prabhu Nityānanda
> Śrī Advaita Gadādhara
> Śrīvāsādi Gaura-bhakta-vṛinda.

Swāmi Bhaktivedanta offers the following translation: "I offer my obeisances unto Śrī Kṛṣṇa Caitanya, Nityānanda Prabhu, Śrī Advaita, Gadādhara, Srīvāsa, and all the followers of Lord Caitanya" (*International Society for Kṛṣṇa Consciousness,* 1970:81).

After they repeat this several times, intermediate chants of different kinds may be introduced. A common one is: "Jagaṅnātha-Śvāmi/nayana paṭhagāmi/bhavatu me," which has been translated: "Oh Lord of the universe, please be visible unto me" (*International Society for Kṛṣṇa Consciousness,* 1970:83).

Thus Krishna receives the intercession of at least the spiritual master and Chaitanya before he himself is honored by his own special chant. The *mahāmantra* or Hare Krishna *mantra* begins slowly. As the tempo is quickened, the sound of the *mṛidañga* drums and the finger cymbals reverberate into a crescendo, which continues louder and faster until the three blasts of the conch shell signal the end of the first part. The power of this chanting should not be underestimated. The enthusiasm of the devotees leaping in ecstasy with upraised arms before the shrine can be contagious for many.

Of all the various chants, each of which has its own tune, the *mahāmantra* is certainly most important:

Hare Krishna, Hare Krishna,
Krishna Krishna, Hare Hare,
Hare Rāma, Hare Rāma,
Rāma Rāma, Hare Hare.

In this invocation "Rāma," a descent of Krishna according to the Gauḍīyas, is another word for Krishna. "Hare" is said by Swāmi Bhaktivedanta to be the vocative case of Harā,* which represents Krishna's energy, Rādhā. Giving her name first makes her an intercessor herself, although she and Krishna are actually one. When the *mahāmantra* is chanted, the devotees consider that there is no difference between the form of Krishna and his name. Krishna is not only present, but the chanter himself is regarded as transcending the material platform or plane. To recite the *mantra*—or even to hear it chanted—is considered purifying. Through this purification process, the *māyā* is gradually loosened from the conditioned soul, opening the way for closer and closer fellowship with Krishna.

Hare Krishna Festivals. The festivals of the Hare Krishna Movement form an important part of devotion to Krishna. Chaitanya's birthday, which marks the first day of each year in the Vaishṇava calendar, has been celebrated in Berkeley even since the closing of the temple there. In 1970 it fell on March 24. Devotees from temples in all the western states congregated to celebrate. The event was marked by a parade down Telegraph Avenue, led by devotees carrying a giant figure of Chaitanya. Accompanied by the sounds of the *mahāmantra* chanted by hundreds of devotees and other participants, the parade moved on to Willard Park about a mile away. There a skit was performed dramatizing events in Chaitanya's life, a full *ārati* was held, and a feast of *prasādam* was offered to all. At the conclusion of the celebration in the park, *saṅkīrtans* were continued all evening in the local temple.

In June, the bathing celebration of Lord Jagannātha takes place.

* It may equally well be taken to be the vocative case of "Hari," another name for Krishna.

At this celebration, the deity is removed from his shrine. To the chanting of the *mahāmantra,* the devotees circle round him and one by one pour a spoonful of water over him and then prostrate themselves in obeisance. At the conclusion of the ceremony and during the love feast, it is announced that Jagaṅnātha has caught a severe cold and is ill. The Ratha-yātrā Festival, which is held in July in San Francisco and elsewhere, marks the complete recovery and outing of the deity. The Jagaṅnātha Festival emulates the celebration held at Purī in India each year. In the Hare Krishna Movement the event marks the outing of the three deites, which are enshrined in three gigantic carts and pulled through the streets of the city. This festival, which is also similar to the one for Chaitanya, concludes with a free feast for all present after the parade.

Although there are many other holy days marking the birth and disappearance of the numerous Vaishṇava saints, most are not generally celebrated by the devotees in the United States.

The Organization of ISKCON. The Hare Krishna organization has one supreme head, Swāmi A. C. Bhaktivedanta Prabhupāda, who appoints a governing body of twelve commissioners. Each commissioner is responsible for the maintenance of standards and important decisions in a particular sector of the world. Commissioners determine whether new temples should be opened or others closed within their areas.

Under them are the appointed presidents of each temple, who maintain the standards of worship and discipline therein, and see that the devotees are properly cared for. Each temple has a secretary and a treasurer who are responsible to the president. There is also a temple commander or coordinator who assists the president in seeing that the devotees chant their required rounds, get up in the morning at the proper time, take their proper baths, and so forth. He assigns special duties to devotees, works closely with them, and is responsible for keeping the temple spotlessly clean. In larger temples there is a *saṅkīrtan* leader in charge of five or six men forming a party, a head *pūjari* and his assistants who are in charge of the deity worship, and a head cook and his assistants.

CHAPTER SIX

HARE KRISHNA AND THE COUNTERCULTURE

Chapter 5 points to the nature of the alternative life style of the Hare Krishna devotees. Since for most devotees this represents a change from the hippiedom of the counterculture, the nature of that counterculture is examined briefly in this chapter. Some attention is paid to the reasons for the protests and to how the devotees may be considered to have formed part of it.

The Changing Scene. "Counterculture" signifies "a set of beliefs that is contrary to the very roots or foundation upon which the dominant culture rests" (Westhues, 1972:10). It presently applies to an alternative culture that differs from the predominant American culture, or from what is commonly referred to as "the establishment." As originally used by Theodore Roszak in his *Making of a Counterculture* (1969), it described the "contemporary youth scene," although even at that date it did not by any means represent all youth. Some social researchers have aptly broadened its denotation to include older historical movements, such as the Shakers, the Dukhobors, and the Mormons in their early history, as well as the Brethren of the Free Spirit, Christian monasticism, and other movements (Westhues, 1972:8–12). In this book, however, it refers primarily to hippiedom in the largest sense, as it is from that group that the majority of the Hare Krishna devotees studied have been drawn into their new faith.

The hippiedom of the 1960s has been like a drama played with ever changing scenes. It reached its climax in 1969, but even yet has no clear denouement. By 1969 hippiedom had reached the end of its first phase, to be later described, and than waned rapidly in most American cities. Places where the street people had gathered in large numbers now often show little or no signs of them.

Few hippies are now to be seen in Haight-Ashbury district of San Francisco, which was one of hippiedom's greatest havens. The remaining hippies moved their center of activities across the bay to Telegraph Avenue in Berkeley beside the University of California. But even here the scene is changed. The street people who formerly had their love-ins with no visible signs of financial support have now opened their own sidewalk businesses on both sides of the avenue. There they offer every kind of handicraft from fancy leather belts and beads to ornamental rings with semiprecious stones. Just beyond, at Sproul Plaza, fiery student orators not long ago incited demonstrations and riots that became the signal sounded by the news media for similar occurrences elsewhere. The scene has again changed. There are still some speeches, but they are delivered to a placid audience. The speakers are now more likely to represent some religious group, such as the Unified Family or the Jesus People. The temper is different, too. At the noon hour one may pause and listen to any number of small musical groups within the space of a couple hundred yards. Among them are found the Hare Krishna devotees chanting and dancing for Krishna.

Classes of Hippiedom. Hippiedom is an amorphous phenomenon that has represented several types of persons. While not delimited by age, the term "hippie" has been applied primarily to youth—and not just in the United States since it has no national boundaries. We encountered hippies in India from various countries in the summer of 1973, but most were going home. Nepal still had quite a few, but that will change since a law forbidding the sale of hashish has been put into effect.

Hippiedom may be divided into several classes, which are based on the extent of involvement in the counterculture. One division, known by some as "heads" (Westhues, 1972:74), refers to hippies in the truest sense. These persons left their homes to live in the society of others like themselves and to devote full time to their alternative life style. They deviated from the views and standards of the dominant culture in many ways. As unfavorably characterized by the news media, these ways included departure from "established" sexual morality, heavy drug abuse, disregard for law and order, and sometimes violence. Another division, often called "the weekenders," practiced similar ideas only part time while generally leading "straight" lives. "Plastic hippies" or "teeny-boppers" refer to beginners, who had the external characteristics such as drug abuse and long hair (Westhues, 1972:74). Among the last two groups must be included many who were attending college or high school, or who were employed.

These varieties of hippies constituted only one expression of a more universal youth revolt, which during the 1960s often recruited young people during their first year at college, when former cultural ties were weakened. Often separated from their families, they found new sources of authority among their countercultural peers.

The restlessness of American youth in the 1960s became a worldwide phenomenon, which often erupted in revolt. Such explosions among students and other young people provided the background of the Second International Seminar on Youth Policy in Vienna, Austria, in 1968. The topics studied and statements made as part of the program showed a new awareness and demand for action by youth all over the world.

As a result of the twentieth-century population explosion, more than one-third of the world's population is estimated to be below twenty-five years of age. Never before in history have youths been so widely educated. Increased communication through radio and television via satellite also helped unify the concerns of youth by cutting across national boundaries, political ideologies, and races and creeds. Leaders were often created by the news media as messages of revolt were reported throughout the world. The youth revolt in the United States often quickly found widespread sympathetic expressions in South America, Western Europe, India, Japan, and even Czechoslovakia and Poland. The demonstrations of young people in various countries who joined their American counterparts in protesting President Johnson's Vietnamese War policy were examples of this effect of our advanced communications systems.

As might be expected, however, the youth rebellion has varied from country to country. In the developing countries, youth has carried the banner of the struggle for liberation. In the newly independent countries of Africa and Latin America, young people have spearheaded freedom movements and have found places for themselves in most of the political parties. The students of France, like those in America, demonstrated for university reforms and for a voice in university affairs. Thus the cry of "Power to the people!" promoting a participatory democracy has not been only an American dream. The collapse of the De Gaulle government was due to some extent to student power. Student rebellion in Indonesia has also been credited with choice of a new government compatible with its demands. Such events clearly demonstrated as never before the impact of youth as a force for social change.

Social change has, however, been stimulated by youth groups in the past. In the 1840s the Italian patriot Mazzini organized his Young Italy youth movement to seek Italian independence. He later championed nationalism throughout Europe, founding two other youth organizations, Young Europe and Young Switzerland. Russia and Germany also experienced youth rebellions in the nineteenth century. The Chinese student movement achieved importance in its effort to break down the old traditionalism and mediaeval social order and accept a Western liberalism. Like those in Europe, the youth protests occurring in the Latin American countries were largely political. The spread among youth of Marxism in Europe gave rise to communist communes when economic opportunities became scarce in the postwar world (Ahluwalia, 1972:1–19). The Young Communist League in America also played at least a minor role in youth dissent earlier in this century.

Although the present American counterculture has not been the first expression of youth rebellion here, it has nevertheless had its own distinct character. If it has at times demonstrated against government policies and thus played a political role, it has also made a deeper protest against the present *practices* of our "American way of life."

Beginning with the sit-ins in the South in 1959, young people rallied to the Civil Rights Movement, and student organizations promoting greater human dignity and freedom began to mushroom. Most authorities agree however that the Vietnam war united more young people in protest than any other factor. This protest cut across lines that had formerly separated countercultural youths from others. Every delay in terminating the conflict was met with stiff resistance, marked by sit-ins, demonstrations, and riots. The extension of the war to Cambodia brought further reprisals, and was met with worldwide student demonstrations. More violence occurred in various cities of the United States, and student strikes closed a number of institutions of higher learning.

And yet protest against the Vietnamese War, important as it was, was only the rallying cry for youth to unite in rebellion against more deeply engrained cultural problems. As this is the phase that most concerns hippiedom, it is our chief interest here.

Interpretations of the Counterculture. In recent years many social observers have projected great changes in the organization of our society. Moreover, investigators have described the appearance of the counterculture as a crisis in our social system. Some theorized that it marked the beginning of a new culture. There has been a general unity of opinion concerning the broad causes of the counterculture. Differences of opinion are found when authorities attempt to explain those causes.

The insights of Philip E. Slater regarding these causes are well suited for interpreting the data from the Hare Krishna Movement. Slater postulates that there are three basic human desires that must be fulfilled in order to have a stable culture. But these desires—the needs for community, engagement, and dependence—are frustrated in American society. Although these desires and their opposites are present in all people, when one is emphasized too greatly over the other, discomfort occurs. As our culture has slowly developed, they have been thwarted and frustration has occurred.

The desire for community is the wish to live in close fellowship and cooperation with others in a collective unity. For example, although some form of collectivism that subordinates the individual to the welfare of the group has been the more usual way of mankind, our emphasis upon individualism in a competitive life has taken precedence over the desire for community, according to Slater. At an earlier period in our history we had close associations in business and fellowship with those who were our friends in the neighborhood, but this time has passed. Among other reasons, changes brought about by technology, the growth of the cities with their tendency to cause anonymity, and the mobility that allows our automobiles to separate us have helped break our ties to family and community.

The desire for engagement is the wish to deal directly with social and interpersonal problems. Slater believes that America has had the tendency to avoid direct confrontation with chronic social issues. Too often we have been satisfied with filing a report, establishing a commission to study a social issue, or passing a law. We have employed short-range solutions instead of making the lasting adjustments necessary to remedy the problems. We do not want to be personally involved.

The desire for dependence is the wish to share with others the responsibility for controlling one's impulses and guiding one's life. Although any training that emphasizes to an extreme either dependence or independence will cause discomfort, Americans have stressed the latter. The ensuing discomfort in our society appears as a desire to escape responsibility for making decisions. Although authoritarian submission would lessen our problem, our deep-seated ideas of democracy keep us from achieving this end. In stable societies the control of an individual's impulses is usually the responsibility of the group. In changing societies such as ours, however, the controls tend to be internalized and less dependent on the enforcement of the group.

The suppression of community, engagement, and dependency can be traced to our commitment to American individualism. We have believed that we could be the masters of our fate and thereby have been forced to become emotionally detached from our social and physical environment. We come at times to feel some guilt about our competitive life and our indifference to others, since our childhood training also emphasized cooperation and sharing. Extreme individualism denies the importance of interdependence, the repudiation of which technology itself supports. Technology has sought to free us and to make us more independent from others, but the more it succeeds, the more lonely we become (Slater, 1970:5–26).

Many commentators on the social scene agree with Slater that the counterculture is part of an inevitable revolution in social values that will ultimately lead all people in the United States and in other industrial nations to a new society and an alternative way of life. They believe that the present social system is obsolete. They also agree that people are suffering a loss of selfhood due to their alienation from themselves, from others, and from their environment. The basic cause of this impending transformation in our civilization is seen as the growth and power of our technology. Through advertising, we are continually led to wish for more and more possessions, the fruits of technology. This problem is in turn related to the competitive nature of our individualism, as Slater and others have claimed.

In giving free rein to technological change, we have precipitated social change. We have in effect abdicated the control of our environment to the "whimsical deity" of technology. The changes brought by technology are so great that the desire for social change based on human needs rather than on those of technology has appeared as another disruptive force (Slater, 1970:44, 71).

The current energy crisis may put a rein on and redirect our technology. It may force our industries to manufacture items in accord with basic needs rather than stimulated desires, and thus transform one ideal of the countercultural revolution into a reality.

Our very prosperity gained through technology has often influenced our system of values. We have equated our ideal good with material success. Our educational system is designed to equip us for achieving that goal. A Protestant Christian ethic, which has been said to measure our "heavenly standing" in proportion to our material success, has given it moral backing (Leonard, 1972:27). Perhaps to the regret of those belonging to the establishment, youth who have grown up within this social system have seen its inconsistency and done something about it. A conflict has sprung up between the ideal of being free to enjoy life in a world of plenty and the true reality, the domination of technology in a competitive system.

Our predicament has been pictured as a conflict between two cultures, the old and the new. In their polarized extremities they represented respectively "the far right—authoritarian, puritanical, punitive, fundamentalist" against "the New Left, with its emphasis on equalitarianism, radical democracy, social justice and social commitment" (Slater, 1970:98).

The new culture was characterized as not being homogeneous, however. Slater among others noted the split between the militant activists and the nonactivists. The former stressed political confrontation and revolutionary action to try to bring about changes in the structure of society; the latter renounced society in order to find inner experiences and "pleasing internal feeling states" (Slater, 1970:114). The latter group best characterizes the hippie.

To what extent has a new consciousness developed? Consciousness may be defined as "the total configuration in any individual, which makes up his whole perception of reality, his whole world view" (Reich, 1970:14).

Have we outgrown one type of life that represents the spirit of American individualism, the support of our competitive free enterprise? Our Constitution, in declaring that each individual should be the source of his own fulfillment and achievement, has fostered this system. It has been said that the competitive self-interest thus fostered gave rise to corruption. Unable to change with the times, it continued to teach that material success was due merely to hard work. Further criticism has said that as the market system grew, man's labor and environment became commodities valued as money to permit competitors to profit from the exploitation of labor and resources. This meant that scientific techniques were to be developed and applied for greater efficiency.

In dictating specialization of labor and mass production, technology has threatened our pursuit of happiness by limiting our opportunities. The growth of technology has made its impact felt not only through pollution and the careless use of natural resources, but also through the creation of large cities with their ghettos. It has effected changes in our traditions, family relationships, and even in our religions. Most of all, it has alienated human beings from their environment, from others, and from themselves. Work is no longer self-expression. Man has more and more become a cog in a machine, dominated by one desire—money (Reich, 1970:21–30).

These specific conditions have been said to have contributed to the present counterculture. May we not generalize and say that every culture has an ideology that embraces knowledge of everything those in the society must have in order for them to behave in conformity to its norms? This includes not only instrumental knowledge of how things should be done, but also knowledge of the society's structure of value, its ideas of right and wrong. Accordingly, each member of the society is instructed to think in a certain way so that he may be able to conform to expectations of behavior and contribute to the furtherance of the society's ideals. The culture will then continue as long as its members can explain events through this system of meaning. Where such experiences contradict and do not reinforce these principles substantially, countercultures arise (Westhues, 1972:25–28).

What the social researchers mention as specific causes are but examples of things which countercultural youths have felt in varying degrees to be realities conflicting with an ideal. They have abandoned the established culture to create a new one. In so doing they have tried to develop a culture that will conform to the experienced realities of this time and place. They hope thereby to recover or discover a meaning for their life.

The conditions discussed also correspond essentially to the ethical deprivation theory of Charles Y. Glock, whose studies in this area are an extension of H. Richard Niebuhr's hypothesis concerning the origin of religious groups. Glock's theory is able to account for the growth of the Hare Krishna Movement, which is not a derivative of a primary religion of the culture. Ethical deprivation, according to the theory, is "exemplified by the person who becomes satiated with the economic and social rewards of life and with the efforts to obtain them, and who seeks some alternative system of values which will inform him as to how he should act." The Krishna devotees fit this part of his typology, but are an exception to its full expression. According to Glock, a secular response reflects "a rejection of the general value system" of the society, while a religious response represents "an alienation from the dominant religious system" (Glock, 1964:25, 28, 31).

The Hare Krishna Movement is a religious response that includes a rejection of the established American secular culture as well as the established religions that form part of that culture. It incorporates countercultural secular values into its religious philosophy.

It may be of interest to note that as religious responses to the established churches, the recent development of the Hare Krishna Movement, the Jesus People, and the increase of occultism may be contrasted with similar religious protests growing out of the latter part of the nineteenth century. I refer particularly to such "metaphysical" sects as the New Thought healing groups, including the Churches of Divine Science, Religious Science, the Unity School of Christianity, and Home of Truth. We have also noted that the occult explosion in the last few years had its counterpart in the last century with the development of organized Spiritualism and Theosophy, the occult wing of the metaphysical movement. While representing religious responses to what their members considered the sterility of American churches, the metaphysical sects were not countercultural. By and large they met the crisis of the nineteenth century's conflict between science and religion by postulating a God of scientific law. Their philosophies became religious sciences, whose laws they believed to be demonstrated experientially for one's better health, prosperity, happiness, and welfare. They were mirrors of American culture, as I have shown elsewhere (Judah, 1967).

The healing sects in particular expanded their goals beyond physical healing. Even in their early development they offered material prosperity and all the pleasing benefits of the American ideal. At a time when many churches were freshly involved in the struggle between religion and science occasioned by the new theories of Darwin, they felt no conflict. The good things of life would be given to them by a God of Science, who as Principle could be known and utilized. As part of a different religious protest against the established American churches, the Pentecostal sects began to emerge as movements toward the end of the nineteenth century. While they have been fundamentalist in viewpoint and have placed an emphasis on the religious experience of speaking in tongues, they remain strongly within the Christian tradition.

By contrast, however, although the "metaphysical" sects have varying associations with Christianity, their basic philosophy, which developed out of the milieu of American Transcendentalism, is more often akin to the monistic view of the Hindu Vedānta or dualistic Gnosticism. The "metaphysical" sects have certain points in common with the Hare Krishna Movement, insofar as they share to some extent a common historical heritage, in addition to accidental correspondences. Both exhibit a type of panentheism in which God is believed to be all and in all. They both believe the soul of man contains a spark of divinity; man's individual self continues in a future life after death; matter exists, but is a lesser reality. Jesus is revered as a great divine teacher, but stands in a lower position than ultimate reality. The cause of evil is finally due to one's ignorance of his true nature and relationship to God; ultimate salvation of all is eventually assured. In both groups, validation of the principles of the faith by some form of religious experience internalizes an entire way of life, whether according to the ideals of the establishment in the former case, or the counterculture in the latter example (Judah, 1967:13–17).

One may however find differences between the metaphysical sects and the Pentecostals, and the Hare Krishna Movement and the Jesus People of our present countercultural era. Although the two recent movements have entirely different religious backgrounds, their ideologies and ways of life reflect similar countercultural features. The protests that both are making will be later outlined in the case of the Hare Krishna Movement, including antipathies toward the established organized churches and synagogues. Essentially, however, both the Hare Krishna Movement and the Jesus People represent revolts against the established culture in similar ways. Both are seeking to validate an alternative style of life—a new culture and a new set of values—a new consciousness through meaningful shared experience in religious context.

Two Stages of a Counterculture. Students of the countercultural movements have noted two divisions in development: a charismatic beginning followed by an organized stage. Although Max Weber applied the term "charismatic" generally to individuals, it is also applicable to movements such as hippiedom. The first stage of hippiedom in our present counterculture was marked by its entry into the various Bohemian sections in larger cities. This occurred during the 1960s in districts like Greenwich Village in New York and Haight-Ashbury in San Francisco. In such places its adherents cast off the social roles, rules, and views that marked them as belonging to the predominant culture. This emotional, essentially irrational stage was often marked by personal religious experience through the use of drugs. While characterized also by "lofty ideals like love, freedom, and peace" (Westhues, 1972:193), hippiedom's use of drugs signified its experience of joyful freedom from the establishment.

The second stage of organization occurred, according to Helen Constas and Kenneth Westhues, through the commercialization of the movement and the simulation of the hippie by the establishment in the lengthened hair styles. As a result, the self-expression and uniqueness was lost and the external characteristics became a mass phenomenon. In the late 1960s, hippies who wanted seriously to continue their alternate way of life began separating themselves from others who seemed too "freaky." By 1970 the charismatic stage had ended and the organized stage was well under way. By 1972 as many as 5000 communes and communal arrangements were estimated to be operating in the United States and Canada (Constas and Westhues, 1972:191–194).

The first phase of the counterculture had within itself the seeds for its own transformation. Loosely united by protest songs, rock concerts, and mass media coverage of its demonstrations, it was more of a protest than the presentation of a unified positive philosophy. The freedom to do one's own thing is not highly suited for achieving a common culture, which was in any case not necessarily desired. While the first phase of the counterculture presented some common ideas that represent a different way of looking at life, a new consciousness, which tangentially the data from the Hare Krishna Movement seem to support, there were psychological reasons for its failure.

First, the data seem to indicate that the counterculture lacked a single charismatic leader who could give it a unified authority for a viable alternative way of life. Leaders like Timothy Leary too often demonstrated in their own lives the lack of survival value of some of their ideas, as we shall later see.

Second, a close fellowship with others of similar ideas and experience was missing during the first phase. The various successful communes of the second phase of the counterculture originated with groups that had similar ideas and goals. The communes allow these various groups to live together in alternative cultures of their own liking. As Gregory Johnson has discovered concerning the devotees of Krishna in the Haight-Ashbury District, the Hare Krishna temple became for them the alternative community thay had hoped to find. Such community could not be experienced, however, in the larger context. The devotees felt that they could not pursue the quest for a chemically-induced transcendence in the context of a materialistic drug culture. The disparity of goals and ideas prevented the creation of "community," defined as the close fellowship and shared experiences of like-minded people with common purposes and ideals. As one devotee said (Johnson, 1970a:[1]):

> I really believed in community in those days. I expected to live in a place where there were completely new forms of living . . . Many different things were written about it. Well, such a place didn't exist then and it doesn't exist now . . . everybody was just kidding himself, if they thought a community existed. I did not know what it was until I joined Krishna Consciousness.

Third, not only was a close fellowship missing, but there was no common routinized experience. After all, as another devotee said: "The dropping of acid can be a lonely experience." He was referring to the fact that the experiences originating from ingesting LSD are individualistic even though a group may take the drug at the same time. Each may have his own experiences that are unshared by others; it is as though one were entirely alone. We note later the variety of phenomena, a variety in marked contrast to the routinized shared ecstatic experiences in the worship of Krishna, in which a contagious religious enthusiasm of similar content rises to the rhythmic chanting and dancing.

Fourth, the initial phase of the counterculture lacked a common purpose to unite its followers. When asked why he believed everybody thinks the Haight-Ashbury is falling apart, another devotee contrasted the communal life with the larger, more chaotic counterculture of the first phase (Johnson, 1970a:[11]):

> The Haight is disintegrating because it lacks a common purpose. There is nothing people can share . . . There is no possibility for engagement. Every person is bound into their own skins. All they care about is their own needs. They satisfy these needs by consuming something; then they need it again.

While one must recognize the validity of the two-stage theory, the data on the Hare Krishna Movement indicate that the transition from one stage to the other was not an abrupt one. A few of the Krishna devotees had already lived in various types of hippie communes even before they joined the well-organized commune of the Hare Krishna Movement.

The Hare Krishna Devotee as Part of the Counterculture. Hare Krishna devotees, whether remaining for a time in employed positions, going to school, or giving full time to being hippies, typically first became part of the counterculture principally because they were looking for meaning they could not find in the world of the establishment. They were, therefore, willing to experiment with an alternative style of life, which they hoped would liberate them from feelings of alienation that stemmed from conflict with and rejection of the established culture. If not working or going to school, they had previously experimented with other aspects of the counterculture. Some joined communes and lived in mountainous areas or on beaches, where they practiced *yoga* techniques for spiritual realization while taking drugs. Others formed part of the floating population comprising the hippie communities in various cities here and abroad. One characteristic of the counterculture's first phase revealed by data from the Hare Krishna Movement was the mobility of its adherents. As already noted, mobility continued among the Hare Krishna devotees in the second phase.

Age and Social Status. In searching for reasons for their dropping out of the established society, one discovers that it was not because they had tried and failed to achieve the American dream of material success. They had not really started. Of those surveyed, 85 percent were twenty-five years old or younger at the time of the survey; only 3 percent were above thirty.

It was also not due to financial deprivation, because they are largely upper-middle-class youth. Their fathers, mostly in business or professions, were making an average annual salary of $17,000, with a median range between $12,000 and $15,000. In arriving at these figures, an executive engineer whose salary was reported only as "upper tax range," and a corporation executive whose annual income his son could not estimate, were discounted.

CHAPTER SEVEN

COUNTERCULTURAL "PROTESTANTS"

In the preceding chapter we looked at theories enunciated by social researchers as the basis for the countercultural rebellion. It is now time to discuss the protests that the devotees of Krishna have themselves made against the culture of the establishment. Because of the magnitude of these we are treating the religious objections in a separate chapter. It will also be noticed that in the case of the Hare Krishna devotees, the protests are not only against the established order in favor of countercultural principles, but also in part against some failures of the counterculture itself (see Chapter 6). Their religious objections are treated separately in Chapter 8.

In most cases, the protests of the devotees of Krishna against the establishment represent countercultural attitudes that the devotees currently hold. The extent to which the philosophy of their spiritual master has reinforced their countercultural position will be discussed. In other cases, we shall observe how Swāmi Bhaktivedanta has changed their ideas. It may be significant that elements of the counterculture that might have contributed to its instability as an alternative style of living, such as drugs and promiscuous sex, are forbidden by their new philosophy.

Protest Against a Surfeit of Possessions. The devotees of the Hare Krishna Movement have indirectly supported the attack on technology that social researchers regard as the primary raison d'être of the counterculture. Since most come from upper-middle-class families, they grew up with the advantages and material products that technical knowledge has provided. The majority seems to have questioned the life whose principal aim was material success and the accumulation of possessions. When one devotee expressed himself concerning his life at home before entering the counterculture, he said:

> I was miserable . . . I mean, I have a rich family and everything. Everything was there, but it was a miserable situation.

Some had seen their fathers tied to their work from morning until night, day after day, for what? To add to their surfeit of possessions. They questioned whether this was the meaning of life. As one devotee said in speaking of his father:

> His whole thing is devotion to work, just plain work, and he doesn't realize that they're just going to kick him out in another ten years or five years without a care, so it's just misplaced devotion.

Others, after entering the counterculture, discovered that taking drugs, like the accumulation of possessions, was another form of sense or ego-gratification. This alone was sufficient cause for them to change. One devotee remarked (Johnson, 1970a:[2]):

> It took me a long time to figure out that drugs were just another object of ego-gratification and selfishness. They are illusory objects that are placed in front of you to make you want them and feel important. It makes no difference whether it is a new car, a pretty girl, a meal in a fine restaurant, or the best acid that you can find—they are all the same. They create anxiety because as soon as you have one you want more. The only way out is to give it all up. Not just one or two, but all of them. Then you will realize that you don't need objects to feel important.

Observed statistically, their answers indicate that before they had become devotees of Krishna 35 percent were strongly opposed to the practice of accumulating possessions, 27 percent were moderately opposed, and 23 percent were indifferent. Therefore, 85 percent were opposed, while only slightly more than 7 percent moderately favored and about 5 percent strongly favored the accumulation of possessions. Those opposed were able to carry their protest over into their newfound life in the Hare Krishna Movement. No matter what reasons may have informed their views before, the Movement gives them a unified view, a rationale for continuing their belief, which forms part of their total meaningful world view, their new consciousness.

In accord with their protest, their spiritual master has also criticized the establishment in countercultural terms: "The philosophy is to work hard, get dollars, and enjoy as you like. This is misguidance. Therefore, the young are not happy" (Bhaktivedanta, 1970a:19). He further warns that technology, while continually inventing more and more things for sense gratification, can also endanger the whole world. He writes in his exposition of the *Bhagavad-gītā* (Bhaktivedanta, 1968a:282–284):

> The demoniacs are engaged in such activities as will lead the world to destruction . . . The materialistic people who have no concept of God think that they are advancing . . . They try to enjoy this material to the utmost limit, and therefore always engage in inventing something for sense gratification . . . Such people are considered the enemies of the world. Because, ultimately, they invent or create something which will bring destruction to all . . . The demoniac person thinks: 'So much wealth do I have today, and I will gain more according to my schemes. So much is mine now, and it will increase in the future, more and more.' . . . Such demoniac persons are enamored by the possessions they have already—such as the land, the family, the house, and the bank balance. And they are always thinking to improve such things.

One devotee attacked the establishment's materialism on its own ground. He cited Matthew 9:21, Jesus' words to the rich young ruler to give up all his possessions and follow Him, and also Matthew 6:19–21 concerning not laying up treasures on earth, but seeking spiritual ones (Hayagriva dās Brahmachary, 1966b:15).

This does not mean that the devotees have turned their backs on the fruits of technology. Automobiles, radios, television sets, and so on that should not be used for their own sense gratification may be employed in the service of Krishna to spread Krishna Consciousness.

According to the philosophy of Chaitanya, material possessions are only an expression of illusion. Therefore, they cannot form part of the transcendental spiritual life and truth that the devotees seek and identify as Krishna Consciousness. They regard all property as the possession of Krishna anyway, and consider it sinful to have more possessions than one needs. To be sure, the devotees are not unmindful that money is needed for food, clothing, and shelter. When asked concerning this, however, the answer has always been the same in essence—"Krishna will take care of it." Their trust and unconcern for "tomorrow" is reminiscent of something said by a Galilean almost two thousand years ago.

Protest Against the Vietnam War. The Vietnam war was probably the most significant factor in driving the devotees from the society of the establishment to the counterculture. Of all the protests they have made, none has registered as strong as this. Of those who answered the question (all but 3 percent), 68 percent registered strong opposition to the war, 21 percent were moderately opposed, and 11 percent were indifferent. None expressed any degree of favor whatsoever. Their attitude was probably one reason for alienation from the family. As part of the establishment, the parents had often supported the government's position in the early years of the war.

Once converted to Krishna, devotees became absorbed in the religious discipline and accordingly showed less concern about the war. They felt that they knew its true cause; by their own actions they were striking at the root of this and related problems. Trai dās, one of the devotees, expressed quite well the Hare Krishna Movement's philosophy on this point. When asked whether he was now concerned with Richard Nixon and the war, he replied:

> A little bit, but not with much feeling. We understand the underlying reason for it and that is godlessness, forgetfulness that everything belongs to Krishna. We understand that there is a root cause of all this distress, and so we're going to the root cause of all the problems: pollution, overpopulation, starvation, and wars. All these things are caused by forgetfulness of our real position to render sacrifice to the Supreme Lord. If we forget that, then everything goes wrong . . . If you see a tree and there's a wilted leaf here and there, the materialistic man says, "Let's pour some water on the leaf." But we understand that to help a tree, you have to water the root, then automatically all the leaves will benefit . . . Therefore,

> we are going to that root by reviving everyone's God Consciousness so that they benefit from this society.

Though not generally recognized as such, the devotees consider their program for spreading Krishna Consciousness as the really only effective social program for the ameliorization of society's ills. For them, the desire to serve Krishna is also secondarily a desire to help all humanity.

Protest Against All War. Since 11 percent did not answer the question, it is not possible to give an accurate figure concerning their degree of pacifism before conversion, nor to make a valid comparison with the figures for their protest against the Vietnam war. Perhaps the higher percentage did not answer the question because the pacifist position—probably held by nearly all in varying degrees before their conversion—is no longer valid for them. Of those who did answer, 62 percent had been strongly opposed to war under any circumstance before their conversion; 27 percent, moderately opposed; and 9 percent, indifferent. To the support of my above view, only 2 percent indicated moderate favor of war.

Indeed, the Hare Krishna Movement is not pacifist, although it does not support wars of aggression. Swāmi Bhaktivedanta declared his position on the subject in an interview in May, 1972:

> When Pakistan and Hindustan, that is, India, were preparing for fighting, some reporters came to me to take my opinion and I said that you must fight or there will be great agitation . . . They thought that I was a spiritual man and that I should say "nonviolence." [But I said,] "You must fight!" Just like Krishna said, you must fight . . . Where violence is, there must be violence. But generally we are not violent.

When asked whether he would use violence if his wife were attacked, he replied:

> Yes! . . . We are not of Gandhi's philosophy, which was, "If somebody attacks, I shall lay down my life, and let him kill me." No! We don't follow that philosophy. If somebody comes to attack me, I must protect myself to my best capacity. This is our philosophy. Our philosophy begins in the war field.

Thus to a devotee of Krishna nonviolence refers only to wars of aggression, but does not eschew the right to defend oneself or others.

This nonpacifism accords with the *Bhagavad-gītā*. First, its very setting is a battlefield where Krishna and the hero, Arjuna, are waiting to fight Arjuna's kinsmen. When Arjuna laments having to kill even enemies, much less kinsmen, Krishna chides him by saying that they are fighting a war of defense. He is a member of the Kshatriya or warrior caste, and therefore it is his duty to fight. Second, because there is no birth or death of the soul, the self is never really slain. Third, when Krishna orders fighting, it is for justice. Since Krishna has already ordained the destruction of the enemies' physical bodies, any violence done by Arjuna for justice is not really violence. Therefore, there will be no sinful reaction. Fourth, by not fighting, he would not keep his kinsmen from dying, and yet would be degrading himself for his failure to do his duty. Finally, to fight for Krishna is "transcendental consciousness" and gives no bad reaction. To perform action for the benefit of Krishna and for justice with no expectation of sense gratification is action in Krishna Consciousness (Bhaktivedanta, 1968b:64–78). In a general sense, however, may one legitimately ask whether this last reason is not the ostensible rationale for all religious wars—indeed for all wars.

Protest Against the United States Form of Government. The statistics of attitudes about the United States form of government before the devotees' conversion to Krishna also indicate that the majority held countercultural beliefs; 10 percent failed to answer. Of the remainder taken as a whole, 39 percent registered strong opposition to our form of government, 28 percent were moderately opposed, and 24 percent were indifferent. Only 7 percent were moderately in favor of it, and a little less than 2 percent were strongly in favor.

That some felt they had not had an adequate part in decision and policy making is probably correct, even though few were political activists. "Power to the people" had been one of the most frequent slogans advocating participatory democracy and uniting countercultural youth during West Coast demonstrations in the 1960s. Their protest does not indicate a particular leaning toward Marxism or Maoism. Less than 2 percent of the Hare Krishna devotees surveyed are known to have had Russian or Chinese Communist sympathies, even though their present alternative life represents in its own way a form of communism in action.

After they were converted to Krishna, their spiritual master continued to voice their protests. In an interview, and also during a lecture at the University of California shortly before the national election, he raised serious doubts about the value of voting. He suggested for America a *"Vedic"* four class system consisting of the earlier mentioned four traditional Hindu castes. This does not mean that he seriously advocates a complete change of government; he does suggest, however, that political and economic problems could be solved if politicians and economists were to take the advice of Krishna Conscious people. Mukunda, one of the first of the American devotees, quoted the spiritual master's words: "When the high judges are wearing *tilaka* on their foreheads, then our mission will be successful." Mukunda continued:

> We want to help the politicians to be better politicians, and we want to help the teachers of all kinds to teach people with love, gentleness, and understanding based on Krishna Consciousness.

The above statement points again to the fifth division that Swāmi Bhaktivedanta himself clarifies in his commentary on the *Bhagavad-gītā*. This class consists of Krishna Conscious people, who transcend "the mundane divisions of human society." Accordingly, Swāmi Bhaktivedanta teaches that, unlike many Brahmins who know only the impersonal manifestation of Krishna as Brahman, the Supreme Absolute Truth, Krishna Conscious persons have a knowledge of Krishna as the Supreme Personality of Godhead. These are the Vaishṇavas, the group to which the spiritual master says all Krishna Conscious people belong (Bhaktivedanta, 1968b:120). For him, these are the true Brahmins who alone are intelligent enough to advise on all matters. Thus the highest spiritual status is given to the Krishna Conscious person, even though it is believed that all people in their essential natures are spirit-soul and are equally part of Krishna. The devotee Mukunda summed up their political aspirations:

> We won't become a political party as such . . . The problem is that everyone thinks that unless he gets everything done through politics, he'll not get anything done, because that's

> the most practical thing to do, but we've realized that unless we do something spiritual with Krishna involved, also the spiritual master, then everything becomes not only impractical, but impossible to perfect. So the idea is that the politicians . . . take advice from Krishna Consciousness, [that] they read the books. The idea is that these politicians . . . can perfect their lives with Krishna Consciousness. It's not so much that we have to run, but we have to make it [that is, Krishna Consciousness] available to the people who are running the country . . . Just try to conceive for a moment the potency of a political candidate running for office having spiritual advisors who are telling him that his only goal should be to serve Krishna, not I've got to get this office or step on this guy—no, but the potency of a political candidate who has no other desire than to serve Krishna.

Protest Against the Established Methods of Education. Another characteristic of the counterculture has been its protest against the educational system. This has included not only that system's aims but also its methods. Students have rebelled against required courses and questioned the purpose and content of others. They have objected to the lecture method that prescribes copying down the words of lecturers for later regurgitation during examinations. Instead they have wanted more discussion, practical application, and greater opportunity for creative expression. Moreover, they have decried the competition involved in getting high grades, and have rejected the meritocracy of the grading system.

Some of these dissatisfactions have been evident among those who became devotees of Krishna. When questioned concerning their opinions about the established methods of education, 41 percent stated that they were strongly opposed, 32 percent were moderately opposed, and 21.5 percent were indifferent. On the other side of the scale only 3.5 percent were moderately in favor. Less than 2 percent were strongly in favor of the established methods of education. These figures exclude 12 percent who did not answer the question.

Table 2 indicates that the devotees are above the national average in education. Seventy percent have had some college training, but considering the economic status of most of their families one might have expected an even higher percentage to have completed four years of

Table 2 Educational Dropout Point of Hare Krishna Devotees

Below eighth grade	2.0%
Less than four years of high school	10.5%
High-school graduate	17.5%
One year of college	30.0%
Two years of college	14.0%
Three years of college	5.0%
Four years of college	16.0%
Graduate work	5.0%
	100%

college. Only 37 percent had definite plans for a livelihood before they dropped out of school. Only 24 percent considered their education to have been relevant, although about 31.5 percent simply refused to answer the latter question.

Table 3 indicates that they did not become dropouts because of poor grades. With a margin of error of a little less than 2 percent who did not answer, approximately 54 percent had grades in the A and B range; less than 2 percent were on the D level.

Most devotees of Krishna have asked the question, What is the purpose of education? What does it have to do with man's real purpose in life? They have challenged the materialistic goals of American society—and thus education for material success—because they do not see evidence that material success has brought happiness to their parents.

The following testimony of a Hare Krishna devotee seems to sum up the general attitude. Speaking of his father's ambitions for him, he said:

> He wanted me to be an engineer really badly, and I kind of swerved away from that, so he wanted me to be a great artist.

Table 3 Average Grade Levels of Hare Krishna Devotees at the Time They Dropped Out of School

A	8%
A–B	2%
B	44%
B–C	8%
C	34%
D	2%

> And he still wants me to be something great . . . He always wanted me to be great in the eyes of society. That's the whole thing I'm trying to make him understand isn't the real goal . . . I told him . . . "We're both suffering, we're both in ignorance, we're both in the material world. We've got to get out. There's no safety here." I said: "You're not really happy here doing what you're doing. You're trying to make me do the same thing." And one time he admitted it. He said: "I know I'm not happy, but you let me be in my unhappiness!"

The devotee laughed. "He actually said that." His father holds an executive position in a large manufacturing company.

Another has expressed the challenge of most devotees to what is considered a materialistic education. He wrote (Nayana Bhiram Dās Brahmachary, 1968:31):

> Modern educational systems are generally a failure because . . . the emphasis is on material advancement rather than spiritual . . . despite the wondrous achievements of technology. People are more miserable because any attempt to exploit and lord it over material nature is doomed to frustration and failure.

This is a view that Swami Bhaktivedanta has also frequently expressed.

Although about 12 percent had dropped out of school before graduating from high school, Swāmi Bhaktivedanta has usually encouraged the completion of high school. Nevertheless, he offers a philosophy that appeals to their dissatisfaction with education: first, by emphasizing the importance of devotion over knowledge; and second, by depreciating the importance of material knowledge. The former spiritual master of the disciplic succession. Bhaktivinode Ṭhākur, was quoted by Swāmi Bhaktivedanta (Bhaktivedanta, 1970b:11–12):

> The advancement of material knowledge renders a person more foolish because it causes him to forget his real identity by its glimmer . . . By the advancement of material knowledge people are becoming more and more entangled in material existence.

Being dissatisfied with the public schools, the Society has opened the first of its parochial schools in Dallas, Texas, called Gurukula, "place of the *guru*." There children of devotees may eventually be able to receive a complete elementary and high-school education. At the present time children of the devotees from ages eight to fifteen may attend this innovative boarding school. Under the instruction of trained devotees the students receive instruction in history, geography, and mathematics, together with reading and writing of English and Sanskrit. One teacher is assigned to every twenty students. The teacher gives individual instructions and assignments so that each may advance as rapidly as his or her ability allows. The study period is for six hours a day, six days a week. On Sundays the children are "free to play as they like, imitating the pastimes of Krishna and taking part in the Sunday festival" (Satsvarūpa dāsa Gosvāmi, 1973:19) held in the temple for guests. Their parents are permitted to visit the children on semiannual parents' weekends.

The idea for this unique school originated with Swāmi Bhaktivedanta to counteract what he has considered to be the materialistic training received in the modern educational system, which he feels creates frustrated young people who do not know the purpose of life. He believes that regardless of our scientific knowledge, the products of our present schools lack self-realization and are thus no more than animals. By the time children are twelve years of age they are fully trained to believe that life is only for the gratification of the senses. Therefore, the school of the Hare Krishna Movement aims first to train Krishna Conscious children who will know that they are spirit-souls rather than material bodies. They will be trained to have this realization of pure consciousness. It is taught that this is the only way to real happiness.

This method of training whereby the young student receives individual spiritual instruction from a teacher, the Hare Krishna Movement equates with the *Vedic guru* method. In this system each family among the upper castes has a spiritual teacher to give religious training to its sons. With these methods Swāmi Bhaktivedanta aims to train future leaders of America who will have Krishna Consciousness. Only through such training, the Hare Krishna Movement believes, will responsible citizens emerge. Only through Gurukula will society be improved. The Movement believes that through its training of leaders, corruption, war, poverty, pollution, and other problems can be overcome. Therefore, the student is taught to be kind to everyone, not to be quarrelsome, to be charitable, clean, benevolent, self-controlled, completely devoted to Krishna, and free from material desires. Each is taught that serving Krishna is fun, and that material pleasure is not lasting. The ultimate goal is for each to discover the true meaning of life.

In this training the principal austerity is the requirement for the children to rise at 4:30 A.M. for *maṅgala-ārati,* the early morning worship. They are also encouraged to chant "Hare Krishna" as much as possible, but they are not to be forced or punished. They are to receive discipline with love and affection from only initiated devotees, who will teach the children by their own example (Satsvarūpa dāsa, 1973:10–19).

A person who joins the Hare Krishna Movement understands that his spiritual education will be a continuing effort. Those who are desirous of becoming ministers in the Society are given a curriculum requiring two and one-half years. Past education is not a requirement. If one is illiterate, the Society will teach him to read and to write. Since the study is entirely voluntary, discipline is not a problem. The principal requirements are sincerity and dedication at the time of entering, regardless of one's past history, because it is believed that by practicing Krishna Consciousness, the previous misdeeds will be corrected. Theoretically, completion of these requirements is necessary for formal initiation into the Movement, although in practice some receive initiation in a short time.

The curriculum includes not only the study of the primary scriptures, the *Bhagavad-gītā* and others such as the *Bhāgavata Purāṇa,* the *Brahma Saṁhitā,* the *Iśa Upanishad,* the *Teachings of Chaitanya,* and the *Nectar of Devotion,* but also public chanting and preaching (The International Society for Krishna Consciousness, 1970:21–23).

During classes the devotees sit in a circle on the bare floor or on pillows and take turns reading selections from the scriptures. An appropriate commentary by the spiritual master always accompanies these. Although one devotee conducts a particular class, each person has an opportunity to ask questions and to make his own contribution to the study by noting other relevant ideas of Swāmi Bhaktivedanta. Idle speculation and arguing, however, are unwelcome. In class there is really only one authority—"Prabhupād," their spiritual master. No other interpretation should be introduced into the temple. Therefore, only questions about the teachings as interpreted by the spiritual master are welcomed. When on one occasion a visitor introduced a variant interpretation, he was politely permitted to speak briefly, but his point was quickly challenged. At the conclusion of the session, the president of the temple said rather sorrowfully: "I should not have let that happen. The deities were displeased."

Protest Against the Established Codes of Sexual Morality. The counterculture has been correctly associated with an alternative way of life in which the established rules of sexual morality have often been cast aside either in sympathy or in practice. Among the many changes have been the greater freedom in sexual practices among partners; opposition to monogamous marriages, or even to marriage itself as a rite; and recognition and acceptance of the life style of the homosexual. Such changes, while promoted by countercultural youth, have increasingly become accepted by many of the older generation. These developments have led some social commentators to raise questions about our established moral code and to predict changes in the future culture that is now developing.

Before their conversion to Krishna, the devotees, as part of the counterculture, had shown their opposition to the established codes of sexual morality. When asked their view on the subject prior to their conversion, 10 percent did not answer the question. Of those who did, 31 percent indicated strong opposition to the established codes, about 23 percent were moderately opposed, 37 percent expressed indifference, and only 7 percent were moderately in favor. Less than 2 percent were strongly in favor.

After conversion, however, their viewpoint changed. The ascetic discipline that they adopted for the goal of attaining Krishna Consciousness, like that among mystics in many religions, demands sexual restrictions and a different viewpoint. When asked whether they now believe that extramarital sex is always wrong, their answers showed the transformation. That which they have chosen as their own code, they have universalized for all people. Although 1½ percent did not answer, of the remainder taken as a whole, about 93 percent declared extramarital sex to be always wrong, while only 5 percent felt that it might depend on the circumstances.

Notwithstanding the fact that probably most of those still representing the counterculture would have extremely liberal ideas about sex and sexual freedom, the countercultural youth who have joined the ranks of the Jesus People have also adopted strict sexual regulations. Like our devotees, they too have given up drugs.

The cardinal rule of the Krishna Consciousness Movement against illicit sex means, as we have noted, that for the single men or *brahmachārīs,* and single women or *brahmachāriṇīs* there will be no sexual expression whatsoever. For those who are married, the restrictions against sex are stricter than for the married Catholic layman. When the Krishna Conscious ideal was compared to that which the Roman Catholic Church asks its laity to accept, one devotee reminded me: "Catholics are allowed to have sex at a time when they cannot conceive children; we are allowed to have sex only when we know we can."

The sacrifice they make for their faith was made more poignant when I spoke with a very young wife whose husband of scarcely a year had taken the Order of Saṅnyāsa. Since this complete surrender to Krishna disallows any personal contact between husband and wife, the husband generally moves away to live in another area. When I spoke with some empathy concerning the fact that she would never see her husband again, and would never be able to remarry, she replied quickly: "But my husband is Krishna. Krishna is my husband."

It is difficult for outsiders to understand the relation between man and wife in the Hare Krishna Movement. The young wife explained to me that it recognizes only two kinds of love. One is *kāma* or sexual love, which they practically reject. The other is *prema,* spiritual love—love first for Krishna.

Protest Against Authority. One of the characteristics of the counterculture, particularly in its charismatic stage, was its protest against authority—first, parental; then, in general.

Perhaps it is not a coincidence that countercultural youth appear to have come from families whose parents had the highest ideals of "freedom and liberal values" (Westhues, 1972:28, 32–33). This fact and a better than average education allowed them more quickly and decisively to see the contradiction between the social, political, moral, and legal ideals and their practice. The counterculture includes in its rejection not only the political and social structure of the culture, but also the entire society of the establishment itself for its failure to live by its own ideals. Consequently, its authority comes into question.

To be emancipated from the old rules, however, has meant that the counterculture rejected structured behavior. The proper formula seems to be "old rules—no rules—new rules," as Westhues following Burridge suggests (Westhues, 1972:41). Or to apply it analogously to our situation: first, authority, which is rejected; second, no authority and the type of antinomianism which Nathan Adler suggests occurs in hippies "whose frame of reference is threatened or has been disrupted" (Adler, 1972:78). In this phase, the authority for action lies only in each individual. Each one is a law unto himself. This gives the permissiveness for each one to do his own thing, and is anarchical. Third is the return of authority in the communal stage, if a commune is to be harmonious and enduring.

The devotees of Krishna voiced a repugnance concerning the question of authority in general before their conversion, although 8 percent abstained from replying. Strong or moderate aversion accounted for 57 percent of the remainder taken as a whole, and indifference for 28 percent. Only 15 percent indicated sympathies for authority either mildly or strongly.

When searching for other data that might corroborate and illumine reasons for their opposition to authority, the statistics concerning their relationships to their families are supportive. As might be expected, the devotees expressed more opposition than favor concerning parental authority before their conversion. Their strong or moderate antipathies totaled 51 percent of those interrogated, with 29 percent remaining indifferent. Only 20 percent felt positive in any measure toward parental control. When asked to check a list of attributes which described most closely their relationship to their families, only 25 percent indicated that they were very close; 19 percent considered that their family ties amounted only to mutual respect; 23 percent said that they were critical of each others' attitudes and ideas. Fully one-third, the largest percentage, expressed a lack of communication. This gives a ratio of about 75 percent unfavorable attitudes to 25 percent favorable. Some qualified their answers. One wrote: "My family? I don't even understand them." Another said: "We loved each other, but couldn't understand one another." And still another: "They can't see beyond their own beliefs, hard to talk to them."

The lack of a close relationship between parents and children is further seen in the fact that 34 percent admitted they no longer see their parents at all.

On the basis of the statistics and from conversation with various devotees, the reasons for their disrespect toward authority had been due to their opposition to all expressions of the establishment. Their government, some felt, did not represent them, although I have observed no present antipathy toward it. Still, it had been sending them to fight and often to die in a war they believed to be immoral and senseless—one they could not support. Their parents, as part of the establishment, have often accepted either willingly or reluctantly the goals and policies of the government. Therefore, in many cases their antigovernment stand entailed opposing their parents.

Instead of the authority of the establishment, they accepted the authority of Swāmi A. C. Bhaktivedanta Prabhupāda on their own volition. One should not generalize concerning the entire counterculture from the data gathered only from the Krishna devotees. Still, if these observations are valid, they indicate at least the possibility that many of the youths who revolted against authority in the 1960s were actually seeking an authority by which they might live. They were only dissatisfied with laws that tried to force them into a way of life of which they disapproved.

If the American version of law and order represented by the Hare Krishna Movement seems in one sense to be a closed society, a cultural island, it is still one that its devotees would like to share with the whole world, if only its inhabitants would become Krishna Conscious.

Protest Through Drugs

Protest Against the Established Laws Regarding the Use of Drugs. Although the devotees of Krishna have now given up drug abuse, the Hare Krishna Movement takes a neutral position concerning drug legislation because it does not feel qualified to judge. It also does not censure drug abusers, but suggests Krishna Consciousness as a substitute for what it considers material bondage (Hayagriva Dās Brahmachary, 1967:1). Like others in the counterculture, most devotees had earlier objected to laws regarding drug abuse, although about 6 percent failed to answer the question. Of the remainder taken as a whole, 75 percent had been evenly divided between being either strongly or moderately opposed to the existing laws regarding the use of drugs, about 19 percent were indifferent, 4 percent were moderately in favor of the laws, and about 2 percent were strongly in favor. Even though they may have suffered through the use of drugs, still it resulted in rewarding experiences for many, whether valid or not. Some believe that these experiences spurred them on to seek Krishna Consciousness, even though they may have had their share of bad trips, causing eventual disenchantment with drugs.

Prior Drug Use and Former Occupations of Hare Krishna Devotees. Most of the devotees of Krishna belonged to one of the three classes of hippies before their conversion. Although 6 percent failed to answer one of the two questions concerning their use of drugs and their occupations six months prior to their entering the movement, of the remainder only 6 percent indicated no use of drugs. Of the others taken as a whole, 46 percent would have been classed as heads, who were by definition extensive users of drugs. Those who were either in school or who were working accounted for 26 percent each, while 2 percent were in the armed forces. This means that of those who were on drugs, 52 percent had been either part-time hippies in school or in employment at least six months prior to their conversion.

One survey made in 1967 at a West Coast University demonstrated that from a random sample of 600 students there was a correlation between the degree of adherence to the "hang loose ethic," which rejected traditional society, and the frequency of drug use. Of the sample taken, however, 78.8 percent indicated they did not use drugs (Suchman, 1972:122–123). If the percentage were to be considered a measure of the small minority of college-aged youth who were countercultural, the much higher percentage of drug users among the Hare Krishna devotees before conversion might be the first indication of their countercultural sympathies.

Extent of Drug Use. Since the devotees' former lives showed such heavy involvement in drug abuse no matter what else they had been doing, the complete transformation of their lives and the drug release thereafter shows the effects of their conversion to the Hare Krishna Movement. Before they had entered the order, 91 percent had been smoking marijuana one to twelve years; 74 percent indicated frequent use. Closely following in popularity was LSD, which 85 percent had been taking one to seven years. Of this group, 3 percent did not answer the question concerning their extent of use, but 36 percent admitted to frequent ingestion, while 46 percent were occasional users.

Sixty-eight percent reported having taken hashish from periods of less than a year up to ten years, although a little more than one-half reported having taken it for only up to two years. Of only 61 percent answering concerning the extent of its use, 54 percent admitted to frequent use, and 46 percent smoked it only occasionally. Heroin was used much less. While 17 percent used it for periods up to six years, only 6 percent took it frequently.

The barbiturates and amphetamines had some popularity also, and a small percentage had had some contact in varying degrees with all mentioned drugs. Fifty-two percent took amphetamines; 22 percent took barbiturates.

The answers concerning their actions six months prior to joining the Movement and those concerning their spiritual involvement just before their conversion point out the relationship between the use of drugs and a search for meaning. A majority of 61 percent of all responding testified that they were looking for self-realization and meaning during that period by practicing various forms of spiritual discipline, while still indulging in drugs. Of course, other purposes were also apparent. Some took drugs principally for nonreligious reasons. As one said: "I was taking it because I was bored and I was doing what my friends were doing" (Johnson, 1970b:65).

As Johnson suggests, however, the new philosophy to which they now adhere supplies the explanation, as shown by the continued quote of the same devotee: "But we really couldn't help it, because drugs are merely part of the age we are living in—the age of Kali" (Johnson, 1970b:65). The age of Kali or the Kali Yuga, according to Hindu philosophy, an evil age, and in the Hindu cyclic theory it is the final period before the termination of this particular cycle of illusory material existence.

Still another devotee suggests probably quite correctly that drug use may be part of a protest against the establishment and a desire to escape from the world that the establishment is creating (Hayagriva Dās Brahmachary, 1966a:24):

> No wonder so many young collegiates are trying to flip out permanently on super drugs. Perhaps they sense a part of the truth: that man is not proprietor and lord of the creation, but is a custodian and servitor. Perhaps this is their way of saying, "We don't want any part of this hell you've made for yourselves." So they use psychedelics as a springboard to propel themselves into different realms previously known to mystics. But the drug "flip" is only temporary. It is temporary because it is artificial.

Table 4 shows the detailed correlation between those practicing some spiritual discipline for self-realization while either using drugs or not using them.

Table 4 Correlation between Spiritual Discipline Practice and the Use of Drugs

Practicing spiritual discipline while on drugs	61%
Practicing spiritual discipline, but not on drugs	1%
No practice of spiritual discipline, but on drugs	32%
No practice of spiritual discipline and not on drugs	6%

Religious Experiences Reported While Using Drugs. Excluding 8 percent who did not answer the question, 74 percent of those taking drugs reported that under their influence they had experiences of a religious nature. The importance the devotees attached to the drug induced experiences, however, varied with the individual. Some spoke favorably of at least some of their drug experiences. One said: "All experiences were planned and controlled by Krishna to lead me to Krishna Consciousness." Another felt that the experience showed that the aim of life was self-realization, and this created the incentive to make a serious quest. After having the experience of white light, one decided that "no entity in existence could deter my quest for Truth, or weaken my belief in a higher existence."

Others, however, reacted negatively to the question. One said: "At the time I thought it was a religious experience. Now I can see I was deluded. Actually we can't have a religious experience without the mercy of a pure devotee." This attitude of course denies the validity of any religious experience occurring outside the worship of Krishna.

In order to delineate the types of religious experiences they reported when asked simply to describe them, I have separated those that were drug induced into two categories. These are not mutually exclusive, nor should they be considered to limit those recording them to just those particular experiences. The chief importance of such an outline is to show the variety of experiences through drugs, especially when the experience is not routinized by a common philosophy.

1. The feeling of unity and little differentiated experience may be subdivided according to their various expressions:

(*a*) Eighteen percent reported seeing a white light all around. (Description of reality given by some belonging formerly to Leary's drug cult.)

(*b*) Feeling of union with God, the Void, Nature, or Reality accounted for 17 percent of the experiences of those reporting. (Description of reality akin to a form of monistic Vedānta, which many were following while on drugs.)

(*c*) Thirteen percent felt that they were not a body, but spirit or pure consciousness. (Description of realization of Krishna Consciousness.)

(*d*) Two percent experienced the feeling of eternity.

2. There were also noetic feelings of usually more differentiated experience. All of these had but single examples:

(*a*) Feeling of being able to see "how Nature was working."

(*b*) Feeling that "LSD is the way to happiness and the love of God."

(*c*) Feeling of a "widening of one's concept of reality."

(*d*) Experience of "death and rebirth."

(*e*) Experience of "existing on a different plane."

(*f*) Feeling that "there is a controlling universal consciousness."

(*g*) Knowledge that "beyond the material nature there was God, the Supreme Controller."

(*h*) Feeling of "being the unworthy recipient of kindness and love, whose source I was unable to discern."

(*i*) Feeling of "simultaneous relatedness and diversity of life in everything."

(*j*) Feelings of "separation from God."
(*k*) Experience of "seeing Krishna in the sky."
(*l*) Feeling that one was "clairvoyant and could see spirits."
(*m*) Experience of "seeing one's past lives."

The experience of unity with an Impersonal Absolute, such as the Hindu Brahman, signifies liberation and the achievement of the highest reality for a follower of Śaṅkara. But a Hare Krishna devotee considers this experience to be inferior to his goal. We have called attention before to the belief in the subordination of the impersonal Brahman to Krishna, who is personal. To realize Brahman is to realize only the eternal feature of Krishna, and is therefore not to be sought by the Hare Krishna devotee. The complete truth, according to Swāmi Bhaktivedanta, is the realization of the Personality of Godhead. This is Krishna in his form as a transcendental person. It is the realization of eternity, knowledge, and bliss (Bhaktivedanta, 1968b:30). Perhaps this helps explain why Hare Krishna devotees do not seek the unitive experience through drugs. Because of man's *karma,* there is only one suitable and quick way to eliminate the effects of this evil age and find liberation—by chanting the "holy names of Krishna."

Interpretation of the Religious Experience Obtained Through Drugs. The collected data of Joseph Mouledoux may help elucidate the religious experience that many of the devotees of Krishna had had prior to their conversion, and while still on drugs and practicing some spiritual discipline. He has noted that the "coming down" from a common LSD trip, the reentry into the everyday world, is interpreted from the experience as a reentry into a deficient world. It is a world that "cannot provide the experience and knowledge which have been obtained on the communal LSD trip" (Mouledoux, 1972:118). This view has two sides. First is the apprehension of the world of the establishment as the lesser one. Second is that the true reality is one of transcendental experience, a world that in one's expanded consciousness is indescribable in terms of material experience. It is not subject to logical explanation. One who has had such a religious trip on LSD can more easily accept later the idea of a miraculous reality such as the world of Krishna, because he has already seen a similar one. This is an experience that the majority of people who have not taken psychedelic drugs will never know.

A number of scholars have pointed out that not only in Eastern religious thought, but also in Western history during times of cultural crises, certain viewpoints become popular. For example, the world is seen as sick; life in this world is a living death. Such ideas are often based on an apocalyptic vision of the imminent end of the world. The two responses to this condition have been either to seek to transform the world, or to escape from the world to *real life* in a spiritual world through a transcendental experience. The early gnostics chose this path. In our time, Mouledoux (1972:120) notes that the search for a new life through a transcendental experience by using drugs can be seen as a

> logical response to, a variation on, and at the same time a rejection of the arrogant technological vision which has dominated Western life since the Enlightenment. In making such a retreat from the world the purpose is to escape from the life which is viewed as death and at the same time to come alive.

Transition of the Religious Experience Through Drugs to Krishna Consciousness. If the above is true for those seeking an escape from the material world through drugs, how much more relevant it is for those who later became devotees of Krishna. Their world of reality is also a spiritual one to be achieved through Krishna Consciousness, a world transcendent to this material world of the establishment, a place of unhappiness and illusion. Thus, to depart from the discipline is to be influenced by illusion. To leave the Movement even for a short time is to return to illusion.

There is ample evidence that, even before their conversion, dissatisfaction with the culture and religion of the establishment led many of the later devotees of Krishna to escape first to the transcendental world revealed through drugs. For example, there is the case of the devotee Anahdāsī, who turned to drugs because, as she said:

> I was angry and frustrated. I felt cheated, lost, and was very disappointed . . . After doing some drugs, I was a little less angry, but I still felt cheated, frustrated and was still confused

> . . . I was always very rebellious against any kind of authority, against any kind of restrictions, because I had a feeling—of course in our spiritual identity we are always free—I always felt that any time some difficulty or hindrance came up, it was nonsense. Why can't I do what I want to do? That's my constitutional spiritual position, but it doesn't work so well in the world. Government institutions or anything in particular—I was indifferent. It wasn't worth getting involved with, and *there wasn't any solution that I could see except going away somewhere mentally* or physically. (Italics added.)

This devotee is a good example of the young person who had been dissatisfied with the binding authority of the establishment but who had voluntarily accepted a more severe one—the discipline of the spiritual master. Paradoxically, through the performance of their strict discipline the devotees have found what they often spoke of as their spiritual *freedom* to serve Krishna in loving devotion in his transcendental world of Vaikuṇtha.

The further experience of Anahdāsī reveals perhaps paradigmatically for others also the transition from experience through drugs to Krishna Consciousness. Having first sought to escape from the frustrating and disappointing material world to a transcendental world through drugs, her achievement had one imperfection. This led her to Krishna. But let her tell her own story:

> I had taken a hit of speed. I had taken so much that I was standing there . . . and my body was swaying from side to side. And this girl was asking me questions about the construction of the universe and I was answering her perfectly, completely, about how it all happened, how it was all annihilated . . . and the whole thing. And actually it was pretty correct . . . It was pretty valid from what I remember of it in terms of Prabhupād's teachings. And then she hit me. She said, "Where does love come in? Where does love come from?" And I was totally lost . . . I didn't even know the implications of that question. It just totally floored me. That's why we have to understand it's the Supreme Personality. That's where the love comes from. It's not just atoms and molecules. That's where it's coming from—Krishna, everyone's supreme lover.

Another had experiences with drugs that add to the same paradigm. An interview by Mr. Gar Kellom with Prasutī produced the following taped dialogue:

> "I wanted to find God. I took a lot of LSD one time and I was just living alone and was fasting . . . meditating, reading *yoga* books . . . Then I realized that I just wanted to love God. That's all I wanted to do. I was trying to think, what can I do? I just want to love God. Then something flashed inside. Why don't you get to the Krishna temple? I didn't even know that much about the Krishna temple at all . . . I just went and lived there. I stayed for two months that time. Then I left for four months."
>
> "Where did you go?"
>
> "To *māyā*," she answered.
>
> "Back to the mountains?"
>
> "No," she replied. "I didn't go to the mountains this time—I just flipped out. I was in and out of mental hospitals for about a year and a half."
>
> "Then you came back?"
>
> "Yeah, because it was my real heart's desire. Once you taste the love that's in Krishna Consciousness you can never forget it . . . And giving up all those things like drugs and things for the self—they're not that hard, once you make up your mind you're going to do it. It's gone! The desire! It'll bother you a bit, but it's nothing, if you're determined. It's so much nicer to feel this natural energy."

While the hippie has so often glorified the experience of taking drugs, the foregoing interviews indicate something different. Though many of the devotees had meaningful transcendental experiences, others had become completely dissatisfied. Probably nearly all became disenchanted with drugs before their conversion. They were ready, therefore, for this new experience as devotees of Krishna. Another devotee described life just prior to his conversion as "getting stoned, drinking wine, running around, lying around, and trying to get money for psychotherapy." One of the inducements to join the Movement that has been used by the devotees has been to suggest to hippies that unlike drugs the worship of Krishna produces a continued "high."

Gregory Johnson found in his investigations of the Hare Krishna devotees in the Haight-Ashbury in the 1960s that dissatisfaction with drugs grew after 1967 when they became more accessible (Johnson, 1970a:[l]). People began taking them for sense gratification or for "self-medicated enlightenment," without any sacrifice or commitment. As one of the devotees said (Johnson, 1970a:[9]):

> Somewhere it all changed; acid was distorted into a pleasure trip. It became just sense gratification. People were feeding their heads like they were feeding their mouths. It was used to bring out the human animal nature rather than his spiritual nature.

Finally, there were the very few who wanted and tried, but were unable to change. One such was Richard Grimm, who was in and out of the Berkeley temple for more than a year. His mind had been so addled by LSD that after a final sojourn at the state hospital he ended his life by jumping from the Golden Gate Bridge.

Disenchantment with Charismatic Leaders of the Drug Scene. The adverse affects of drugs often influenced devotees to relinquish them. But there is also evidence that others became less intrigued by drugs when they saw what happened to some of the drug culture's leaders. As has been pointed out, the creation of a counterculture depends on charismatic leaders. They are necessary to displace the concepts of the rejected establishment with the countercultural ideology supporting a new culture (Westhues, 1972:37–39). In the early days of the counterculture, many saw Timothy Leary as a charismatic leader who could help youth drop out of the established society and turn on with drugs. Our evidence, however, indicates that the charisma did not continue for long. Leary dropped out of the scene; drugs took their toll on his associates. They no longer represented the ideal many youths wanted to achieve. The devotee Prasutī is again a case in point. She had belonged to Timothy Leary's Brotherhood, and had known another charismatic leader, a "Professor," and Leary's friend. She said, however, "He was really flipped out. Now I look at him—like his wife, his old lady, I saw her down the street. And I used to look up to those people *so* much, but their consciousness is like a vegetable."

In concluding this section on the general protests that the devotees have made against the establishment, one further observation should be made. The devotees of Krishna comprise largely but not exclusively one part of the counterculture. Slater had distinguished the social and political activists from those who were more interested simply in gaining pleasure from the use of drugs. Our data have indicated that the devotees belonged to this division of the nonactivistic users of drugs. Still it is not correct to lump even the majority in this category without further redividing it. Whereas some devotees took drugs just for pleasure, as Slater's category suggests, we have observed that the majority were simultaneously trying to find meaning through some religious discipline. The fact that the philosophy they followed as well as their experience with drugs were inadequate to their total needs was reason enough to make this phase only an intermediate one. Since the religion of their parents was part of the rejected establishment, the next chapter will consider this religious protest and the reasons for choosing devotion to Krishna.

CHAPTER EIGHT

THE PROTEST AGAINST AMERICAN FORMS OF RELIGION

Decline of Liberal Christianity in the 1960s. The protest against American forms of religion is very revealing. Even though one must take care not to overstate the universality of a protest, in providing meaning to American youth in this period of cultural transition this particular protest does point to problems in the liberal Christian churches and Jewish synagogues.

Today more people seem to be showing a deeper interest in the various forms of religious expression than have other generations for centuries. At the same time, however, membership in our more liberal denominations has declined. Church giving has fallen off. Many congregations are dwindling; some churches are closing. A few of the respected Christian seminaries in both Europe and America are discontinuing their work; in certain cases their libraries are being broken up and their books sold. Some Christian theologians have already spoken pessimistically of the period as the Post-Christian Era, and many occultists have termed this the beginning of the new age of Aquarius.

Dean M. Kelley, a United Methodist minister and Director for Civil and Religious Liberty of the National Council of Churches, has made a careful study of the present decline of the liberal Christian churches. The rapid loss in membership in the 1960s reverses a 200 year trend among the major denominations. The statistics show a rapid decline in adult membership, and an even greater loss in church school attendance. After the liberalizing tendencies of Vatican II, even the Roman Catholic Church showed in 1970 its first drop of membership of this century. By contrast, the conservative churches such as the Southern Baptists, Seventh Day Adventists, Pentecostal churches, and the Mormons, are growing at increasing speeds (Kelley, 1972:1, 2, 33). Figures 2 through 6 show the decline in the 1960s of four major denominations, which reflect similar declines in smaller churches, compared with the increase of the Southern Baptists and other conservative churches.

Some of the reasons Kelley offers for these changes are supported by our evidence from the Hare Krishna Movement. The decline can in part be traced to the growing alienation of young people from the liberal Christian churches. Martin Marty of the University of Chicago has noted that whereas the courses in religion are full, the college chapels are becoming empty. A Gallup poll of college students in 1970 discovered that only 42 percent of the students answered affirmatively to the question, "Is organized religion a relevant part of your life?" (Nordin, 1972:1, 14). In a survey made in 1966 of 2200 youths at the tenth grade level, 60 percent said they attended church at least once a month and 53 percent said they went to church once a week. A poll of the same age group four years later indicated that only 26 percent were going to church each week. This is a decline of more than 50 percent in just four years. In spite of this abandonment of the churches, 54 percent of the youths polled in 1970 considered religion to be very important.

A pessimistic report issued by the Board of Education of the American Baptist Convention (Northern Baptists) confirms and augments this information. It speaks of the crisis in the church school, and it questions whether by 1980, its one hundredth anniversary, such schools would still exist. The statistics showed that its church school membership decreased from 1,000,000 to 670,000, or about 30 percent, in just four years (Winters, 1971:1–2). The reasons offered—the greater mobility of the population, increased recreational and sport attractions, and the lack of interested church school teachers—are at best only partial explanations for this rapid decline. While these factors do play their part, the evidence points to the failure of the churches to answer to the needs of their contemporary membership. The burgeoning numbers of youth and others joining the many non-Christian movements and forms of noninstitutional Christianity such as the Jesus People offer mute testimony to the real truth: the church has failed to reach the religious needs of youth and other age groups. At the same

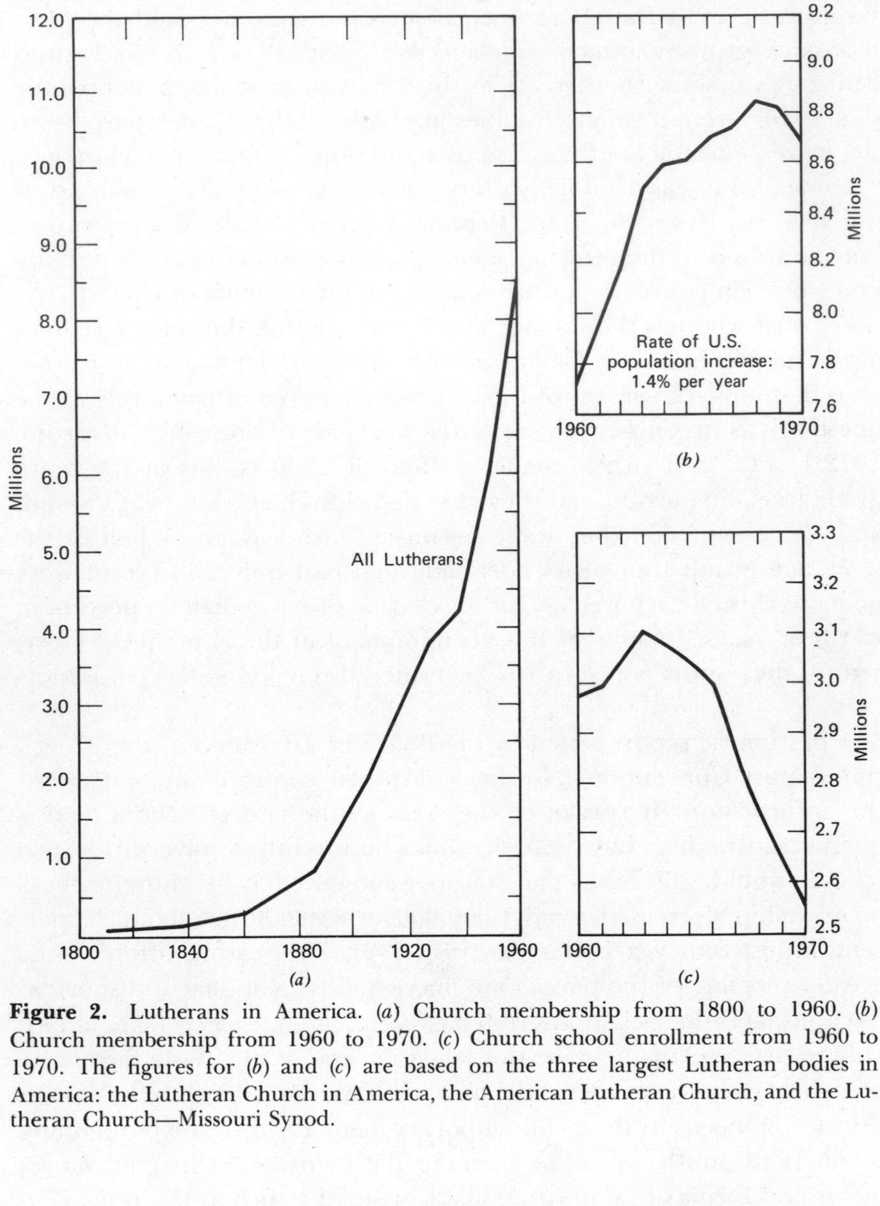

Figure 2. Lutherans in America. (*a*) Church membership from 1800 to 1960. (*b*) Church membership from 1960 to 1970. (*c*) Church school enrollment from 1960 to 1970. The figures for (*b*) and (*c*) are based on the three largest Lutheran bodies in America: the Lutheran Church in America, the American Lutheran Church, and the Lutheran Church—Missouri Synod.

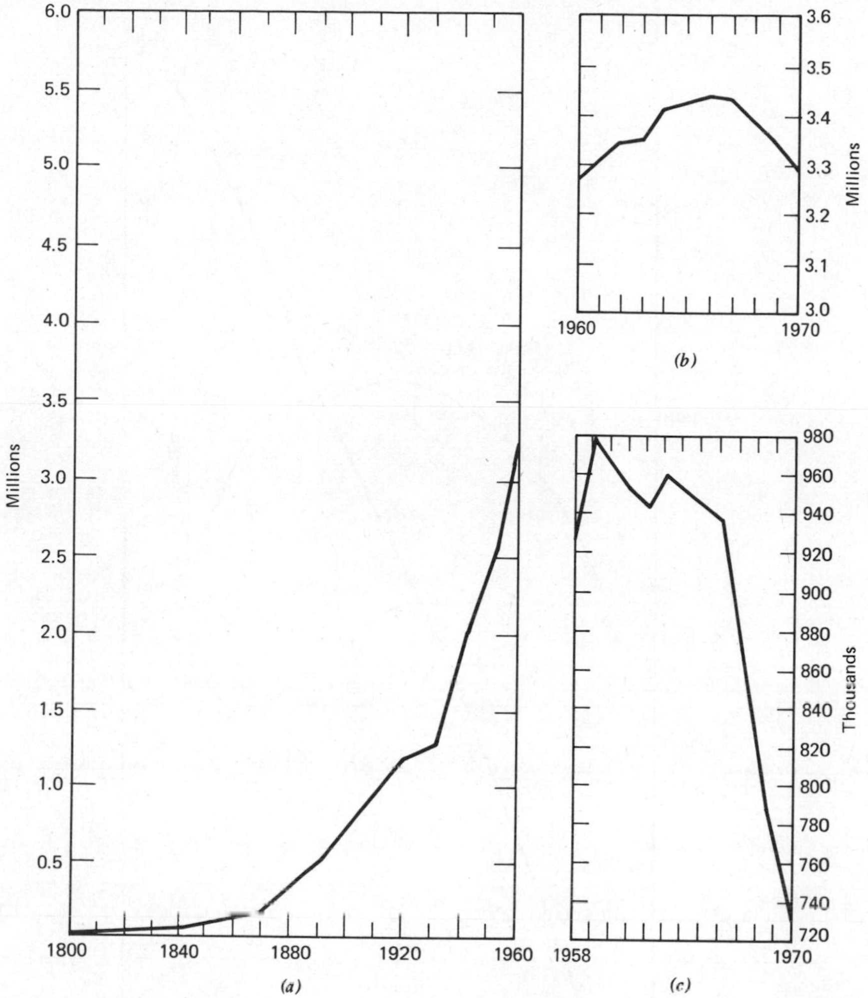

Figure 3. Episcopalians in America. (*a*) Church membership from 1800 to 1960. (*b*) Church membership from 1960 to 1970. (*c*) Church school enrollment from 1958 to 1970.

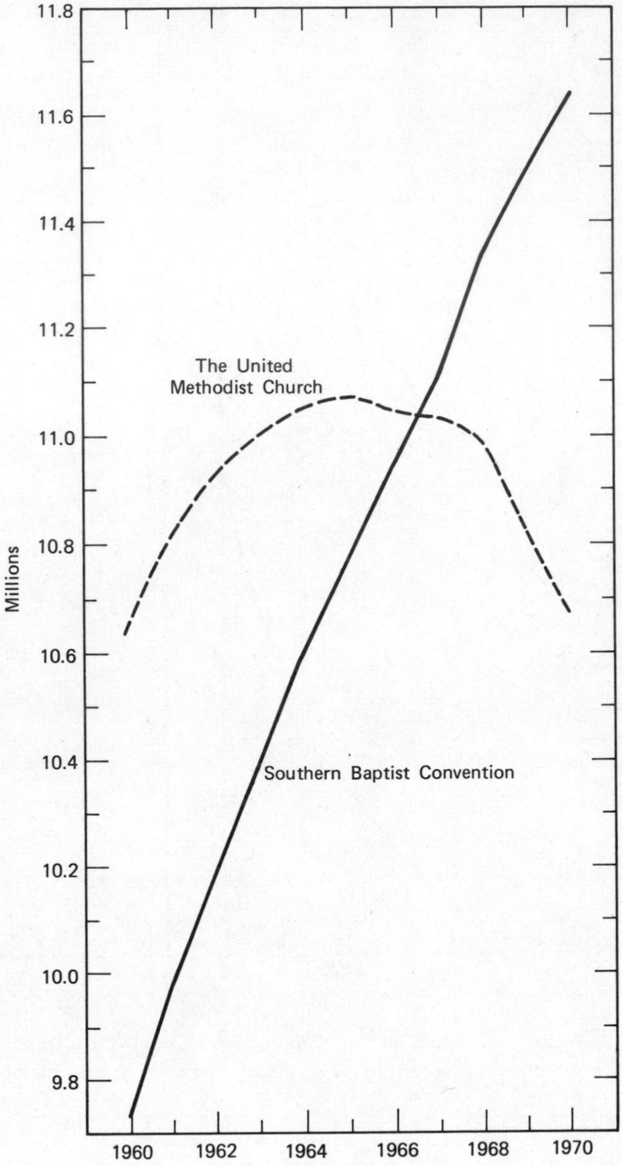

Figure 4. Membership of the United Methodist Church compared with the Southern Baptist Convention from 1960 to 1970.

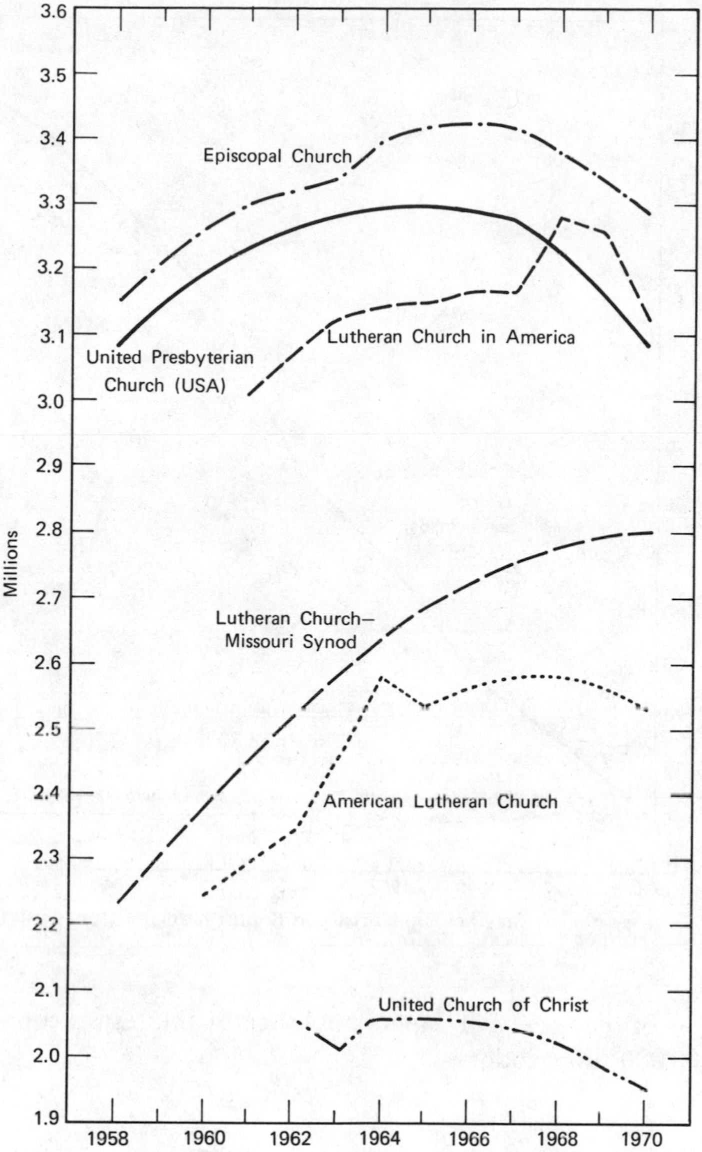

Figure 5. Membership comparison of six churches from 1958 to 1970.

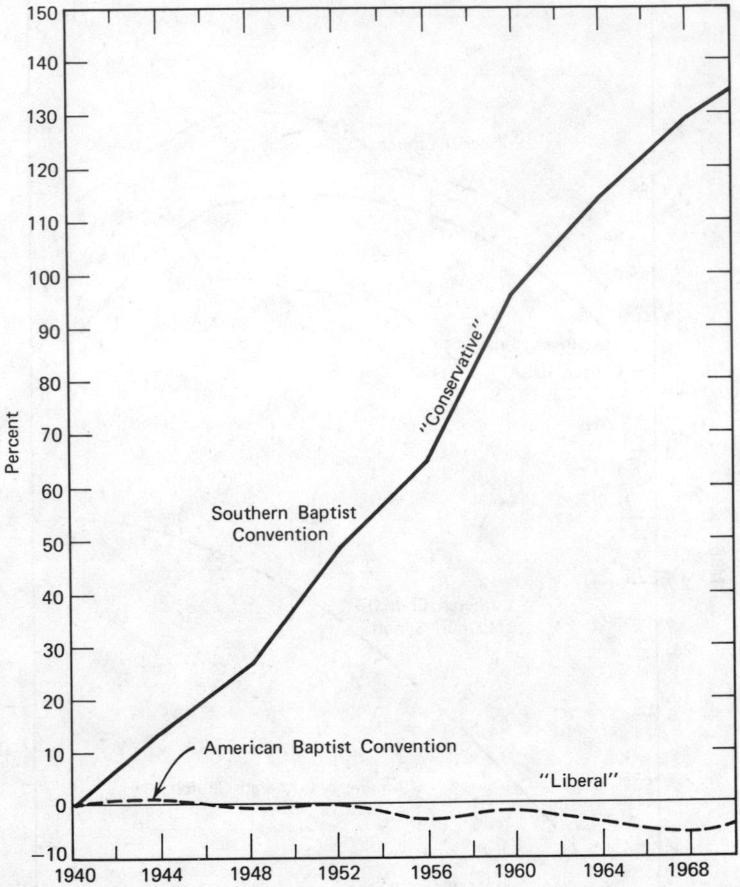

Figure 6. Proportionate membership increase in Baptist branches from 1940 to 1970.

time, one of the dozens of papers published by the Jesus People claims over 400,000 subscriptions.

Factors in the Decline of American Liberal Churches. Kelley notes five characteristics of liberal Christian churches as reasons for their decline (1972:vii–viii). These form a common denominator found neither among the thriving conservative churches nor in the Hare Krishna Movement.

1. The liberal churches are reasonable and receptive to outside criticism. This is not true of the Hare Krishna Movement. Although the devotees of Krishna are courteously silent when ridiculed publicly, in their temples they never leave unchallenged any variant to their views, nor are they interested in what scholars might contribute through literary or historical criticism.

2. The liberal churches are "democratic . . . in their internal affairs." Although there is a certain amount of freedom concerning ways in which the devotee may serve Krishna, the Society is autocratic. If the temples show any signs of participatory democracy at the local level, they are few. The invested powers increase from those of the local temple presidents to those of the spiritual master. Obedience is expected if the devotee hopes to develop maximum Krishna Consciousness. Even though one's particular abilities and desires are taken into consideration, the rationale is that one should be willing to do whatever is necessary in the service of Krishna.

3. The liberal churches are "responsive to the needs of men (as currently conceived) and will work cooperatively with other groups to meet those needs." The Hare Krishna Movement is also answerable to the needs of people but within the context of its own philosophy. It urges that above everything people need Krishna Consciousness. Since it believes that social activism gives only temporary relief and does not get to the root of problems, the Hare Krishna ministry is highly personalized. It relates to individuals as persons rather than to the social groups that many of the more liberal denominations emphasize.

In pursuit of its goal of Krishna Consciousness the Society does not cooperate with outside organizations. The explanation is that other groups do not have the proper qualities. Karandhar dāsa Adhikāri, the head of the Western District of ISKCON, declared that cooperation would be tantamount to corporate merger. He said:

> Quality is more important than quantity. Actually it's explained that one pure devotee is better than ten million churches . . . So one devotee can change the course of the whole world . . . Look at Lord Buddha, Lord Jesus Christ, Lord Krishna, or great devotees! . . . Because they were Krishna Conscious, they have changed the lives of millions.

4. Liberal churches tend to be relativistic. They recognize that no one person or church has a monopoly on truth. They also believe that

religion is only one way to an individual's fulfillment (Kelley, 1972:82). In contrast, the devotees believe that Krishna Consciousness is their *only* way to complete self-realization and fulfillment. While recognizing that Krishna may be worshiped under many different names in various faiths, final salvation is ultimately to be realized *only* when full fellowship with Krishna is attained. As Karandhar stated, "there is not even an alternative. Alternative means you have a choice. There is no choice. Either Krishna Consciousness or finished. That's all."

5. Liberal churches are interested in dialogue with others of differing views in the spirit of ecumenism and with the hope of deepening their own understanding (Kelley, 1972:82–83). The devotees are not only disinterested in listening to other viewpoints, but are also dogmatic about their beliefs. They see their view as being the whole, entire truth. That which varies from their view on any single point falls short of the truth. One must appreciate that these are youths who had rejected the culture and the ideology of the establishment. They were searching for a new basis for an alternative life style. They feel they have found it, and that it expresses the truth. Consequently any dialogue seems meaningless to them, and only threatens their security. Similarly, converts to Christianity in a country where Christianity is a minority religion are often more dogmatic and conservative in belief than other Christians.

6. I should like to add that unlike liberal churches, the Hare Krishna Movement adheres to a literalistic interpretation of its scriptures and emphasizes the importance of religious experience. Other countercultural religious groups such as the Jesus People, the Children of God, and the underground churches that are being organized in the United States and England resemble the Movement in these characteristics. And like the Hare Krishna Movement, these other religious groups incorporate certain countercultural elements. Whenever possible they seek scriptural support to validate their alternative ways of life. These are then internalized and given meaning as tenets of faith through the routinized experience shared by all in the common worship.

In a period of cultural change and consequent insecurity and alienation, many find greater need for an authoritative scripture that will give them ultimate values. These will be interpreted by a human authority and applied to their particular situation. Many therefore feel that absolute truth requires the literal acceptance of the scriptural words.

Organized Religion and the Counterculture. In light of the reports concerning church decline, the data on the Hare Krishna devotees should be relevant. Most devotees are young and have just recently left their former religions. But although our evidence is important for its wider implications, generalizations should be made with care unless supporting evidence is obtained from other sources. Furthermore, our information must be examined within the proper context: it concerns youths who come usually from one part of American society and who have had the experience offered by the life of the counterculture.

About 70 percent of the parents of the Krishna devotees are members of one of the established churches or synagogues, with a margin of possible error of less than 2 percent failing to answer the question. Almost two-thirds (64.5 percent) of their children had attended their parents' church regularly. When asked to identify the denomination or religion to which their parents belonged, the margin of possible error rose to 6.76 percent. Not only do most of their parents belong to an organized church, but almost 81 percent of those whose parents have a religious faith had training in that faith. Table 5 shows the denominations and religions indicated. It corroborates Kelley's observations and is of interest to our investigation. The large liberal Protestant churches, whose church school attendance declined even more during the 1960s than their adult membership, (Kelly, 1972:1–10) contribute most to the membership of the Hare Krishna Movement. Twenty-nine percent of the devotees stated that they had belonged to a Protestant religious denomination. If one adds also the representation from the Roman Catholic Church, the percentage of Jewish members,

Table 5 The Religious Affiliation of Parents of Hare Krishna Devotees

Roman Catholic	18.0%
Methodist	13.0%
Presbyterian	7.0%
Episcopal	5.5%
Congregational	4.0%
Mormon	2.0%
Jewish	14.5%
Jehovah's Witnesses	3.5%
Other	7.0%
None	25.0%

and those from other churches of the Judeo-Christian tradition, this amounts to approximately two-thirds of the total sample. Of the rapidly growing organized religious groups, only the Jehovah's Witnesses and the Mormons, totaling a little more than 5 percent, are represented. The largest Protestant church in the United States and one that has experienced rapid growth—the Southern Baptists—is not represented in the statistics of the Hare Krishna membership, nor are any of the rapidly growing Pentecostal groups.

Table 6 Ages at Which Hare Krishna Devotees Abandoned Their Parents' Religion

Age group 6–10	12.04%
Age 6	3.44%
Age 8	5.16%
Age 10	3.44%
Age group 12–14	25.80%
Age 12	5.16%
Age 13	5.16%
Age 14	15.48%
Age group 15–17	22.36%
Age 15	10.32%
Age 16	8.60%
Age 17	3.44%
Age group 18–20	10.32%
Age 18	6.88%
Age 20	3.44%
Those who felt they had not abandoned their Christian religion	6.88%
Those who felt they had not abandoned their Jewish faith	1.72%
Those whose parents at the time had no religious faith	17.20%
Those who had never accepted the religion of their parents	3.44%
TOTAL	99.76%

With a margin of possible error of about 8 percent, Table 6 shows at what ages the devotees abandoned their parents' religions. There were also those who had never accepted their parents' faith, or who felt they had never abandoned it, or whose parents had no faith at the time for them to abandon. But before considering the reasons given by the Krishna devotees for leaving their former faiths, we should observe that the devotees' actions reflect in their own way the problem of American religions in an established culture when the culture begins to show signs of transition. The data on the Hare Krishna Movement indicate that when the cultural pegs holding one's world view begin to weaken, a routinized personal experience shared with others may validate a new set of ideas, a new *Weltanschauung,* a moral basis for one's acts, and a new faith embracing these elements.

Some first experienced a drug-induced consciousness-expanding experience of union with Reality. This probably gave them limited validation, for reasons already shown. Others were moved by the experience of chanting "Hare Krishna." Still others, for example those who have found a renewed faith in Jesus Christ with the Jesus People, have had meaningful religious experiences that internalize countercultural elements similar to those of the Hare Krishna devotees. Some are seeking new meaning through various types of encounter groups. Finally, some find moral or religious satisfaction through secular demonstrations of social activism. For those who participate, these demonstrations may become an important experience; the participants become as it were members of a religious congregation, and their signs and slogans become the validating liturgy.

Krishna Consciousness and Former Faiths. There is no general agreement among the devotees concerning whether they have indeed given up their faiths on conversion to the worship of Krishna. Some, as might be expected, declared that they had never discarded their beliefs. Just how they reconcile their Judeo-Christian faiths to the worship of Krishna they do not often say in their reports. Still, Swāmi Bhaktivedanta recognizes Jesus Christ as God, albeit in a lower form than Krishna. He has also invited Christians to chant the "holy names of Krishna," declaring that in doing so they will become better Christians. So in his mind also there would be the possibility of simultaneously having two faiths, so long as one recognizes the preeminent position of Krishna. Since only a little more than 40 percent gave the "teachings" of their former faiths as the reason for leaving them, this would indicate that, like the Jesus People, the revolt is more against the churches and the culture they represent than against the teachings. As the devotee Sidheśvar said:

> I was a Methodist. I am a Methodist . . . The whole idea is that you don't give up your previous religious training . . . you expand upon it to its perfectional degree. There is just one God and he takes from all these various cultures; it's just putting it all into one pot. I can chant "Hare Krishna" and still believe in Jesus.

One young woman had abandoned her Jewish tradition and now believed in Jesus Christ. When asked whether she minded relinquishing her Jewish heritage, she replied:

> "No! As a matter of fact, my father asked me, 'What do you think of Jesus Christ?'
> 'Well, we accept Jesus Christ as a pure devotee of God, a Son of God,' I answered and he got—I thought he was going to start crying over the phone.
> 'You accept Jesus Christ? Oh! I just can't talk about it now,' he said.
> "And I was so innocent, because I didn't realize that I had said anything strange."

This bit of dialogue shows the extent to which this age is for some no respector of long-hallowed traditions. The testimony of youths joining the Hare Krishna Movement reveals in many cases that both Christian and Jewish traditions, which we ordinarily associate as part of American pluralistic culture, have little or no meaning for them. As Lochan, who had been raised as a Roman Catholic, said when asked about giving up family traditions, Western traditions such as Christmas, "It's all nonsense. I don't have any qualms at all." In replying, he laughed, and his Jewish wife, Krishna Vilasinī, added: "Like Prabhupād says, we can't artificially renounce anything. Actually we're replacing all of these things. We've tasted something better."

The next questions should be, Why did these youths abandon the traditional faiths, and what did they find in the Hare Krishna Movement which they did not find in their churches or synagogues? Table 7 gives part of the answer.

The percentage of devotees marking each of the possible reasons seems to indicate the high degree of alienation they have from the traditional forms of their former religions. I suggest that their feelings toward them are due at least in part to a different consciousness, the different way youth of the counterculture look at the world. Their former churches are composed of "people of the establishment who are just not with it," as one of the devotees expressed it. In their view, the churches are associated with a decadent culture, which must give way to a new one. Therefore, youth seeks new expressions of religion, new revelations to validate a new and meaningful world view.

Table 7 Reasons Why Hare Krishna Devotees Abandoned Their Former Faith *

1. Its incapacity to develop an experience of God	76.0%
2. Its incapacity to give a larger meaning of life	67.5%
3. Its incapacity to develop a close meaningful fellowship	62.5%
4. Its incapacity to give security	52.0%
5. Its religious teaching	40.5%
6. Its hypocrisy	32.0%
7. Its racism	32.0%

* The devotees often marked several as reasons.

The greatest needs shown in Table 7 are for religious experience and discovering a larger meaning to life, even though by illogical means. Failure to find a close fellowship and feelings of security were also reasons given by the majority of devotees for leaving the organized religions of their parents. The needs for fellowship and security are often felt by people who do not fit into a given culture; when such needs are felt by a group, countercultures may arise. The sad rejection of blacks by whites in America has led them to build their own culture in which "black theology" plays a prominent part. This theology generally supports a religion of enthusiasm, in which religious experience is important. Following O'Dea and Poblete, Westhues has pointed to the anomie and the need for community among former Roman Catholic Puerto Rican immigrants of New York City, who found themselves in a culture that did not reinforce their former world view. Consequently they were ready for the development of storefront churches and Pentecostalism that gave meaning to their new urban experience (Westhues, 1972:30–31). Robert Merton defines anomie as "a breakdown in the cultural structure, occurring particularly where there is an acute disjunction between the cultural norms and goals and the socially structured capacities of members of the group to act in accord with them." In a healthy society, conformity that accepts the ideals of the group and acts in accord with them is normal (Woods, 1971:180–181).

The disintegration of cultural norms may occur when people move to a country of divergent culture, as in the case of Puerto Ricans moving to New York. It may also happen during a period of transformation in an entire sociocultural system, and is in fact occurring in the United States due to rapid technological changes and their related effects, such as ecological and urban problems, more rapid transportation and communication, and the possibilities of alternative styles of living. During such times of alienation, religious enthusiasm is one expression of this need for security and wholeness. Richard Woods quite correctly views our present condition as responsible for the resurgence of occultism during recent years, as well as for the emergence of the Jesus People and the Hare Krishna Movement (Woods, 1971:181–186).

The devotees of Krishna found themselves in an established culture that had been defended by logic, but that did not fit their world view. As the devotee Mukunda said:

> I was in high school and began to perceive things in a different light due to various influences—a lack of being able to understand my environment, meaning the world in general . . . and found throughout my high-school happening I set so many stupid goals . . . . and when I attained the goals it just really was a drag . . . My conception of the world and how the world worked was constantly changing. So it's as though you build up a picture frame of exactly the way you see the world, and all of a sudden something comes along and knocks out one of your picture frame pieces.

Like Mukunda the devotees thus experimented in many ways while searching for meaning in a common culture of their liking.

Table 8 shows the principal reasons for joining the Hare Krishna Movement, and should be compared with Table 7. The predominant reason given was the sound of the *mantra,* Hare Krishna, which they considered the source of their religious experience. Fellowship with the devotees who represent other members of the counterculture was a close second. They are kindred spirits who had passed through and transcended the drug experience. They too had been on the same search for an alternative and fulfilling style of living. The reasons for leaving their former faiths they have found answered and fulfilled through the worship of Krishna. The shared religious experience gained thereby also produces the feelings of wholeness and security

Table 8 Reasons Why Devotees Were Attracted to the Hare Krishna Movement *

1. Sound of the Mantra	58.5%
2. Warmth and friendliness of devotees	52.0%
3. Philosophy of the Movement	41.0%
4. Prasādam (sacrificial food served)	30.0%
5. Power of the Spiritual Master	19.0%
6. Opulence of the temple	5.0%
7. Deity worship	5.0%

* The devotees often marked several as reasons.

they had lacked. They have discovered a countercultural way of life that is to their liking. Unless a suitable countercultural surrogate is to be found, to abandon the Movement would be to risk alienation again. This helps to explain why some who have left the Movement subsequently joined the Jesus People.

The percentage of Jews in the Hare Krishna Movement is second only to the percentage of Roman Catholics. At a recent national conference of the B'nai B'rith on the Jewish family, there was general agreement that drug abuse among young Jews who had entered the counterculture had its origin in the disintegration of the Jewish family. As they have left their ghettos, where they had no problem of self identity, Jews have become dispersed into American society. Problems in the family have resulted—the assimilation of the Jewish youths to the American way of life also has tended to weaken the Jewish traditional values that center in the family (Reed, 1972:1–5). The evidence from the Hare Krishna Jewish devotees, although mixed, by and large supports this view. For example, a young Jewish man gave as one of his reasons for leaving Judaism: "It was mainly social and didn't give any substantial realization." Another said: "Jews identify themselves too much as Jews."

For 78 percent of the Jewish devotees, the main attraction to Krishna Consciousness was the warmth and fellowship among the devotees. Eighty-nine percent said that they abandoned their synagogues because of the inability of their former faith to give a larger meaning to life. An equal percentage cited its incapacity to provide an experience of God. Two-thirds also said that it failed to give security. The strength of these reasons seem to indicate once more the breaking of traditions in cultural change and the need for shared experience with others having similar countercultural experience to give a valid meaning and security in an alternative style of life.

The Meaning of Conversion to Krishna Consciousness. This discovery of meaning and security has been one of the strengths of the devotees' worship of Krishna, who becomes the epitome of all that is meaningful. Having been converted largely through the close fellowship with others and by recitation of the *mahāmantra,* their lives have been transformed. All their actions are now devoted to learning more about Krishna and serving him. When asked about the meaning of the worship of Krishna, one devotee revealed her Methodist heritage in a new context: "It has given my activities and life meaning. I have experienced sanctification. It is a happy, natural way of life." Another wrote:

> Before, my attitude was generally cynical and I experienced a sense of despair and hopelessness concerning the future. My attitude now is very hopeful, and consequently I am developing a greater sense of responsibility. Krishna Consciousness is a way of life. It permeates one's whole existence. *It offers full meaning* and engagement for every man. (Italics added.)

When asked how Krishna Consciousness surpassed her former religion, she replied:

> In every way [there is] a sureness in my heart that this is the only way available for the complete satisfaction I longed for. Even from the first grade my religion seemed to be lacking, hypocritical, insufficient. It seemed to me that the teachings could be accepted as being true in essence, but that there must be more that we humans couldn't understand that wasn't in the Bible. *I felt that security would come from knowledge of God,* and that, though incomplete, the Bible had the most to offer at that time of my experience. (Italics added.)

Another said:

> My former belief was only a belief. No knowledge—only sentiment. The preachers didn't do as they preached, so it was not so convincing . . . Of course, the basic teaching, love God, is right.

And still another:

> Before entering Krishna Consciousness, I had the feeling that the world and all its goings on were a gargantuan mistake and the only way to live with any meaning was to see that life has no meaning outside itself. In this light any plans to enable a person to "win" the struggle for existence could only be seen as meaningless . . . Krishna Consciousness has meaning and permanent results.

Another fulfilling characteristic of Krishna Consciousness for many is that it offers them an active life in service to Krishna and to others in the context of their philosophy. When asked the reason for attraction to Krishna Consciousness, one replied: "It was my desire to serve. I discovered that Krishna Consciousness begins where all other movements, such as Yoga, etc., leave off." This desire of the devotee to serve Krishna cannot be underestimated. It is first evident in the word "*dās*" or "*dāsa,*" the second part of the Hindu personal names many of them have received. It is translated as "servant." Regarding themselves as servants of Krishna, moreover, marks the second stage in the development of Krishna Consciousness.

Serving Krishna, that is, doing that which the devotee considers to be a spiritual activity, often becomes a substitute for work in the material world of the establishment. The devotee Trai dās, answering the question concerning whether he had pursued a career before his conversion replied:

> Oh no! I wasn't doing anything because one can see the fruitlessness of working in material life. For instance . . . many people who come to Berkeley are the type of people who see that material life, working hard for a job to enjoy yourself, to work harder . . . hasn't made their parents happy. Their parents are fighting and miserable . . . So the young people can see that that's not making them happy. So they have to look for something else. And this is Krishna Consciousness. The enjoyment of the spiritual is what they are looking for—spiritual activity, because they have to have some activity. They just can't stop . . . They have to have some engagement, either material or spiritual engagement. If one sees that material engagement is not satisfying to . . . his spirit soul . . . then he has to seek out some kind of spiritual engagement. Krishna Consciousness is perfectly what I wanted, because it's the only full engagement of the spirit-soul.

Even more pointed are the words of the Saṅnyāsi Hanuman, who said:

> We can really help people . . . We are the only ones who give an opportunity, really, for an individual to cop out of the crazy game of material existence. And copping out, we can engage in Krishna Conscious activity.

In summary, we can list eight ways in which Krishna and Krishna Consciousness epitomize the values for which the countercultural devotees search:

1. The philosophy that Swāmi Bhaktivedanta has given them directs them to surrender themselves completely to Krishna. In doing so they are able to feel dependent upon him for everything, and thereby find a security that individuals striving for themselves in a competitive economy may not have.
2. This security is further enhanced by the belief that one is doing

nothing for his own sake. All that he performs represents an effort made in the service of Krishna. One has therefore everything to gain in Krishna Consciousness and nothing to lose.

3. This desire to serve, which seems so important to some, implies here the belief in a transcendent, personal, loving deity whom one may serve as the highest expression of reality. As data given by the devotees seem to indicate, such service is not possible in the same way nor is the security so great if the ultimate reality is thought to be impersonal. Moreover, the philosophy of Krishna Consciousness not only permits one to serve Krishna, but also to serve all mankind by propagating the knowledge of Krishna.

4. The philosophical belief that everything belongs to Krishna and that all efforts should be made only for his pleasure supports the countercultural rejection of accumulating possessions for one's own pleasure.

5. The Hindu system of *āśramas* or stages of life that the Hare Krishna Movement accepts allows for variation in one's life style while one is still deepening his or her Krishna Consciousness. As a *brahmachārī,* an unmarried devotee or student may pursue a full-time religious vocation connected only with temple life, and eschew any business, profession, or trade associated with the outer world of the establishment. As a *gṛihastha,* or householder, he may marry, raise a family, and follow any work he desires while living outside the temple, just so long as the effort is in the service of Krishna. Although the third stage, the *vānaprastha* or anchorite, is not practiced in the Society, much is made of the fourth stage, the *saṅnyāsi.* This is a role similar to that of the upper-caste Hindu who renounces the world, wife, and family to give full expression to his search for God. He is also one who usually travels from temple to temple with added duties. His main function other than deepening his own Krishna Consciousness is to teach and correct any mistaken interpretations of the philosophy, as well as to make sure that the discipline is being strictly followed.

6. ISKCON's interpretation of the caste system, rather than restricting a person to one type of work according to his birth, permits freedom to choose according to his desires. Moreover, it allows one the possibility of attaining the highest spiritual status—that of a Krishna Conscious person—while disavowing any material status that the devotee would associate with the illusory world.

7. The philosophy not only supports a countercultural way of life acceptable to the devotee, but the Society makes it possible for him to follow it. Consequently the devotee escapes from the anomie that he suffered in the culture of the establishment and also from what he considered to be the hypocricy of the establishment. Now for the first time he may experience as a unity the complete collocation of religion and culture.

8. This very service to Krishna in whatever form it takes becomes an escape from the work and life of the establishment, considered to be *māyā* or illusory, because the service to Krishna is spiritual, and therefore transcends the materiality of the illusory world. Therefore, Krishna and Krishna Consciousness are the epitome of meaning for the devotee.

CHAPTER NINE

FROM THE COUNTERCULTURE TO CONVERSION TO KRISHNA

This chapter is in part a summary of preceding data rearranged to show the steps leading to conversion to Krishna. It also contains new material indicating further the relevance of the Movement's philosophical tenets to the devotees' needs, and adds suggestions concerning the import of chanting in the process of conversion.

In this inspection of the data I adapt the model constructed by John Lofland and Rodney Stark, who used it to explain the process of conversion to a deviant perspective. They develop their view from their studies of Divine Precepts, a millenarian Korean Christian movement, which is now rapidly making converts in this country under its new names, the Unified Family or the Unification Church. Since the Hare Krishna Movement exhibits a greater degree of religious enthusiasm than the Unified Family, differences between our data have become apparent, but the model has been useful as a basis of comparison. Lofland and Stark's definition of conversion as the process of giving up one world view and system of ultimate values for another is particularly applicable to the devotees of Krishna (Lofland and Stark, 1965:862–175). The first predisposing condition in their model is tension.

Tension. Our study generally concerns only those countercultural youth of upper-middle-class families who have been disenchanted with the established culture. This alienation is the predisposing condition that creates their tension, and is the first step in the formula for conversion. The discrepancy between an ideal of the way things ought to be and the real state of affairs caused them to feel that there were new truths to be learned and new ways of living. Many believed that the culture of the establishment had run its course and needed to be replaced. They wanted freedom to build their own new world in another design. Their parents, like the older adults in the organized Christian churches and Jewish synagogues in which they had received religious training, represented variant views to theirs. In this sense they had a different consciousness from that of their parents and the other older adults, with consequent alienation from the culture and generally from their parents. This alienation created the counterculture of the Krishna preconvert.

Type of Problem-Solving Perspective. Many members of the counterculture became social activists and participated in demonstrations to try to change conditions, but very few of those who later became devotees of Krishna had engaged in such activism. Those who had were active for a short time, but had given up the game as a losing one. Some tried to solve their problems by escaping from them through drugs while remaining employed or in school. Others left their jobs or dropped out of their educational programs. They left their families usually to join the "street people" in the large cities, to wander alone, or to live in a commune. Some, alienated and frustrated, tried to solve their problems by turning to psychiatry either before or after taking drugs. This, however, accounted for only a surprisingly low 20 percent (only 3 percent did not answer the question). These solutions are all represented by the seekers who eventually became converts to Krishna. Note however that *this model does not apply to others in the counterculture who may have been or appeared to have been in similar conditions and circumstances,* but who have perhaps solved their problems in a different manner.

Seekership. Having once plunged into the world of the counterculture, the Krishna preconverts took many paths in search of an alternative style of life with new meaning. Some sought hedonistic gratification through drugs and sex. Most searched after truth in mind-expanding experiences through drugs, while still practicing a spiritual discipline. Many followed various types of *yoga*. *Kuṇḍalinī-yoga* of Yogi Bhajan, *haṭha-yoga, kriyā-yoga* of Yogānanda's Self Realization Fellowship, and Transcendental Meditation taught by Mahāṛishi Mahesh Yogi were among the favorites.

By this time all had rejected the culture of the establishment and its forms of religion and were looking for meaning in a new way of life. The old precepts of the establishment based on logic and bolstered by the organized religions were found wanting. Most sought first to build their new foundation of meaning on ultimate truth that would transcend the logic of the establishment and would be based on personal experience. Through religious truth that each might share with others, they desired to form the basis for a world view that would be compatible with the needs of our times. Thus the devotees' search for meaning in life has contained, not necessarily in the order given below, three elements that the Hare Krishna Movement later provided them:

1. They sought an authority to give them a satisfactory alternative way of life and a world view, when all other authorities had failed.
2. They searched after a suitable way to validate and sacralize this perspective by means of personal experience. This would give their *Weltanschauung* ultimate and absolute meaning.
3. They looked for a close fellowship with others who would have the same countercultural background and the same needs, and who would reinforce each other in a routinized shared experience of this reality.

For only 6 percent the Hare Krishna Movement was the first religion in which they would search for this truth. The majority of these upper-middle-class youth searched for meaning by using drugs while practicing some form of religious discipline. This experience, which two-thirds of them had in some form of Hinduism or Buddhism, made easier the transition from their former religions to Krishna Consciousness. This was true even though, as indicated earlier, some have never felt that they had actually left their former faiths. They have only found a new interpretation in a larger context. Of these, again, the majority had had some kind of religious experience through drugs that made them believe absolutely in a transcendental reality.

During their countercultural stage, if not before, most had already begun to accept such ideas as reincarnation, *karma,* and other doctrines that the Hare Krishna Movement has in common with the popular nondualistic philosophy of Vedānta. While both philosophies rely on and interpret some of the same basic texts, the followers of Chaitanya now consider the latter as illusory doctrine. They are quick to point out their difference in belief. They argue against the belief that the Brahman alone is the final ultimate reality. They criticize its doctrine of man's final absorption and loss of identity in Brahman, preferring to believe in the preservation of the individual self in loving fellowship with Krishna. It is an interesting fact that although the *advaita* philosophy has been India's chief philosophical export to the West and is accepted by many of India's intellectuals, the religion of the majority favors some form of theistic worship.

Therefore, the conversion to Krishna meant for most of the devotees a change from a belief in an impersonal deity to a belief in a highly personal one; for some at least it was an introduction to a personal deity whom they had never before known.

The Turning Point. Before considering the factors in their turning to Krishna, let us note first the manner in which they first contacted Krishna Consciousness, as shown in Table 9.

With a possible margin of error of 4.5 percent (those who did not answer the question), the results seem to indicate rather clearly the importance of the Movement's method of proselytizing. It has attracted

Table 9 Circumstances of Devotee's First Encounter with Krishna Consciousness

Attended a public *saṅkīrtan* (public chanting)	38.18%
Contact with a devotee in the street	28.22%
Went to a love feast at a temple of Krishna	6.64%
Read about the Movement in its magazine or in newspaper	8.30%
Went to visit a temple	8.30%
Learned about it through a friend who was a devotee	3.32%
Attended a Hare Krishna Ratha-Yātrā Festival	3.32%
Other circumstances	3.32%

the attention of many by its practice of chanting the Hare Krishna *mantra* in public. During these public ceremonies, other devotees sell the literature and engage the curious in conversation about Krishna.

After their initial contact, almost 24 percent decided to surrender to Swāmi Bhaktivedanta immediately or during the following first week. Eight percent joined within a month of the first contact, 61 percent were devotees by the end of six months. Eleven percent waited up to a year before joining. Thus most were converted within six months of the initial contact. These figures must be considered only as minimal, however, since a completely accurate percentage could not be taken from the data. Some had interpreted the meaning "time you decided to surrender" to represent the end of the actual gradual process toward full Krishna Consciousness. For example, one devotee who had been initiated into the Movement four years before answered the question by saying, "Soon, I hope."

Why did they turn to Krishna Consciousness? The data indicate that it may be possible to separate the situational factor that is dependent on their mental or psychological condition when contacting the Movement from other, more directly instrumental factors.

The Situational Factor

Crisis in Personal Distress. In a large number of cases, and I suspect in most, the Krishna devotees had not discovered a satisfactory life in the counterculture. These converts, like those in the Lofland-Stark model, had reached a "turning point in their lives." They had already left the establishment with which they had been dissatisfied some time ago. They had a number of countercultural ideas that they could use to form an alternative way of life, but somehow this adventure did not give them the satisfaction they expected. They had experienced a disruption in their pattern of living, often combined with a time of distress, unhappiness, and loss of meaning often approaching despair. For many, drugs had taken their toll. Although their effects may have included some mind-expanding experiences, they were ready to find relief from drugs. As Lofland and Stark point out, timing is important in the case of situational factors. They had reached a turning point. They were ready for another change. One said, "At the point of suicide I was offered the *mahāmantra* as a last resort." This twenty-five-year old female devotee had left her Roman Catholic faith gradually while attending a parochial school because of what she felt was the church's hypocrisy, lack of close fellowship, and failure to give a greater meaning to life. She had been searching through drugs and religion. She had used LSD off and on for two years, hashish for four, and had meditated in a forest commune. She said she was attracted to the worship of Krishna by the "transcendental vibrations" of the chanting, and because of the friendliness of the Hare Krishna devotees.

Another devotee, a twenty-five-year old male college graduate, whose answers in the questionnaire indicated strong countercultural beliefs, had taken LSD frequently for two years. He had abandoned his Methodist heritage on account of its failure to enable him to experience God or to develop a feeling of community. After practicing meditation with another spiritual master, he encountered the Hare Krishna Movement at an Allen Ginsberg poetry reading in 1965. Six months later, after a mild crisis, he decided to surrender to "Prabhupād." He wrote: "I arrived at the decision jointly with a friend *when the situation in Albuquerque became intolerable.* Our residence became a hangout for junkies, and our coffee house prospects dissolved when the heads took aversion to our constant chanting" (italics added).

A female devotee testified that she had been frustrated, confused, and angry at the world and its authority, against which she had rebelled, and from which she had escaped into drugs. When asked what had drawn her to Krishna Consciousness, she explained:

> I was getting crazier and crazier each year, and more and more frustrated . . . *so what brought me to Krishna Consciousness was complete, overwhelming, undeniable and irrevocable distress.* There was nothing I could do. I was even considering going through psychotherapy . . . I can't begin to describe how empty I was feeling. I had no association; I was seventy or eighty pounds overweight. I had no money. I considered myself completely mad. I had no education, no skills, no friends—I had nothing . . . I had never been to a feast, but somehow I had heard of Krishna and I called him by name . . . I said, "Hare Krishna, here I am." Like Arjuna said, "I am a soul surrendering unto you. Please instruct me!" I said,

> "If you please, tell me what to do! I'll do it, I promise. OK, you've got me Lord, now what?"
>
> So I went over and picked up the book [I Ching], a Chinese classic used in divination, and held it for a few seconds in meditation, and opened it at random. A verse called "The Mountains," about how the mountains stand together . . . It was obviously an instruction to go join the deities . . .
>
> I went down to the temple and asked to move in, and the president said: "What is your name? Have you read the books? [Those written by Swāmi Bhaktivedanta] Yes, you can move in." So I did. (Italics added.)

Another devotee described her life before conversion as a life of "traveling around in search of some kind of enlightenment." After studying under various *gurus,* she turned to Krishna and entered the temple. She spoke of a personal crisis that occured just prior to her conversion.

> You know . . . there was something else that happened that affected my moving into the temple . . . I had split up with my boyfriend that I was very attached to. It was like a very nice security trip for about three and a half years.

Some joined the Society at a time when they were trying to get money for psychiatric help. One was prompted by relief from extreme hunger because of food offered at the Hare Krishna love feasts.

Instrumental Factors. The instrumental factors, which are not exclusive of the situational factors, give still other reasons for turning to Krishna where direct evidence of the conditional factor is sometimes absent.

Finding Religious Experience and Community. The chanting of the Hare Krishna *mantra* and the friendliness and close fellowship with the devotees are the two factors that most devotees said were the initial attractions to the Movement. That for which they were seeking became instrumental to their conversion when found. These two reasons accounted for 58 percent and 52 percent respectively of those polled concerning the principal attractions to the Movement. One must conclude that in this case the combination of the two is most important. It is the shared experience of chanting together in close fellowship the *mantra* and other chants glorifying the spiritual master, Chaitanya, and Krishna.

We have noted that conversions required varying intervals of time. It is possible to be converted to different degrees, which Lofland and Stark call the verbal and the total convert. The total convert to Krishna may be defined as one who believes Krishna is the Supreme Personality of Godhead, who accepts Swāmi Bhaktivedanta as his spiritual master, follows the regulative rules of the discipline, and guides his life according to the teachings, which he fully accepts. He becomes initiated, receiving his Hindu name, and devotes his life to serving Krishna. If unmarried, he lives in the temple. He is to be distinguished from the larger number of those who follow the regulative rules to a lesser extent or not at all, but who participate in the Sunday devotional services at the temple, partake of the *prasādam,* listen to class discussions of the philosophy, and have greatly varying degrees of belief. These are not considered to be devotees, but some will later be converted and will enter the temple for a probationary period before being initiated. The term "verbal convert" used by Lofland and Stark does not seem to fit exactly the data here. They apply it to the stage of conversion of those who, while verbally assenting to the principal tenets of the faith, are not yet willing to "put their lives at the disposal of the cult" (Lofland and Stark, 1965:873).

In a sample taken of those who attend the Hare Krishna temple services on Sunday but are not total devotees, the reasons for their status varies. Probably most significant was the statement of one:

> I have met a lot of people who are very sympathetic with the Movement, who for one reason or another can't take temple life. I don't think I have found anybody who is an exception to it. They all really like to chant the *mantra,* whatever else their trip might be. A lot of people help economically too, small donations on the side.

When asked whether he chanted regularly his sixteen rounds of the *mahāmantra* he replied:

> No I don't. I did for a long time . . . Sometimes in spiritual life, just like in everything else you try and you reach a certain plateau and then you drop from it. The same thing in developing Krishna Consciousness . . . I stopped doing rounds altogether for about a week, and now I am doing five or six a day.

When questioned whether he had ever stayed in the temple, he answered,

> I lived here about a week, but I didn't feel very comfortable in the temple. We're all individuals; we have different tastes and inclinations.

His feelings about Swāmi Bhaktivedanta, however, were quite warm:

> He's the only spiritual master I've seen whom I accept as capable of delivering one from this cycle of birth and death. Each time I see him now I develop a deeper appreciation for what he's teaching . . . It's not that I'm such a great devotee of his either . . . I don't have the love or the ability to surrender to him, but the appreciation is there.

Another stated that he came on Sunday to engage in the services in order to purify himself slowly so as to eventually have an intimate relationship with Krishna, but otherwise he did not follow the regulative rules strictly. He said also:

> It's like my Christian friends who stop me and say, "I see you have given up Christ." Who said I'd given up anything? I still have a lot of devotional feelings for Christ. Hinduism incorporates everything.

Another, when asked why she came to the temple on Sundays, replied:

> I guess I consider myself a devotee. I haven't been a real faithful one lately . . . I still chant at home . . . I live in a commune; I've been very involved in it lately.

She had never lived in the temple, but had stayed overnight once. "I really wanted to move in, but it didn't seem like the right thing . . .

Maybe I will sometime." At present she is living in a commune in which her sister lives.

> I've gotten just really involved where I live, just working on my relationship with people there. I think I'm going to be getting involved again here, but I sort of go in cycles. I feel very close here.

Another when questioned about her relationship to the Movement replied:

> I enjoy chanting, but I'm using it to add to my other spiritual path which is Ananda Marga Yoga. I feel that Krishna Consciousness is beautiful, but other paths are as necessary.

Notwithstanding the fact that there are differences in degrees of conversion among those who only attend the Sunday services, there appear to be gradations perhaps among those who are full-time devotees. The problem lies in the connotation of "conversion." I suggest that differentiation be made between intellectual conversion and the religious experience of conversion. There is evidence that intellectual conversion to Krishna has occurred at least in some cases even before the devotee enters the temple to live the discipline. The data also indicate however that sometimes the experience of conversion occurs before an adequate knowledge of the religious ideas has been obtained. Nevertheless in such cases the discipline of the Movement has been accepted and the converts consider themselves devotees.

This phenomenon has also been cited by Gerlach and Hine in their studies of Pentecostalism. They note that an emotional experience of conversion through the speaking of tongues has sometimes occurred before the convert has become acquainted with the particular views of the church (Gerlach and Hine, 1970:117–118).

While the general statistics on the length of time between initial contact and conversion have been given already, we should break these down even further. Of the more than 23 percent who said they had decided to surrender to the spiritual master during the first week after initial contact with the Movement, almost 8 percent indicated immediate conversion—that is, within the first hour. I suggest that this was the experience of conversion rather than intellectual conversion in most cases. Even though most had a common countercultural background and some knowledge of Eastern philosophy, a firm belief in Chaitanya's philosophy sometimes seems to take a period of time after the experience of conversion. The example of one devotee submitted by Gregory Johnson illustrates this point. The devotee described his conversion experience from the moment he first attended a Hare Krishna devotional service. (Johnson, n.d.:53–53) He said:

> Because of certain feelings, I did not join in—at first. However, I saw the devotees chanting, and those magic words, magic words, "Hare Krishna, Hare Krishna, Krishna Krishna, Hare Hare/Hare Rāma, Hare Rāma, Rāma Rāma, Hare Hare!" So I finally gave in and joined them, repeating over and over again. It certainly felt good afterwards.
>
> Two days later I went to *kīrtana* [*saṅkīrtan*] at the devotee's private house. This time it hit me? I was lost in bliss, divine bliss! Soon, I learned all the devotees' names, Mukunda, Janaki, Shyamsundar, Malati, Gurudās and Yamuna. They invited me back again, and after only four days since I first experienced chanting, they invited me to perform with them. I was overwhelmed! Now Krishna Consciousness really had a hold on me, and I can't believe it's all happened so fast! Tomorrow I am going to move in with them, as Mukunda told me. So for someone just entering into Krishna Consciousness, association with devotees is very important. I have shaved my head so I am complete with *śikhā,* and I hope you can understand how happy I am feeling at this moment. *Although I know very little about Krishna or His life, I am so eager to learn.* (Italics added.)

Even when the full belief is intellectually known, it may still require time before it is totally accepted. The devotees say that complete acceptance and understanding is a matter of degree dependent upon one's self-discipline in chanting and following the regulative principles. Another devotee showed quite clearly this connection between chanting and the development of faith and understanding. He said:

> Prabhupād is giving us this . . . and everything is so complete. Everything is fitting into place for me . . . *Although we may not understand something when it is given to us, it comes to us through faith.* It's revealed to us through our continuing efforts in chanting. (Italics added.)

The pastimes of Krishna, which all devotees accept as being true, contain value not only in giving the devotees a knowledge of Krishna, but also in helping manifest his spiritual presence during their worship. The biographical information of the converts shows that understanding and acceptance of the pastimes are not immediate, but increase the more they chant and follow the discipline. Chanting creates faith and faith gives understanding. Chanting is the primary requisite. A case in point is the older devotee whose other experiences we related earlier. While confessing to his lack of complete conformity to the discipline, he answered the question, "Are the stories of Krishna literally true?"

> That's hard to say, really . . . both the wife and I, and my children as well, ran into snags, at least in the very beginning . . . To those who don't know Krishna Consciousness, they appear as myths. They do to lots of people. Now with us, we can see things now more clearly than we could six months ago when we first came to Krishna Consciousness. And the stories fit in; they're plausible now. Whereas in the beginning they were more like fiction.

As Guru Basar once said to me: "If the pastimes seem difficult, just chant more and you will understand them. They are transcendental, and chanting the holy names of Krishna is a transcendental vibration." He meant that chanting puts one on the "spiritual platform," the transcendental plane where the pastimes eternally occur.

My colleague A. Durwood Foster has recently observed that faith preceding understanding is also a part of the Hebrew-Christian tradition. Augustine commenting on Isaiah 7:9 said: *Credo ut intelligam,* "I believe, in order that I may understand." This referred to the abovementioned passage in the old Latin version: *Nisi credideritis non intelligeris,* which one may translate, "unless you shall have believed, you will not understand." This same thought was voiced by Anselm's *Fides quaerens intellectum,* "faith seeking understanding."

Finding a Viable Authority. Besides a faith in which to believe and a means by which it may be obtained, it is evident that the authority is also important. Many in the counterculture were looking for a new standard. In the transitional period of Krishna's devotees their countercultural leaders had lost their appeal, and the followers' lives had become empty. They found what they wanted in the person of Swāmi Bhaktivedanta. He gave them a reinforcing countercultural philosophy, which was modified meaningfully. He offered them security. Devotees were questioned concerning Swāmi Bhaktivedanta: "What about his authority? You have no difficulty at all accepting the fact that he's the Supreme Authority? And that he can tell you exactly what to do with your life?" One replied:

> No! No question at all! When you accept the spiritual master, it is understood that you will follow perfectly the dictates of the scripture. Everything he says should be backed by scriptures.

"Did you realize that that was what you needed in your life?" was the next question. The answer came quickly: "O yes, definitely."

For some his charismatic presence and words caused an immediate emotional conversion. One such convert described that moment by saying: "Tears came to my eyes: Prabupād spoke to my heart. For the first time I was able to accept that I am not the doer. Krishna is in control."

One devotee from the counterculture had abandoned his Protestant faith during high school. He felt the church was neither able to engender a feeling of close fellowship, nor to give meaning to life. When he heard Swāmi Bhaktivedanta, he was able to say:

> From the first time I heard him speak, I knew what he expressed was true and natural, and it was the only time I'd heard anyone express it . . . Before, my attitude was generally cynical and I experienced a sense of despair and hopelessness concerning the future . . . Krishna Consciousness has given meaning in darkness.

Another said, when first seeing Swāmi Bhaktivedanta: "It was indescribable. It was like seeing the sun after being in the darkness." Still another replied: "My mouth hung open, and I was almost in a trance." Others described their feelings as being "ecstatic," "filled with awe," and "inconceivable."

Only 19 percent, however, indicated that the "potency" of the spiritual master had contributed to their initial attraction to the Movement, but then slightly fewer than 25 percent had even seen him before they were converted to Krishna Consciousness. Therefore, one cannot say that the charisma of Swāmi Bhaktivedanta's physical presence had been a significant factor in many initial conversion experiences. Still, his importance in the later stages is evident. The data indicate that 86 percent of the devotees upon seeing him for the first time, whether before or after conversion, expressed their feelings concerning him in words denoting his power.

To his devotees Swāmi Bhaktivedanta is both the authority for Krishna Consciousness and the "pure devotee," a pattern for their lives. His words are hallowed by the firm belief of his followers that he is God on earth. His devotees prostrate themselves before him in obeisance when first coming into his presence. Swāmi Bhaktivedanta represents the Hindu *guru* in a tradition that demands that the student give the spiritual teacher the respect due to a deity. Bhakti Siddhānta explained that the *guru* is the "Transcendental Mediator" between the Personal Absolute deity and the devotee. As the "Embodiment of Love," he is an absolute necessity as a guide to Krishna and to spirituality. As one serves Krishna through recitation of the "Holy Name," it is the spiritual master's grace that bestows this kind of service. Therefore, one is enjoined first to accept the protection of the teacher and then his teaching.

Swāmi Bhakti Siddhānta said further that Krishna in "the role of Shrī Guru is engaged in Beholding Himself as the Object of contemplation by seeking His own support." Accordingly, one under the protection of the spiritual master is believed to be also under the protection of Krishna. The *guru* is to be served and worshiped just like Krishna (Bhakti Siddhānta, 1967:286–311). Such a philosophy contributes to the charisma of the spiritual master. The chant of obeisance to him that begins every devotional service helps to sacralize all his countercultural teaching. His writings are therefore also important.

Reading the Literature about Krishna. For some, reading the Hare Krishna literature (see Appendix) was instrumental in their conversion. One whose first contact with the Movement had been to attend a devotional service three years before decided to surrender to the spiritual master after reading in his translation of the *Bhagavad-gītā* the passage where Krishna tells the hero Arjuna, "Just surrender to the spiritual master!" The strong countercultural feelings that his questionnaire revealed are probably the reason why he left his Jewish faith. He ascribed the cause, however, to his need to experience God. He complained also that Judaism had given him neither security nor meaning. After completing four years of college he had entered the counterculture, turning first to the practice of *yoga,* while occasionally taking LSD and hashish for nearly a year.

About 42 percent of the other devotees cited the philosophy of Chaitanya as one of the initial attractions. A few claimed that they were converted after reading the magazine *Back to Godhead.*

Finding a Personal God to Love. There seems to be still another basic reason for turning to Krishna Consciousness rather than remaining in or turning to another of the religious practices offered by the counterculture. Other religious groups have had their countercultural devotees, and some have impressive records of curing drug abuse. Even though the majority of Krishna's devotees had already been following some sort of unitive Eastern discipline, examples already given reveal that one element had been missing—love for a personal deity as the basis of love for all and everything. This need for the expression of love in worshiping and serving a personal, living deity is probably a predominant factor uniting all devotees of Krishna.

The *saṅnyāsi* Mukunda had left his Jewish faith. He said he had been mistakenly taught that God was a force, and not a person like Krishna. He continued:

> You can love what you think is God maybe, but we know from practical experience that you can't love even air, sky, or music. You have to love a person. This is what love is all about. It requires reciprocation. It requires two entities, one on each side.

Mukunda further explained:

> When the *mṛidaṅga* plays faster and the *kartālas* clang, it helps me open up. That love of Krishna is within us all, but when we're with a group of people we can open up more and

> express our spiritual emotion . . . So unless we can devote that loving relationship with God, we cannot even love one person as much as we love ourselves. But if we can devote that loving relationship to God, we can love not only all men, but animals and plants equally. Our spiritual master said once that "if you are actually in Krishna Consciousness, you will become a lover of the universe . . ." When it's reposed in Krishna, then brotherhood has meaning. But if we simply try to impose the United Nations or some other brotherhood society, but in our hearts we don't feel the same about a man down in Mississippi as we do our own brother or wife . . . then it ultimately has to deteriorate.

The devotee Trai dās also spoke against the impersonalism of much of Eastern philosophy:

> I had been reading Eastern literature, but it is missing something . . . that personal feature. So Krishna Consciousness fulfilled everything—that feeling of being at home, that personal shelter, that relationship with the supreme personality and actual detailed knowledge of who he is and how one can render service to him.

Other devotees also indicated that they have felt greater security in the worship of a personal loving God than in a unitive experience of an impersonal reality, such as the monistic Vedānta might provide. They are surrendering themselves to a loving God whom they feel has complete control over their lives. Through the spiritual master he personally takes charge of the welfare of his devotees. To surrender to Krishna is to be relieved from worry and to find shelter and security in a personal deity. The devotee can know him intimately through knowledge of his pastimes, and through private and public devotion.

Finding a Sacralized Countercultural Life Style. All of these instruments to conversion aid in the sacralization of an alternative countercultural life style. A person who has rejected the goals of the establishment finds in the communal life a freedom that the establishment does not offer. His main goal, however, will be the development of a transcendental spiritual consciousness free from the illusion of materialistic desires.

The spiritual master gives the basis for this view in his commentary on the *Bhāgavata Purāṇa.* He declares that the competitive struggle for existence in the material world is due to mankind's desire to lord it over nature. This is the very reason, he says, for the creation of the strong and the weak and therefore the "law of struggle for existence" (Bhaktivedanta, 1965:919). In the spiritual world there is no such difference because everyone there exists eternally. "There is no disparity because everyone wants to render service to the Supreme Lord and nobody wants to imitate the Lord in the matter of becoming a beneficiary" (Bhaktivedanta, 1965:919). Even in his daily life, the devotee seeks only the spiritual plane through constant service to Krishna. The spiritual master teaches that having forgotten that Krishna is the creator, proprietor, and enjoyer of all things, we in the world of illusion are conditioned by the law of the struggle for existence and survival of the fittest (Bhaktivedanta, 1965:919–920). He notes again that engagement in continued work for its rewards of material enjoyment keeps one in material bondage (Bhaktivedanta, 1965:943).

Typical of the devotees' attitude is the following illustration of one convert and his wife who shared his countercultural ideas. He said:

> We both had very good, well paying civil service jobs. Money? There one had it, but we found that money wasn't everything. I said: "Who needs this money, if we have to break our backs, working around the clock; both of us working in shifts to support a house, to support the government which has war after war—Korea, Vietnam—slaughter after slaughter?"
>
> I was in the peace movement up to my ears. In fact, if I didn't pull out of this country when I did, I would have been like the Weathermen. I would have turned to violence myself. I was so frustrated. Yes, we were fed up with society . . . And I still want no part of it.

He took a position in the Movement's incense factory, which he contrasted with the work in the culture of the establishment:

> Having worked in different factory jobs, assembly line and what not, I've found my association at the factory very likable in terms that the association of devotees was such that I was able to take the job and have considerable liking for it. Whereas . . . I still couldn't do that if I had to take my place

in a production line situation in *karmi* society, society of the establishment, with the almighty dollar and everything. Still we did such production quotas there under such blissful surroundings in the incense factory that it was astounding. It was almost unbelievable some of the records that they set with none pushing. . . . That philosophy has helped considerably—it's not to be attached to the results of our work. Of course I get carried away at times too . . . Worry, worry! This needn't be so. By not being attached we know that Krishna is controller of all things and he makes all things equal. As I say, we have no wants or desires. Everything is provided and that's the rut that most people get into. They think they're the controller.

In contrasting his life style with that of the establishment, another devotee offered this justification:

I think there is probably a lot less anxiety living in a temple situation. You're not absorbed in material life trying to compete with everybody, trying to get a lot of money, trying to get so many material possessions, always in anxiety about whether you have this or whether you have that, trying to hold on to so many things. If you're really Krishna Conscious, you know that nothing really belongs to you. Everything belongs to Krishna and you're just using it temporarily. If you're really in that knowledge, then you are free from anxiety. Like Prabhupād says, there is no hankering and no lamenting, no hankering for something you don't possess and no lamenting for something you've lost—when you're free from hankering and lamentation, then you're on the road to spiritual freedom.

He sums up this part of the philosophy in the following:

If you're really in the understanding that . . . whatever you're doing is for the pleasure of Krishna, and give up all of your false ego and your false prestige or whatever . . . then you're free from anxiety. But it's completely different from anything we've ever learned . . . that we're not entitled to the fruits of our labor . . . that whatever I do I do it for God. That consciousness just goes against everything that we've ever learned. I'm not doing it for myself. I'm not trying to get something for myself. Actually when you're acting in that

> consciousness, it's really blissful, if you're actually surrendering to it, but that process of surrendering can be very difficult.

Correlative to the above is the countercultural disdain for material status, with which the spiritual master agrees. The only important status is that of the Krishna Conscious person. Accordingly, devotees offer a respect to one another in ways other than to outsiders, since all devotees are striving for Krishna Consciousness. So when two devotees first meet each other after a long separation, say, at the Ratha-yātrā Festival, both may prostrate themselves before one another. At the same time they offer two set *mantras* to Krishna. The same type of obeisance is offered to a *saṅnyāsi* when he first comes into the presence of other devotees, or when he is departing. This action gives recognition to his spiritual wisdom and consciousness, but not to any material status. Thus the Movement honors the principal protests that he among other countercultural youths had made.

One other instrument toward complete faith should be mentioned. This is the devotee's witness to his belief through public chanting and preaching on the streets. In the Hare Krishna Movement the importance of this device is seen by the policy of getting the new converts into the *saṅkīrtan* parties as quickly as possible. Public demonstration of one's belief is not only a means of gaining new converts, but also a way of strengthening one's own faith. One devotee quoted Karandhar dāsa Adhikāri as saying:

> It's important for boys and girls who come into the Movement when they're new to do a lot of street *saṅkīrtan.* It's very, very helpful. It really fixes you up in Krishna Consciousness so that later if you end up having responsibility . . . where you're not directly on the street . . . still you have control of your mind—thinking Krishna Consciousness most of the time.

Jehovah's Witnesses and Mormons have added strength to the faith of their adherents by this means. The Latter Day Saints require missionary responsibilities of each member for a period of time. A friend who was a former Mormon related his experience. Although no longer a believer, he was asked by the president of his stake to perform his missionary duty. When he explained his circumstances the request was repeated. He was told that if he were to perform the missionary assignment he would regain his faith.

Conversion and the consequent transformation in the devotee's life are probably only *apparently* immediate. More generally it is a multifaceted process that continues over a long period, and that includes the validation of a way of life.

Cult Affective Bonds. In the Lofland-Stark model the next important step necessary before full conversion is "some positive, emotional, interpersonal response," generally through a converted friend or a quick rapport with another believer. Their study indicates that this response is needed before the preconvert begins to consider the movement seriously as his personal construction of reality.

The data from the Krishna devotees are in essential agreement with the model. Although the statistics show that a friend in the Movement accounted for only a little more than 3 percent of the initial contacts, a friend or a close relative was sometimes a later factor in the preconvert's residing in the temple for a time, a step that often leads to conversion. More important was the support found in the warmth and fellowship of the devotees.

Extra-Cult Affective Bonds. In agreement with the Lofland-Stark insight, emotional attachments to persons outside the Hare Krishna Movement have been one factor inhibiting the completion of conversion, but this is not as evident for our devotees as in the data on the Unified Family, for at least three reasons.

First, many of the preconverts had been transients for some time before converting to Krishna. Often they had not remained long enough in one place to develop close friendships. The streets were not conducive to community.

Second, most devotees had already left their parents and friends, and at the time of their conversion were often separated from them by some degree of time and distance. We must recall that only about one-fourth of the devotees polled had indicated a close relationship with their parents. Noncommunication, as the largest single category, expressed the relationship of about 33 percent.

Third, all devotees are supposed to give up the company of nondevotees (The International Society for Krishna Consciousness, 1970:27). Association with other devotees reinforces one's faith and Krishna Consciousness. Associating with nondevotees, they say, means that one will be influenced by illusory material desires for sense gratification.

When asked about her friends who live close by, one devotee replied:

> I still have feelings for them, because for so long I tried to shut out these feelings. It's natural to feel feelings for people . . . It's just that you know that to be in association with them, you're gliding downwards instead of upwards. But I still have feelings for them.

A *saṅnyāsi* answered the question concerning whether he corresponded with his parents:

> No, not really. Sometimes they write me a telegram. They want to know where I am so I tell them, but I am a *saṅnyāsi.* We're not supposed to do all these things anymore. Your parents are so temporary. I had millions of mothers and fathers before, so it's all temporary. When I speak to my mother on the phone, it's like a stranger . . . My father is Prabhupād. He raised me. My father didn't raise me. What is a father? A father is one who . . . gave me this material body. But what is that relation? It's a relation of bone and stool and blood. That's all it is. But he didn't raise me. I raised myself in the street as much as I could. I raised myself, but he didn't tell me anything to do. Prabhupād, he raised me. He told me what to do—how to live like a human being, how to elevate myself. My father never told me anything. He didn't know himself. He is not a bad boy, but he didn't know. He had sex life and he had me, somehow or other. So my relation with my parents I just see in terms of blood and stool and meat eating and taking alcohol. My father is Prabhupād and my mother is the scripture.

It should be recognized that this is the extreme position of the *saṅnyāsis,* who ideally are most advanced in renouncing all relationships with the material world. Nevertheless, this is still the ideal for all full-time devotees. The Hare Krishna ideal of love for people is one that is without attachment or detachment. Its primary direction is to Krishna.

Intensive Interaction. Intensive interaction, meaning continual daily and hourly accessibility to other members of the group, is the last step in the Lofland-Stark model for total conversion. The devotees of Krishna would support this with no reservation. In fact they would cite evidence to show that unless one is very advanced, living outside the temple increases the difficulty of advancing in Krishna Consciousness.

Unfortunately perhaps for some, the 1972 directive enjoining the married devotees to live outside the temple has created this problem. According to Ṛishava dās, one of the devotees so affected, this has meant: "We simply have to be even stricter in our discipline." Without intensive interaction among one another in the temple, the practice of the discipline becomes more difficult. Being away from the temple also exposes one more easily to the lure of this material world. Thus the key word that opens the Krishna devotee to faith and understanding and that keeps him from backsliding is discipline. It occupies all his time in the company of others.

Lochan spoke of the devotee who had left the Movement on three different occasions—the last to end in suicide. He said:

> I don't now much about his personal life, but I know he took a tremendous amount of drugs . . . Prabhupād says even a crazy person can be pure by this process if he follows the regulated principles. It will change anybody. There's a case of a boy who joined in New York . . . and he was almost dead from drug addiction. He would just sit in his room in the dark. Now he's one of the most important devotees. He's never taken any intoxicants since he joined. He's very joyful in Prabhupād's service . . . So this is the example of a person who can stick to it. Richard couldn't stick to it. He was here, but *he wouldn't chant the required amount that Prabhupād requested in order to live in the temple. He couldn't follow the other principles either,* because he didn't have the capacity to just stay with it. (Italics added.)

Of course this explanation does not recognize extreme cases of addiction.

Although some who have dropped out of the Movement have expressed reservations about the humility of other devotees, the most prevalent reason for falling away has been the lack of discipline and the allure of the illusory world. A number of devotees have left the Movement for a time before returning. Inevitably the reason given was "*māyā*."

The observed pattern of change in the devotees begins with alienation from and rejection of the established culture and its religious forms. In their search for a new style of life, preconverts then move through the chaotic and confused antinomianism of the drug-infused counterculture. After suffering and disillusionment, they find an alternative style of life that they believe to be fulfilling, and an authority who gives them a way to sacralize it.

CHAPTER TEN

BIRTH OF THE PHOENIX

This concluding chapter opens with a final look at the Hare Krishna Movement from the standpoint of its possible future and as the fulfillment of Slater's psychological criteria for a stable culture. We then examine the Movement as part of the larger counterculture representing the historical climax of a cultural revolution and the end of a historical period. The meaning of this as well as its reason is interpreted in two contexts: the need for myth and a new synthesis. Two illustrations, one secular and one sacred, are used to examine these contexts. The chapter concludes with an analysis of the possible guidelines these give for the liberal Christian church at a time of cultural crisis.

The Future of the Hare Krishna Movement. The discipline the devotees follow for their spiritual requirements in their alternative style of life should impart reasonable stability to the Society. Its flourishing business enterprises will meet the material needs of the devotees. With capable management these businesses should give every devotee the possibility of pursuing his goal of attaining Krishna Consciousness. Nevertheless, two questions should be asked. First, what will happen after the death of the revered and beloved spiritual master? Some Movement leaders have already projected the possibility of controversies occurring at that time. Bhakti Siddhānta's own Gauḍīya Vaishṇavas are a case in point. Schism could be the fate of an organization left without a capable and appointed successor in whom the devotees would develop similar faith.

Second, will the conditions that gave rise to the initial interests in the Movement exist in the future? Certainly hippiedom as we knew it in the 1960s is waning fast. The day of the big protest seems to be past. We have noted the different tempo on the campuses, even in Berkeley. Is the development of a new consciousness, a new culture to be aborted, or will some further development give new impetus to the counterculture? The decline of hippiedom already seems to have slightly reduced the number of Hare Krishna temples. Figure 7 shows the number of temples reported in the issues of *Back to Godhead* from August 1969 to February 1974. It indicates that there has been a small decline since January 1973 (issue 58). Records kept on a number of devotees for 1972 show however that only one out of twenty had dropped out (Kellom, 1973:43–55).

Karandhar dāsa Adhikāri, the Western executive of the Society, gave the following recent directive from the spiritual master: "The theme for now is 'boil the milk!' Instead of adding water to the milk to make it more, we now want to make strong what we have" (Kellom, 1973:55).

The Hare Krishna Movement is filling an important place in American religious history, one that many of the organized churches have

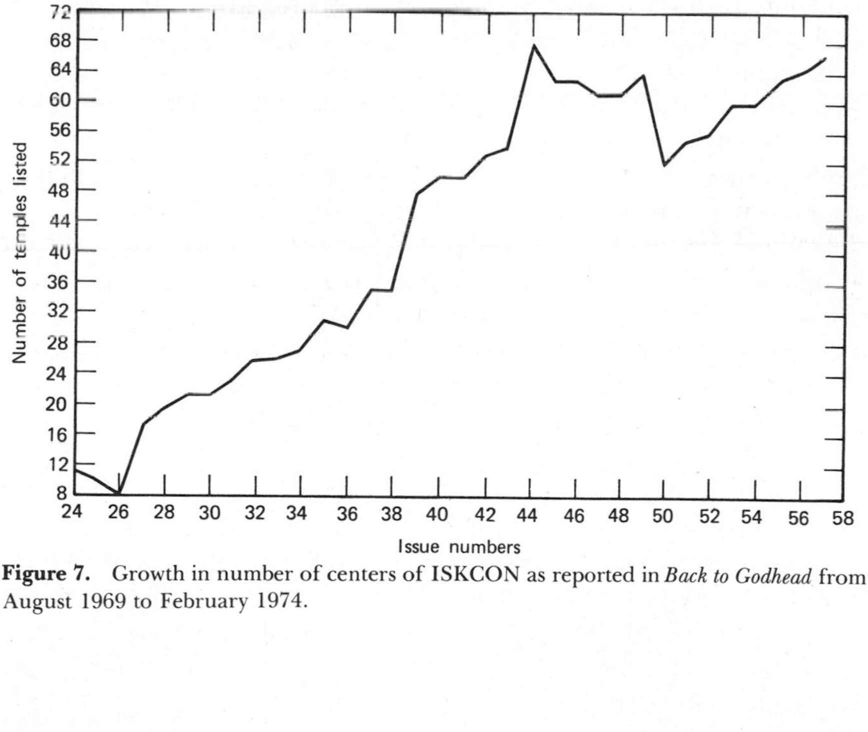

Figure 7. Growth in number of centers of ISKCON as reported in *Back to Godhead* from August 1969 to February 1974.

failed to fill. I therefore expect that those who remain in the Movement will continue with the fulfillment of meaning that they have found. Nevertheless, because of the rigor of the discipline contrasted with the strength of *māyā,* some will succumb to temptation. If they do, and if their involvement with Krishna has seemed to have been only a temporary sojourn or a rite of passage, I feel confident that they will take with them an experience that will continue to give added meaning to their lives. But let us reexamine the Hare Krishna Movement in a larger total context, not only according to the categories which Slater introduced, but also as part of a new structure.

Psychological Elements for Stability. If Philip E. Slater's three necessary characteristics for a stable society—the needs for community, engagement, and dependence—are valid, the Hare Krishna Movement certainly offers greater stability in its alternate style of life than does the "American way." Its communal living arrangement indeed satisfies the first requirement in a way our present culture cannot meet. Individualism and the competitive life of the establishment have been set aside for a belief that nothing should be done primarily for one's own satisfaction but for Krishna's. This philosophy has guided the followers of Krishna to resign from the *competitive* battle of material *self*-achievement in favor of a common fellowship in their temples.

In their own way, as we have seen, the devotees fulfill the requirement for engagement. Theirs is a community, but one with a highly personal message to individuals. They are not viewers of the game of life as so many of us are via the television screen, the sports arena, or the radio. They are participants in it. They engender activity in behalf of others. Their gifts are not of money to impersonal groups such as community funds, Christmas seals, or heart funds, however valuable they may be. Theirs is a gift of time and energy in a personal ministry to individuals. In their association together they stand against a non-understanding world, reinforcing one another in their goal to find Absolute Truth and to help others along the way. They believe that their public witness alleviates world problems. It represents to them the only possible way to peace, stability, and happiness.

Finally, the desire for dependence finds full expression in the philosophy of the Movement. Krishna as the Absolute Controller is the answer Swāmi Bhaktivedanta has given to the protest against the competitive life that so much of the establishment portrays to them. This absolute dependence on the directions of the spiritual master as Krishna's representative is Bhaktivedanta's reply to the spirit of American individualism.

It seems relevant to note that in none of the interviews was technology declared outright to be the major problem of the establishment. The devotees disdain the accumulation of possessions because of their association with sense gratification. They have no aversion to wealth or material things if they are used for the furtherance of Krishna Consciousness.

Only indirectly from the interviews is it possible to induce that the freedom to develop one's own life in business is slowly being closed, and that the development of larger and larger monopolies with ever-widening diversified interests are controlling more and more lives. One can detect a rebellion against being a cog in a business machine. In general however the criticism is against the whole system and its curtailment of freedom. Only the newly acquired philosophy reveals the basic objections that resonate with their feelings. Let us listen in on a dialogue between Gar Kellom and the devotee Krishna Kanti. Krishna Kanti was graduated with good grades from high school in 1963. He then went to a trade school to learn electronics. He received his Federal Communication license and planned to work in radio and television while attending college. This did not work out, and he became discouraged by the time it would take to get his degree. He then began taking drugs, dropped out of college after two years, and was drafted into the armed services. When asked to tell something more about his life before entering the Movement, he said:

> "Just an all-around situation. You can't pinpoint it. I was just aware that every one of us was insane. I found myself being forced to do so many things that I didn't want to do. I think that was what blew my mind, so to speak. Here I was day to day doing things that I didn't want to do—so many people had control. Where I thought I was controlling my life, I found that I wasn't. I saw so much wrong . . . There were political problems, psychological problems, racism, poverty, the whole material world situation. You could see insanity, mismanagement. But where was the root of it? Most youths

have this vision. We're growing up, and this world is really in a mess. And where do you go? Where do you start to solve it? I knew that it had to be solved from within. But it wasn't until I came to Krishna Consciousness that I could actually see a positive program."

"You mentioned war and other people controlling your life. Do you feel now that you are controlled, that you can't do what you want?"

"The point is, we're always being controlled. You can either be controlled by material nature, a cruel master. Or you can be controlled by Krishna. The reason we are here in this material world—we want to be the controller. Only Krishna is the controller . . . When I got into the service, that's when Krishna showed me first that I was being controlled, that I didn't have control over fate and my destiny. I thought I had . . . But if we follow Krishna's will, then automatically we become happy. I recollect how I used to read the philosophy, just the elevated far-out thing, but I couldn't see how it was related to practical things day to day, but now I really do . . . So, until you purify your senses and your mind by engaging them, by eating *prasādam* and chanting, preaching, working for Krishna, then you really don't get to the realization of the philosophy."

The Counterculture as a Cultural Climax. Thomas F. O'Dea views our present countercultural revolution as a revelation resulting from a crisis in meaning and pointing to a severe problem. Given a society based on technology, we have acted out one possible answer to the question: "What is it in man's makeup that is characteristically human and what should he be doing to bring that humanity to realization?" (O'Dea, 1970:4). O'Dea sees our predicament as part of a "Long Revolution" of two centuries, which can be foreseen much earlier in Israel's prophetic religion. Judaism had "introduced a transcendent social morality according to which social and political life could be judged" (O'Dea, 1970:10). It also gave an ethical criterion that would be superior to the interest of rulers and their supporters. Largely through Christianity, these were later introduced to the Western world. Since that beginning the church, which has mingled its thought with that of Greece and Rome, has been forced to rethink its Biblical heritage in each generation. With the discovery of previously unknown cultures and the shaking of the traditional foundations of philosophy by Imannuel Kant two centuries ago, a critical skepticism arose to challenge the congruity between Christian standards, and the character of human nature and the human condition. Traditional religion, which had received the stamp of the more traditional culture, was attacked. The new world that emerged was however still rooted in ideas from Christianity or from other sources that Christianity had preempted. Still this present generation of youth has seen an eclipse of spirituality amid the banality of technical achievement. Youth's protest is against a meaningless secularization, revealing the inadequacy of half-way houses. Its protest is a challenge to our entire civilization (O'Dea, 1970:4–16).

The struggle of modern civilization may again be viewed as the struggle of man to be basically human in the sense that he was created good, while recognizing his polar propensities toward both good and evil. Perhaps the antinomian quality of the crisis in the 1960s is still historically part of the basic problem which the will to power of Nietzsche revealed. But the mystic has always had to pass through the dark night of the soul before the shining light of revelation appears. If the counterculture experienced the nothingness of despair in the 1960s, perhaps as Robert Bellah has said, "the experience of nothingness exposes man as the creator of his own myths and that is not only a frightening, but also an immensely creative experience" (Bellah, 1970:8).

The devotees of the Hare Krishna Movement have found their way through the dark night to the light in their own fashion.

The End of an Age? Do the devotees of Krishna represent one segment of the countercultural hippie movement which Mark Messer suggests has seen the end of a cultural era and the myth upon which it was based? He follows Susanne Langer, who suggests that a myth "is the first form of a new symbolic system, a new dream, a new way of seeing the world" (Messer, 1972:145). The myth in this case is that autonomous man is the measure of all things. With its Faustian characteristics and its submyth, material success, it proposes that mankind can dominate nature. Messer maintains further that this concept was rationalized in the Age of Reason and Enlightenment in the seventeenth and eighteenth centuries as the capitalistic system. It flourished in the second half of the nineteenth-century America, and has now become overripe, as we experience an overdeveloped production.

If we are truly nearing the end of a cultural era, Messer suggests that the current counterculture may be the vanguard of a new mythology, a symbolic transformation (Messer, 1972:145–148). He suggests further (1972:153):

> Men need religion to make meaningful sense of the world in which they find themselves. Traditional Western religious forms made sense of Calvin's fragmented and goal-oriented world, but . . . that myth has run its course.

We can explore this idea further in comparing one conception of myth in relationship to Max Weber's thesis with parallels from the Hare Krishna Movement philosophy. Ironically, the very basis of Chaitanya's thought parallels the philosophy of John Calvin, which Max Weber and others accredit as the moral basis for the Western capitalistic system. Calvinist theology emphasized similarly to Chaitanya's view the sovereignty of God over man, and the later Puritanism has interesting similarities, as we shall see.

Max Weber has shown that capitalism as an economic system in Western Europe and America is a relatively modern phenomenon. He points to its origin in psychological sanctions that came from religious belief and practice (Weber, 1930:97). It was far from the first expression of man's acquisitive nature, however; history gives numerous examples of pecuniary profit motives and their extreme expression as avarice (Weber, 1930:18, 56). Man's desire to acquire property for himself is an innate part of his nature, as is his willingness to share with others. Naturalists have shown that acquisitive and sharing natures exist even among many gregarious animals, whose territorial boundaries are often carefully set and defended, especially in the mating season. The quality of greed seems however to be characteristic of human beings.

All religious thought recognizes the polar opposites of good and evil in man's nature, whether expressed as the Chinese cosmological monad of the Yin and the Yang, or as the Christian attempt to reconcile the Biblical concept of man whom God created good but who has a propensity for evil. Even Charles Darwin, in one of his later works in the 1860s, notes that man's survival depends in part not only on his innate aggressiveness, but also on an opposing quality that he called "sentiment."

If we assume the existence of human psychological antitheses, we can predicate one function of myth to be an expression of man's innate needs and desires. Myth allows us to represent meaningfully the many basic dualities of human nature, such as sharing and acquisition, and good and evil. Myth participates in the domains of both the sacred and the profane. It guides man in his actions and gives meaning to the profane, from which the sacred cannot be separated. The problem for man is to understand myth's polarities and deeper meanings. Myth is in a larger sense the full expression of man's beliefs, both sacred and secular, and is grounded ultimately in his psyche. It is here that some locate the divine; here the Krishna devotees find Vishṇu, the Supersoul.

In this perspective, myth becomes a subjective reality that speaks not of the truth or falsity of any proposition in an empirical objective sense, but of its meaning as apprehended and *believed* by man. It also permits us to observe its expression at any one time in history as fulfilling either one or the other, or even both, of such polar opposites of man's nature as sharing and acquisition. These find expression in individualism and community, and in capitalism and forms of collectivism. If either is carried to its extreme with no opportunity for some manifestation of the opposite expression in man's personality, it becomes psychologically unfulfilling and self-destructive.

Western capitalism's association with the Protestant ethic provides an illustration. Weber showed how capitalism and the acquisition of wealth became sacralized as part of the Protestant ethic originating from sixteenth-century Calvinism. He viewed the individualism of this ethic as a product of Calvinistic Puritanism, as seen in Bunyan's *Pilgrim's Progress*. This popular work pictures its hero, Christian, one of God's elect, as being in the world for one reason—the glorification of God. After receiving God's call to go as a pilgrim to the celestial city, he responds as a Puritan by obeying the divine call to one of the elect. Stopping his ears with his fingers and crying "life, eternal life," he staggers from the city on his pilgrimage, abandoning his wife and children who try to cling to him (Weber, 1930:107). His actions are reminiscent of the guidance engendered by Krishna's grace, which commands the devotee to forsake all others who will not take his same path to Krishna Consciousness. Although the Hare Krishna Movement does not proclaim such a doctrine, the doctrine of election is implicit in the use of Krishna's grace, since Krishna is as much a controller as Calvin's God.

In Puritan ethics, the principal objection to wealth was the danger of idleness and the material temptations it might create as a distraction from the religious life. The highest good in this ethic became the calling to earn more and more money, while avoiding all spontaneous pleasure (Weber, 1930:157, 53). The parallel in the philosophy of the Hare Krishna Movement is explicit.

In the Puritan conception, work was for the common good or for one's own good, if not injurious to anyone. God's hand is to be seen in any action of the elect, and thus if one of the elect sees a chance to profit, he must not neglect the opportunity. As the Puritan, Richard Baxter (cited in Weber, 1930:162) said:

> If God show you a way in which you may lawfully get more than in another way (without wrong to your soul or to any other), if you refuse this, and choose the less gainful way, you cross one of the ends of your calling, and you refuse to be God's steward, and to accept His gifts and use them for Him when He requireth it: you may labour to be rich for God, though not for the flesh and sin.

Wealth became the sign of a reward which God made to his chosen people for their obedience; it could indicate a condition of grace (Weber, 1930:163–164, 170).

The Puritan belief that man is only a trustee of the goods he acquires (Weber, 1930:170), echoes Chaitanya's conviction that God alone is the owner of material goods. Both the Puritans and the devotees of Krishna disallow the use of acquired property for one's own sense gratification (Weber, 1930:170). It is to be used for the glorification of God or for advancing Krishna Consciousness. The consumption of goods was limited by the Puritan ethic, as it is in the Hare Krishna Movement. The result was in the one case and will be in the other the accumulation of capital through the compulsion to save.

As Weber notes, John Wesley, the founder of Methodism who enjoined work and the frugal life, saw the real danger: "I fear, wherever riches have increased, the essence of religion has decreased in the same proportion (Weber, 1930:175). Therefore he felt that a revival in religion would not endure long. He realized that the frugal and active life of work might increase pride, anger, and the desire for material pleasure, as well as wealth. Nevertheless he was able to "exhort all Christians to gain all they can, and to save all they can; that is, in effect, to grow rich" (Weber, 1930:175). Weber notes, however, that Wesley follows this advice by exhorting Christians to give all they can, so as to grow in grace (Weber, 1930:176).

As religious pietism slowly faded, utilitarian worldliness gradually replaced the search for the Kingdom of God. The growth of a bourgeois economic ethic followed. God's grace was seen through one's visibly correct moral deeds; objections concerning the use of wealth subsided, and unequal distribution was attributed to God's grace. The idea of duty passed too, so that Weber noted that in the United States (Weber, 1930:176–177), "the pursuit of wealth, stripped of its religious and ethical meaning, tends to become associated with purely mundane passions, which often actually give it the character of sport" (Weber, 1930:182).

Other reasons contributing to this change of attitude and the present results in the countercultural revolt are not difficult to find. In a lecture entitled "No Direction Home, Religious Aspects of the Present Crisis," Robert Bellah points to the collapse of the belief that this world is only a temporary dwelling place. Our American ancestors believed that their real home was their Father's in heaven. "Gradually over the course of several centuries, that upward course has become truncated. The heavenly home in which it ends is a split level in suburbia supplied with all the latest electrical equipment." The pleasures once reserved for the hereafter are now expected here on earth, through the happiness sought in the products of technology. Wealth for the pleasure it is supposed to bring has become an end in itself. This is the aspect of the accumulation of money that has produced the strong protest of the Krishna devotees. Their Puritan ancestors would have reacted similarly. The former reject this ideal because they do not feel that it has brought the expected happiness to their parents. Like Paul Bunyan's Christian, they are turning to the search for the Kingdom of God.

Weber also noted that anyone born in a modern capitalistic economy is bound by its unalterable order of things, and must conform to its rules. More than forty years before the countercultural revolt he observed that this capitalism, which dominates our economy, educates and selects its needed subjects "through a process of economic survival of the fittest" (Weber, 1930:55). With this also our youth would agree.

One may well ask whether unimpeded capitalism is reaching its final constriction? Have American individualism and man's acquisitive nature been carried to such an extreme in our system that equal opportunity for the pursuit of life, liberty, and happiness is becoming limited to only the fittest few? By witnessing the threatening ecological problems that rugged unrestricted individualism has caused, our young people have seen the limitations of the belief that man is the master of his fate. Man is not only wasting his resources but is in danger of destroying himself and his world through his boundless efforts to produce more and more wealth.

The counterculture is a visible sign of needed changes and the search for a new freedom. Times of stress and change often give birth to new religions; they produce apocalyptic expectations of a new saviour and of a new era. The devotees of Krishna are endeavoring to usher in a new epoch of Krishna Consciousness, an epoch of peace and happiness. The Jesus People are looking toward a second coming of Christ and the millennium. The occultists, to echo the popular song, call this the dawning of the age of Aquarius.

According to the Theosophists and other occultists, the Piscean Age, the age of Christianity, is now ending. In the 1920s the Theosophists declared that there were already signs of the return of some souls who were the forerunners of the new root race to develop in the Aquarian Age. The Theosophists predicted that the new root race would find its beginning in California, the site of much of the recent revolutionary turmoil. Alice Tingley, one of the leaders of a schismatic Theosophical group, built her short-lived and ill-starred Theosophical City at Point Loma in San Diego. There she thought the two millennia of Aquarius would begin. Madame Blavatsky predicted almost a hundred years ago a revival of the "Ancient Wisdom" of the East and the triumph of occultism, to be brought about by a new savior who would appear in 1975. Other occultists have identified our youth culture, with its antiestablishment position and its predisposition toward various forms of occultism and mystic philosophy, as one that presages the Aquarian Age.

If this new age were coming to pass, what would this mean for organized religion? We have shown that the protest of the Hare Krishna devotee is directed not only against the culture, but also against the liberal organized religions that were perceived to be supporters of this culture. The data indicate that the liberal Christian churches have been found wanting. Countercultural youths do not find community in these institutions, which they see as related to a rejected culture. Furthermore, these churches, through demythologization and growing secularity, are in danger of losing the possibility to impart the types of religious experience that many people, and particularly youth, need to make the symbols and philosophy of faith meaningful in the widest context. The expressions of religious enthusiasm that occur in times of uncertainty and alienation are necessary for the wholeness of individuals. Because many always have such needs, there must necessarily be avenues for such integration. Without them, violence has been and will be the answer.

That the basic symbols of Christianity still have some efficacy is indicated by the data from the Hare Krishna Movement. Some of the devotees themselves still consider themselves Christians. Swāmi Bhaktivedanta, as we observed, preaches that chanting the *mahāmantra* can make even a Christian who is not a devotee a better Christian. The testimony of some who have left the movement indicates that there is a latent clinging to the symbols of Christianity. Statistics are lacking concerning the number leaving the Hare Krishna Movement to join the burgeoning Jesus People, but apparently there are quite a few. Their testimonies indicate that there may be a few doubts about worship of Krishna among the devotees.

One of the broadsides distributed by the Jesus People to those watching the Hare Krishna Festivals gives the testimony of David Hoyt, a former Hare Krishna devotee. He said that as a devotee in the San Francisco temple, over and over in his mind came the Biblical thought that there was only one Mediator between God and man, "Christ Jesus." This former devotee confessed that he had been in youth institutions for six and a half years, finally ending up in a federal penitentiary for smuggling narcotics. There he tried to find God through meditation, chanting, and abstention from meat. He had studied the philosophy of the Self-Realization Fellowship as well as Transcendental Meditation and the Vedānta of Vivekananda. After becoming a hippie in the Haight-Ashbury he joined the Hare Krishna Movement. Later his Catholic training came back to him. He felt he was going through meaningless rituals as he did when he was an altar boy. Then one night in bed he had a vision of a multitude of people of all races in a marketplace. Suddenly there was a great noise and then complete silence. Next with arms raised to the sky they all began to sing and were lifted physically off the ground. He said (Hoyt, [n.d.]):

> Then I looked up and as big as the sky I saw the arms and face of Jesus taking all his children home. Wow! It was at that moment I got the largest shock of my life for I saw my feet were on the ground along with many others who had been deceived. I had always believed that Jesus was the greatest Guru or Avatar of the Ages, but now I realized that he must have been more.
>
> I can honestly say that this was the first time in my life when I actually began to pray. I didn't have words, or my own idea, but I inwardly pleaded and asked God if He would please show me the Truth at any cost.

He soon came to believe "that the blood of Jesus was now my righteousness, and His Resurrection from the dead was my Victory!"

The polemical broadsides issued by the Jesus People against the Hare Krishna Movement reflect once more a protest against all oriental philosophies, as well as a protest against the organized churches. One of them (Christian Information Committee, 1972?) cites Nathan Adler's remark that such religious enthusiasm as they display happens frequently in history "during periods of apocalyptic political crises and crumbling institutions." The testimony states further:

> Whenever that faith of man to control his destiny is lost, and when political chaos threatens to wipe out any rational meaning in the universe, it is tempting to escape into the psyche to discover the meaning mystics have found throughout the ages. The same thing happened about the time Christianity was sweeping the Roman Empire.

Comparing the present scene with earlier times of crisis, the commentator continues:

> Techniques for finding the "God within" are proliferating.
>
> All this is happening at the same time that Christianity, the traditional religion of the West, is losing its grip. This is in

> contrast to its overpowering growth during the decline of the Empire. The contrast is understandable when we note that the institutional "Christian" Church has strayed so far from its roots that it hardly bears even resemblance to the family [*sic,* faith?] of the early Apostles. (Institutional degeneration seems to be the rule in religious history.) On the one hand, the Church is under the sway of bondage to an outdated (or at least unpopular) morality and mythic ritual which has lost its power, and on the other hand it has accepted an empty rationalism which in the end degenerates into mildly platitudinous morality. The Brother and Sister of Christianity, the Protestant and Catholic Churches, are sacrificing themselves while fighting each other for the allegiance of the masses.
>
> Out of their death may come a new life. In fact, Christianity is being imitated in various quarters. The followers of meditation are claiming it for their own by reinterpreting the words of Jesus so that they appear to have been the words of a small town Buddha . . . Jesus himself said that he was "the way" and that no one could approach God unless they came "through him."

After giving a well reasoned apologetic, the anonymous writer continues:

> Jesus' message may sound improbable. You can't know this other being, you can't prove that he exists, you can only MEET him. Meditation won't introduce you to him, and you can't take a pill to find him, because he is beyond your consciousness, just like I am. But he will meet your consciousness when you are willing to meet him, when you open your mind enough to admit his possibility and take a blind step of asking him to introduce himself. You must have the courage to overcome your anxiety. It is the same anxiety which you feel consciously or unconsciously when you meet any other person. The solitude of the ego must be broken . . .
>
> The surrender of the ego explains why the metaphor of marriage is often used in the New Testament to describe the relationship between a human consciousness and this God beyond. The spirit of Jesus which meets us is described as the groom, and the human spirit as the bride. This Divine Marriage is the union of two spirits, and it requires the kind of feminine receptivity which Jung describes as the striving for completeness. In contrast to the masculine drive for perfec-

> tion, the feminine urge is not a kind of self-assertion, but a yearning to become complete in another being. The oneness with God which Jesus talks about is not any monologue with the soul—it is not spiritual egotism. It is a marriage of two individual and complementary spirits. It is a union of love. It is utterly unique.

This message emphasizes the importance of the religious experience of meeting Jesus. This encounter is not within the context of a Eucharistic service. For these youths, the meaning of this ritual has been lost by its association with the culture of the establishment, or its connotation has often been so demythologized that it becomes a memorial service for a dead Jesus who on one commemorative occasion broke bread and took wine with his disciples. Instead, the Jesus People respond to a myth that is also Biblical: the encounter of Jesus, the groom, with the bride. This mythical application is placed into the rewarding and psychological Jungian context of the feminine in man yearning for completion in a masculine deity to achieve wholeness.

The psychological relationship between this use of myth and the analogous one of the Hare Krishna Movement is obvious. As we have seen, the Hare Krishna Movement's philosophy is based on the historically recorded longing of Chaitanya as Rādhā for Krishna, the Beloved, thus setting the pattern and highest goal for the devotee's achievement of Krishna Consciousness. That which has been termed here as "myth" is actually the highest subjective reality to the devotee. It is the vehicle carrying him to inner integration. Man can only live without "myth" at his peril.

A new theology is not what the liberal churches need for a revivification. As Russel Barta says, a new theology would only result in a new rationalization. He maintains that the real need is "for a powerful mythic statement about man and his world." It has been the saints and other charismatic leaders who have periodically revitalized the church. Barta suggests a reappropriation of the mythic dimension of belief in the church's revitalization of itself. One must dethrone "the objective rational consciousness as the only definitive mode of apprehending the real" (Barta, 1972:118–120).

In this manner those in the Hare Krishna Movement, the Jesus People, and underground churches, as well as many following other oriental religions, are making myths real in an experiential way. But what are the liberal churches to do?

Part of the challenge is how to accept the empirical world of scientific reasoning in its widest sense while still allowing for a transcendental reality that exists in the world of "myth." Experiencing this reality, illogical though it may appear, may give psychological wholeness. Let us recall that Krishna Kanti, in his admitted alienation from the culture of the establishment, believed himself and the world to be insane. He was no different from thousands of others who have similar feelings, and who strike out in terrible violence. As a devotee in the Movement, this youth has found wholeness and an escape from his alienation through the practice of Krishna Consciousness.

A second part of the challenge is more difficult. If the church is to continue, it must have young members. But how can there be real community among those of the counterculture and the establishment when the gap has become so large, unless there is a ministry to them? And for this, the old ways are not satisfactory. New myths, new liturgy, new music are necessary, as they were at the time of the Reformation. Later, Puritanism also ushered in such changes to revitalize the church.

But in the final analysis, the question may be purely academic. Its answer may be conditional on other questions—Is the counterculture still continuing? Is the culture of the establishment slowly changing? If so, in which direction will it go? Many of the counterculture are now indistinguishable in outer appearance from those of the establishment. Some have shaved their beards and are now wearing short hair, so outward appearances may be deceiving. I am reminded of two recent experiences. Perhaps they were rare coincidences. On two successive days in December, 1973, when I was walking from lunch on the University of California campus, I overheard snatches of conversations that struck me. On the first occasion as two nicely groomed students passed me, one said to the other: "I understand the Aquarian Age will actually begin in 1980." On the second day, I passed two others who were walking slowly and carrying a load of books. One said: "I agree with you entirely that the myth of Christmas ended in the sixties." And I recalled Lochan's words on the subject of giving up family and Western traditions—"It's all nonsense!"

The phoenix is born, but where will it fly?

REFERENCES

ADLER, NATHAN

1968 "The antinomian personality: The hippie character type." *Psychiatry* **31:**325–338.

AHLUWALIA, SAGAR

1972 *Youth in revolt.* New Delhi, Young Asia Publications.

Back to Godhead (the magazine of the Hare Krishna Movement)

1967 "Bhakti Siddhanta Prabhupada," (editorial). **II,** 1:28.

1974 "Centers Around the World." 58:2.

BARTA, RUSSELL

1972 "Demythologizing theology." *America* **126:**118–120.

BHAKTI SIDDHĀNTA SARASWATĪ GOSWĀMI

1932 *Shree Brahṁa-Saṁhitā* (fifth chapter), with commentary by Shree Shreemad Jeeva Goswāmi and translation and purport by Shree Bhakti Siddhānta Saraswatī Goswāmi. Madras, Tridandi Swāmi Bhakti Hriday Bon.

1967 *Shri Chaitanya's teachings.* Edited by Tridandi-swāmi Shrimad Bhakti Vilās Tirtha Goswāmi Mahārāj. Madras, Secretary, Sree Gauḍīya Math.

BHAKTIVEDANTA, A. C., SWĀMI PRABHUPĀDA

1965 *Śrimad Bhāgwatam.* Third part. Delhi, The League of Devotees.

1967 "Lecture, September 4, 1966." *Back to Godhead* **I,** 9:7–8.

1968a *The teachings of Lord Chaitanya: A treatise on factual spiritual life.* New York, ISKCON Press.

1968b *The Bhagavad-gītā as it is,* with introduction, translation and authorized purports. London, Collier-Macmillan, Ltd.

1970a *Kṛṣṇa, the reservoir of pleasure and other essays.* Boston, ISKCON Press.

1970b *The nectar of devotion: A summary study of Śrīla Rūpa Gosvāmi's Bhaktirasāmṛta-Sindhu.* Boston, ISKCON Press.

1970c *I Kṛṣṇa, the Supreme Personality of Godhead: A summary study of Śrīla Vyāsadeva's Śrimad Bhāgawatam.* Boston, ISKCON Press.

1970d *II Kṛṣṇa, the Supreme Personality of Godhead.* . .

1972a Interview with Mr. Gar Kellom taped at the ISKCON Temple, Los Angeles.

1972b *Bhagavad-gītā as it is.* Complete edition with original text, roman transliteration, English equivalent, translation, and elaborate purports. New York, Collier Books.

1972c *Śrimad-Bhāgavatam.* First Canto, "Creation," Part Three, Chapters 13–19. New York, The Bhaktivedanta Book Trust.

1972d *Śrimad-Bhāgavatam.* Second Canto, "The cosmic manifestation," Part One, Chapters 1–6.

BON MAHĀRĀJ, B. H., SWĀMI

1973 "Śrī Caitanya's concept of finite self." *Indian philosophy and culture* **18:**47–69.

CHAKRAVARTI, SUDHINDRA CHANDRA

1969 *Philosophical foundation of Bengal Vaiṣṇavism: A critical exposition.* Calcutta, Academic Publishers.

CHRISTIAN INFORMATION COMMITTEE

1972? *Transcendental brain-bust.* Berkeley, California. [a single sheet broadside]

CONSTAS, HELEN, and WESTHUES, KENNETH

1972 "Communes: The routinization of hippiedom." *Society's shadow: Studies in the sociology of countercultures,* Kenneth Westhues, ed. Toronto, McGraw-Hill Ryerson, Ltd.

DASGUPTA, SURENDRANATH

1940 *A history of Indian philosophy.* Volume 3. Cambridge, The University Press.

1949 *A history of Indian philosophy.* Volume 4. Cambridge, The University Press.

DE, SUSHIL KUMAR

1961 *Early history of the Vaiṣṇava faith and movement in Bengal, from Sanskrit and Bengali sources,* second edition. Calcutta, Firma K. L. Mukhopadhyay.

DIMOCK, EDWARD C., JR.

1972 Foreword. In A. C. Bhaktivedanta Swāmi Prabhupāda, 1972b.

ELIADE, MIRCEA

1959 *The sacred and the profane: The nature of religion.* New York, Harcourt, Brace.

GERLACH, LUTHER P., and VIRGINIA H. HINE

1970 *People, power, change: Movements of social transformation.* Indianapolis and New York, Bobbs-Merrill Company, Inc.

GLOCK, CHARLES Y.

1964 *The role of deprivation in the origin and evolution of religious groups.* Berkeley, University of California, Survey Research Center. Reprinted from *Religion and social conflict,* Robert Lee, ed. New York, Oxford University Press.

HAYAGRIVA DĀS BRAHMACHARY

1966a "Flip out and stay." *Back to Godhead* **I,** 1:24.

1966b "The process of surrender in God realization." *Back to Godhead* **I,** 4:15.

1967 "Psychedelic drugs and Krishna Consciousness." *Back to Godhead* **I,** 7:1.

HOYT, DAVID [no date singlesheet broadside]

Only one way? How narrow minded!

INTERNATIONAL SOCIETY FOR KRISHNA CONSCIOUSNESS

1970 *The Kṛṣṇa Consciousness handbook.* Los Angeles, ISKCON Press.

JAISWAL, SUVIRA

1967 *The origin and development of Vaiṣṇavism: Vaiṣṇavism from 200* B.C. *to* A.D. *500.* Delhi, Munshiram Manoharlal.

JOHNSON, GREGORY

1970a "The Krishna movement: Its emergence from the 'Counter-Culture.' " A research paper on the Hare Krishna movement in San Francisco, written in preparation for the Ph.D. degree, Harvard University.

1970b "Personal transformation in the Krishna movement." A paper based on research for the Ph.D. degree at Harvard University.

[n.d.] [Pages from an untitled paper of an unknown date]

JUDAH, J. STILLSON

1967 *The history and philosophy of the metaphysical movements in America.* Philadelphia, The Westminster Press.

1974 "The Hare Krishna Movement." In *Religious movements in contemporary America,* Irving Zaretsky, ed. Princeton, Princeton University Press.

KAVIRAJA, SRI SRI, KRISHNADĀSA GOSWAMI

1959a *Sri Sri Chaitanya Charitamrita.* Adilila I. Translated by Nagendra Kumar Ray. Revised by Dr. Satish Chandra Ray. Second edition I. Puri, Nagendra Kumar Ray.

1959b ———. Madhyalila, Part 1, II:1.

1959c ———. Madhyalila, Part 2, II:2.

1959d ———. Madhyalila, Part 3, II:3.

1959e ———. Antyalila, Part 1, III:1.

KELLEY, DEAN M.

1972 *Why conservative churches are growing: A study in sociology of religion.* New York, Harper & Row.

KELLOM, GAR E.

1973 "The Chaitanya movement in America." M.A. thesis, Pacific School of Religion, Berkeley, California.

KENNEDY, MELVILLE T.

1925 *The Chaitanya movement: A study of Vaishṇavism of Bengal.* Calcutta, Association Press; New York, Oxford University Press.

LEONARD, GEORGE B.

1972 *The transformation: A guide to the inevitable changes in humankind.* New York, Delacorte Press.

LOFLAND, JOHN, and RODNEY STARK

1965 "Becoming a world-savior: A theory of conversion to a deviant perspective." *American Sociological Review* **30:**862–875.

MAJUMDAR, A. K.

1965 *Bhakti renaissance.* Bombay, Bharatiya Vidya Bhavan.

MESSER, MARK

1972 "Running out of era: Some non-pharmacological notes on the psychedelic revolution." In *Society's shadow: Studies in the sociology of countercultures,* Kenneth Westhues, ed. Toronto, McGraw-Hill Ryerson, Ltd.

MOULEDOUX, JOSEPH

1972 "Ideological aspects of a drug dealership." In *Society's shadow: Studies in the sociology of countercultures,* Kenneth Westhues, ed. Toronto, McGraw-Hill Ryerson, Ltd.

MUKHERJEE, DILAP KUMAR

1970 *Chaitanya.* New Delhi, National Book Trust.

NAYANA BHIRAM DĀS BRAHMACHARY

1968 "The knowledge implosion." *Back to Godhead* No. 20:31.*

NORDIN, KENNETH

1972 "How youth of U.S. looks at religion." *Oakland Tribune* (California), July 30, 1972.

* This magazine discontinued numbering by volumes, and distinguishes issues only by numbers, with individual paging.

O'DEA, THOMAS

1970 "Youth in protest: Revolution or revelation?" Salt Lake City, Sociology Department, University of Utah.

PRATT, JAMES BISSETT

1926 *The religious consciousness: A psychological study.* New York, The Macmillan Company.

RAY, BENOY GOPAL

1965 *Religious movements in modern Bengal.* Santiniketan, Visva-Bharati.

RAYARĀMA

1969 "Contemporary education in the West." *Back to Godhead* No. 23:12.*

REED, ELAINE

1972 "Can the Jewish home survive?" *Oakland Tribune,* (California), July 30, 1972.

REICH, CHARLES A.

1970 *The greening of America.* New York, Random House.

ROSZAK, THEODORE

1969 *The making of a counter culture: Reflections on the technocratic society and its youthful opposition.* Garden City, Doubleday.

RUKMANI, T. S.

1970 *A critical study of the Bhāgavata Purāṇa, with special reference to bhakti.* Varanasi, The Chowkhamba Sanskrit Series Office.

SATSVARUPA DĀSA (ADHIKĀRI) GOSVĀMI

1972 "Second birth." *Back to Godhead* No. 45:20.

1973 "Gurukula, new hope for humanity." *Back to Godhead* No. 54:19.

SLATER, PHILIP E.

1970 *The pursuit of loneliness: American culture at the breaking point.* Boston, Beacon Press.

SUCHMAN, EDWARD A.

1968 "The "hang-loose" ethic and the spirit of drug use." In *Society's shadow: Studies in the sociology of countercultures,* Kenneth Westhues, ed. Toronto, McGraw-Hill Ryerson, Ltd.

WEBER, MAX

1930 *The Protestant ethic and the spirit of capitalism.* Translated by Talcott Parsons. Foreword by R. H. Tawney. New York, Charles Scribner's Sons.

WESTHUES, KENNETH

1972 *Society's shadow: Studies in the sociology of countercultures.* Toronto, McGraw-Hill Ryerson, Ltd.

WINTERS, CHESTER T.

1971 "The death of the Sunday school." *The Torch.* XII, 4:1–2.

WOODS, RICHARD, O. P.

1971 *The occult revolution: A Christian meditation.* New York, Herder and Herder, Inc.

SELECT BIBLIOGRAPHY FOR FURTHER STUDY OF VAISHṆAVISM

The following annotated bibliography is added for two reasons. First, since *bhakti* is presently enjoying a renaissance in India, many new and interesting books are being published. Second, since I have tried to present the beliefs of the Krishna devotees as exactly as possible, I have avoided either a detailed literary or historical critical approach. I have therefore offered the second subdivision of the background materials representing books written by those outside the Hare Krishna Movement. These will often have a broader approach, including literary and historical criticism, and will be of use to those who wish to study Vaishṇavism in general more widely.

The list is not to be considered in any way exhaustive. It aims merely to suggest titles that I have found useful in my own study of Vaishṇavism.

Source Materials for the Hare Krishna Movement

Back to Godhead (the magazine of the Hare Krishṇa Movement)

1966 Boston, ISKCON Press. Most important source for ongoing history of the Hare Krishna Movement. Articles on all phases of Krishna Consciousness written largely by the devotees of the Movement. Although the back file is out of print, a copy on microfilm is available at the library of the Graduate Theological Unión, Berkeley, California.

BHAKTI PRAJNAN YATI MAHĀRĀJ, TRIDANDISWĀMI

1968 *Gita Darsan as Bhakti Yoga as a Chaitanyite reads it.* Madras, Sree Gauḍīya Math. A commentary of the *Bhagavad-gītā* by the secretary of the Gauḍīya Math at Madras, representing the point of view of the Gauḍīya Vaishṇavas.

BHAKTI SIDDHĀNTA SARASWATĪ GOSWĀMI

1932 *Shree Brahma-Saṁhitā* (fifth chapter), with commentary by Shree Shreemad Jeeva Goswāmi and translation and purport by Shree Bhakti Siddhānta Saraswatī Goswāmi. Madras, Tridandi Swāmi Bhakti Hriday Bon. This work is of singular importance, since the main commentary is by the spiritual master of Swāmi Bhaktivedanta, and is a link between his thought and that of the Gauḍīya Vaishṇavas. This part of the Brahma Saṁhitā is one source of the philosophy of Chaitanya.

1967 *Shri Chaitanya's teachings.* Edited by Tridandiswāmi Shrimad Bhakti Vilās Tirtha Goswāmi Mahārāj. Madras, Secretary, Sree Gauḍīya Math. Probably the most important work by Swāmi Bhakti Siddhānta to appear in English. Because it contains a collection of writings and lectures by the one who was the spiritual master of Swāmi Bhaktivedanta, its words should be most authoritative for both the Gauḍīya Vaishṇavas and the Hare Krishna Movement.

BHAKTI VILĀS TIRTHA GOSWĀMI MAHĀRĀJ

1964 *Sri Chaitanya's concept of theistic Vedānta.* Madras, Secretary, Sree Gauḍīya Math. This is interesting for comparison, since it is the work of the current president of the larger faction of the Gauḍīya Vaishṇavas.

BHAKTIVEDANTA, A. C. SWĀMI PRABHUPĀDA

1968 *Teachings of Lord Chaitanya: A treatise on factual spiritual life.* New York, International Society for Krishna Consciousness. The most important work written by Swāmi Bhaktivedanta concerning the teachings of Chaitanya, upon which the Hare Krishna Movement bases its philosophy.

1969 *Śrī Īśopaniṣad: The knowledge that brings one nearer to the Supreme Personality of Godhead, Kṛṣṇa,* with original Sanskrit text, roman transliteration, English equivalents, translation, and elaborate purports. Boston, ISKCON Press. The only commentary by the author on one of the few theistic *Upanishads,* in which he expresses his Vaishṇava philosophy.

1970 *Easy journey to other planets* (*by practice of supreme* yoga), third edition. Boston, ISKCON Press. An introduction to the *bhakti yoga* in which the basic rules are outlined briefly for attaining a degree of spiritualization according to the Vaishṇava philosophy. A brief primer.

1970 *The Kṛṣṇa Consciousness Movement is the genuine* Vedic *way: A cogent discussion between A. C. Bhaktivedanta Swāmi and Dr. J. F. Stall* (Professor of Philosophy and of South Asian Languages, University of California, Berkeley, California). Boston, ISKCON Press. An article in the *Los Angeles Times* by Professor Stall was the occasion for a published exchange of letters by Professor Stall and Swāmi Bhaktivedanta. Of interest for its contrast between Eastern and Western scholarship.

1970 *Kṛṣṇa Consciousness: The topmost yoga system.* Boston, ISKCON Press. Another brief primer on *bhakti.* Of interest for its explanation of the *mahāmantra.*

1970 *Kṛṣṇa, The Supreme Personality of Godhead: A summary study of Śrīla Vyāsadeva's Śrīmad-Bhāgavatam,* Tenth Canto. 2 volumes. Boston, ISKCON Press. This is a commentary on the most important *Purāṇa* for the study of the life of Krishna, according to the Hare Krishna Movement. An uncritical narration of the pastimes of Krishna, the cowherd deity of Vṛindāvan from his birth to his disapparance.

1970 *Kṛṣṇa, The reservoir of pleasure and other essays.* Boston, ISKCON Press. A brief paperback containing four essays, including a brief biography of Swāmi Bhaktivedanta.

1970 *The nectar of devotion: A summary study of Śrīla Rūpa Gosvāmi's Bhaktirasāmṛta-sindhu.* Boston, ISKCON Press. The most important and thorough treatment of *bhakti yoga* in the tradition of the Gauḍīya Vaishṇavas: A commentary by the author on the work of one of Chaitanya's closest disciples and a formulater of his system of devotion.

1972 *Beyond birth and death.* New York, ISKCON Press. Another brief paperback of five essays.

1972 *Bhagavad-gīta as it is.* Complete edition with original Sanskrit text, roman transliteration, English equivalents, translation, and elaborate purports. New York, Macmillan, Inc. Undoubtedly his most important single-volume work. It not only gives a good exposition of the philosophy of the Hare Krishna Movement in the form of a commentary, but the index is extensive and makes the work very useful for reference.

1972 *Śrīmad-Bhāgavatam of Kṛṣṇa-Dvaipāyana Vyāsa.* New York, Bhaktivedanta Book Trust. The most ambitious and detailed treatment of this important work for the Movement. Six volumes have already been published; it is projected that the complete work will require over forty volumes. As with his other works, it represents an uncritical exposition of its contents as well as translation, but is highly important for those seriously interested in the philosophy of the Movement.

Indian Philosophy and Culture (a quarterly)

1973 *Special issue: Sri Caitanya* (**18**,1, March 1973). Published by the Institute of Oriental Philosophy. Vrindaban, Shri Harbinani Press. This special number on Chaitanya contains a number of informative articles by important Vaishṇava scholars of the Gauḍīya school, including Thākur Bhaktivinode, Bhakti Siddhānta Saraswatī Goswāmi, and Swāmi B. H. Bon Mahārāj, the editor of the journal.

The Institute of Oriental Philosophy, Vrindaban

1963 *Jiva-atma or finite self: The concept of the individual finite self in twelve different systems of philosophy.* Edited by Swāmi B. H. Bon Mahārāj. Vrindaban, The Institute. An interesting comparative study of the self according to various Hindu philosophical systems by Hindu scholars.

International Society for Krishna Consciousness

1970 *The Kṛṣṇa Consciousness handbook.* Boston, ISKCON Press. A most valuable paperback handbook giving briefly the essential teachings concerning the philosophy and devotion, the brief history and organization of the Movement.

1971 *Vyās pūjā: The appearance day of our beloved spiritual master, his divine grace, A. C. Bhaktivedanta Swāmi Prabhupāda, founder-ācārya of the International Society for Krishna Consciousness.* Brooklyn, ISKCON Press. A paperback that attempts to let each of the Hare Krishna temples express in its respective way the extreme love and veneration they have for their spiritual master.

1972 *Transcendental teachings of Prahlād Mahārāj.* Brooklyn, ISKCON Press. Five brief essays in a paperback concerning our purpose in life, our foolishness in spoiling our lives, the illusion of family happiness, and the love for Krishna are given as the teachings of an ancient devotee of Krishna.

KAVIRAJA, SRI SRI KRISHNADASA

1959 *Sri Sri Chaitanya Charitamrita.* Translated by Nagendra Kumar Ray; revised by Dr. Satish Chandar Ray. Second edition, 6 volumes. Puri, Nagendra Kumar Ray. Because of the close contact of the author with the 6 Goswāmis at Vṛindāvan, this is the best single source for the study of the life of Chaitanya dating from the sixteenth century. Officially recognized by the Gauḍīya Vaishṇavas as the basis of their belief.

Background Sources for the Study of Vaishṇavism by Authors Outside the Hare Krishna Movement and Gauḍīya Vaishṇavism.

BANERJEA, J. N.

1966 *Paurānic and Tantric religion (early phase)*. Calcutta, University of Calcutta. Gives in part the background for the development of Vaishṇavism from literary and archeological sources.

BHANDARKAR, SIR RAMAKRISHNA GOPALA

1913 *Vaiṣṇavism, Śaivism and minor religious systems* (Grundriss der indo-arischen Philologie und Altertumskunde). Strassburg, K. J. Trübner. One of the older critical and scholarly works that still has some importance. Promotes the distinction in tradition between the Gopāla Krishna and Krishna Vāsudeva.

CHAKRAVARTI, SUBHINDRA CHANDRA

1969 *Philosophical foundation of Bengal Vaiṣṇavism: A critical exposition.* Calcutta, Academic Publishers. One of the best scholarly treatments of the Chaitanya school of philosophy in all aspects giving attention to the ideas of Jīva Goswāmi, one of the chief formulaters of the philosophy.

DASGUPTA, SURENDRANATH

1932–1955 *A history of Indian philosophy.* Cambridge, University Press. Volumes two to four offer excellent treatment of the various doctrines in the different schools of Vaishṇavism.

DE, SUSHIL KUMAR

1961 *Early history of the Vaiṣṇava faith and movement in Bengal, from Sanskrit and Bengali sources,* second edition. Calcutta, Firma K. L. Mukhopadhyay. Probably the most definitive treatment of Bengal Vaishṇavism utilizing the native literary sources.

DUTT, KANAI LAL

1963 *The Bengal Vaishṇavism and modern life.* Calcutta, Sribhumi Publishing Company. An interesting work that promotes the idea that Chaitanya's Vaishṇavism is the type of utopia needed in our complex changing cultures, and that it establishes the validity of human emotions in a religious context.

EIDLITZ, WALTHER

1968 *Kṛṣṇa-Caitanya: Sein Leben und seine Lehre.* Stockholm, Almquist and Wiksell. Of special interest only to scholars who want to study the thought and life of the Chaitanya school on various subjects that can be examined from translated excerpts from sources nearly contemporary with Chaitanya. The author's intent as he explains it is to weave together for the first time a complete picture of the life and work of Krishna Chaitanya.

JAISWAL, SUVIRA

1967 *The origin and development of Vaiṣṇavism: Vaiṣṇavism from 200* B.C. *to* A.D. *500.* Delhi, Munshiram Manohalal. A revision of the author's thesis at Patna, which presents in a scholarly manner the early development of Vaishṇavism.

KELLOM, GAR E.

1973 "The Chaitanya movement in America." M.A. thesis, Pacific School of Religion, Berkeley, California. Of particular value concerning the Hare Krishna Movement in America. Derived from extensive interviews with the devotees.

KENNEDY, MELVILLE T.

1925 *The Chaitanya movement: A study of the Vaishṇavism of Bengal.* (The religious life of India.) Calcutta, Association Press; New York, Oxford University Press. Still a well-rounded treatment of the Chaitanya Vaishṇavism, its teachings, and the history of the Movement up to modern times.

LAL, KANWAR

The religion of love. Delhi, Arts and Letters. A delightful popular treatment that deals with the love aspects of Vaishṇavism; nicely illustrated.

MAJUMDAR, A. K.

1965 *Bhakti renaissance.* Bombay, Bharatiya Vidya Bhavan. A brief introduction to the modern revival of *bhakti* in India with very brief descriptions of the most important movements.

MAJUMDAR, BIMANBEHARI

1969 *Kṛṣṇa in history and legend.* Calcutta, University of Calcutta. An excellent critical treatment of the chronological problems connected with Krishna and a study of Krishna in the various literary sources including mediaeval literature.

MISHRA, KANHU CHARAN

1971 *The cult of Jagannātha.* Calcutta, Firma K. L. Mukhopadhyay. An important scholarly contribution concerning the history, philosophy and worship of Jagannātha at Purī.

MUKHERJEE, DILIP KUMAR

1970 *Chaitanya.* (National biography series.) New Delhi, National Book Trust. An excellent introduction to the life of Chaitanya and the development of his thought by the Goswāmis. Includes material on the Movement in Bengal and Orissa.

MUKHERJI, SHYAM CHARD

1966 *A study of Vaiṣṇavism in ancient and mediaeval Bengal up to the advent of Caitanya.* Calcutta, Punthi Pustak. A revised thesis submitted to Calcutta University, studying the development of the Movement through examination of archaeological and literary data.

RAY, BENOY GOPAL

1964 *Religious movements in modern Bengal.* Santiniketan, Visva-Bharati. Informative presentation of material on all modern religious movements in Bengal, and important *gurus.* Because of their number, the articles are brief.

RAYCHAUDHURI, HEMEHANDRA

1936 *Materials for the study of the early history of the Vaishṇava sect,* second edition, revised and enlarged. Calcutta, University of Calcutta. A critical survey of the development of Vaishṇavism in India.

RUKMANI, T. S.

1970 *A critical study of the Bhāgavata Purāṇa, with special reference to bhakti.* Varanasi, The Chowkhamba Sanskrit Series Office. A critical study of this most important *Purāṇa* for Gauḍīya Vaishṇavism, at times unfortunately marred by the author's attempts to explain by logic various pastimes of Krishna.

SINGER, MILTON, ed.

1966 *Krishna: Myths, rites, and attitudes.* Chicago, University of Chicago Press. Contains eight articles by different scholars giving scholarly treatment to much that is pertinent to a study of modern day Vaishṇavism. Studies on the social teachings and archaism of the *Bhāgavata Purāṇa,* Bengal Vaishṇavism, and the Rādhā-Krishna *bhajanas* in Madras and other places in South India are included.

SIRCAR, D. C., ed.

1967 *The śakti cult and Tara.* Calcutta, University of Calcutta. A series of lectures largely on the subject of Śaktism. Of interest to the student of Vaishṇavism because of its material concerning the relationship between Vaishṇavism and Śaktism.

GLOSSARY OF IMPORTANT NAMES AND TERMS

Āchārya (*ācārya*) *

Spiritual master or teacher.

Achintya bhedābheda (*acintya*)

See *bhedābheda.*

Achyutānanda (Acyutānanda)

Literally, imperishable bliss. Name of one of the six Dāsas of Orissa who popularized Chaitanya's philosophy through their poems and songs.

Advaita

Literally, having no duality. It represents the Hindu type of Vedānta philosophy popularized by Śaṅkara. It declares the identity of the ultimate reality or Brahman with the *jīvātman* or the individual soul, and the phenomenal world of matter to be the result of *māyā* or illusion.

Advaitāchārya (Advaitācārya)

Name of one of Chaitanya's disciples, whom the Gauḍīya Vaishṇavas and those of the Hare Krishna Movement consider to

* Words spelled with a "c" rather than "ch" and appearing in parentheses represent the more original Sanskrit spelling, which has been anglicized in the text as "ch" for use in pronunciation.

be an expansion of Krishna as part of his descent (*avatār*) as Chaitanya. He is also identified with Māhā-Vishṇu according to the *Caitanya Caritāmṛita.*

Advaitin

A follower of the *advaita* Vedānta philosophy. See also *advaita.*

Aghāsura

A demon in the shape of a serpent. Conquered by Krishna as one of his pastimes.

Aham̐ brahmāsmi

Literally, "I am Brahman," which is the *Upanishadic* sentence identifying the real self, the *ātman,* with the Brahman, or Absolute Reality.

Aham̐kāra

The empirical or "false ego," which is as much a product of *māyā* or illusion as is the material body. It is to be distinguished from the real self or *ātman,* or the *jīva* or soul.

Ahirbudhnya Sam̐hitā

One of the most important texts of the *Pañcharātrā* literature.

Aiśvarya

The state of being sovereign. Here it represents one aspect of Krishna, his majestic power as distinguished from his beauty and from his loving nature. This aspect is often identified with the deity, Nārāyaṇa, whom the Gauḍīya Vaishṇavas and Hare Krishna Movement consider as an expansion of Krishna.

Alvars

A group of *gurus,* living perhaps during the period between the seventh and ninth centuries A.D. in the Tamil-speaking part of

South India. Their works influenced the philosophy of the later Vaishṇavas.

Ānanda

Literally, bliss. This is the bliss that here is not only part of Krishna's nature, but is the promised state of mankind when Krishna's ecstatic principle is realized through Krishna Consciousness.

Ananta

One of the six Dāsas of Orissa who popularized Chaitanya's philosophy through their poems and songs.

Ananta Śeshanāga

Name of one of the *nāga* or snake deities whose history probably goes back to the pre-Indo-European period of Indian religion. He is here regarded as a plenary expansion of Vishṇu and appears as a great cobra with millions of heads holding all the planets of the cosmos. He is also identified with Saṅkarshaṇa and with Balarāma (Baladeva), Krishna's brother.

Aniruddha

Here one of the four *vyūhas* or expansions of Krishna who is identified with the third Purusha, a manifestation of Māhā-Vishṇu for purposes of creation. In the *Vishṇu Purāṇa* he appears also as the son of Pradyumna and the grandson of Krishna.

Āraṇyakas

A class of literature known also as the forest *Brāhmaṅas* or guides for the Brahmin in the *vānaprastha* or third stage of life, when he goes into the forest to meditate. As literature they mark the intervening stage between the *Brāhmaṇas* of the sacrificial tradition and the *Upanishads* of the more philosophical one. A few, however, like the *Bṛihad Āraṇyaka* are already to be classed as an *Upanishad*.

Ārati

The usual dialectical spelling for *ārātrika.*

Ārātrika

The name of the daily temple ceremonies in praise of the spiritual master, Chaitanya and Krishna. During the various chants the temple deities are offered food, incense, flowers, a handkerchief, a fan, and an offering of flames.

Archā (*arcā*)

A form of incarnation of Krishna, in which he appears in visible form, for example, the Jagannātha deities in the temple. Although appearing in the form of an image, the deities are not to be considered as material, but rather as being in spiritual form. Because of our materially contaminated senses we see only the material likeness, according to Swāmi Bhaktivedanta.

Arjuna

The hero in the *Bhagavad-gītā* who conducts the philosophical dialogue with Krishna, his charioteer, just before the famous battle at Kurukshetra in which Arjuna and his brothers fight against their cousins, the Kauravas.

Āśramas

The four traditional Hindu stages of life recommended originally for the Brahmins: student, householder or married stage, the "retired," and renounced life. In the traditional view, the "retired" stage is the *vānaprastha* stage, when the Brahmin went into the forest to meditate.

Atharva Veda

The fourth and latest of the four *Vedas,* the *mantras* of which were often used in magical incantations.

Ātman

The real spiritual self as distinguished from the empirical or "false ego." It is that part of an individual entity which continues in various material forms through reincarnation until the self receives liberation, according to the Hare Krishna Movement.

Avatār

Here, a "descent" or manifestation of Krishna (Vishṇu) in one of many forms, usually to help mankind in a time of crisis.

Āveśa

A type of *avatār* of Krishna (Vishṇu) in which the deity takes possession of a person in order to inspire him as a prophet.

Avidyā

Literally, ignorance and here the root cause of one's sinful life of sense gratification. Liberation is through transcendental knowledge of one's relationship to Krishna as his eternal servitor.

Avikṛita-pariṇāmavāda

Literally, the doctrine of transformation without change (in Brahman, the Absolute Reality). Because of the doctrine of *bhedābheda,* according to which Krishna was both one with and yet separate from his energy (*śakti*), it was doctrinally possible for the world to be created by Krishna's energy without any change in Brahman (Krishna). In earlier Vaishṇava schools, such as Rāmānuja's, Brahman was considered to be modified during creation.

Balabhadra

See Balarāma.

Baladeva

See Balarāma.

Balarāma

One of the six Dāsas whose poems and songs, composed in Orissa during the seventeenth century, contributed to a revival of Chaitanyaism.

Balarāma or Baladeva or Balabhadra

Krishna's older brother, the son of Vāsudeva. He is also as Saṅkarshaṇa-Baladeva, one of Krishna's *vyūhas* or emanations for creation. As one of the Jagaṅnāth deities, he is frequently called Balabhadra.

Bāṇa

Seventh-century author of the *Harsha-caṛita.*

Bhagavad-gītā

The famous philosophical treatise forming an episode of the Hindu epic, the *Mahābhārata,* in which occurs the dialogue between Arjuna and Krishna, his charioteer. This marks the first important treatment of *bhakti-yoga* or salvation through devotional surrender to Krishna.

Bhagavān or Bhagavat

Name of Krishna expressing his personal aspect of Ultimate Reality as distinguished from his impersonal character as Brahman, and as *paramātman,* the Supersoul.

Bhāgavata Purāṇa

The most important *Purāṇa* for the Hare Krishna Movement and the Gauḍīya Vaishṇavas, which contains the pastimes or sports of the young Krishna as the cowherd deity of Vṛindāvan.

Bhāgavatas

One of the early sects of *bhakti-yoga,* to which the *Bhagavad-gītā* has been ascribed.

Bhakta

One who practices *bhakti-yoga.*

Bhakti, or *bhakti-yoga*

The way to salvation by loving surrender to a personal deity, which here is Krishna, the supreme personality of Godhead. By the discipline one achieves Krishna Consciousness, the knowledge of one's original nature as an eternal servitor of Krishna.

Bhakti-rasāmṛita-sindhu

Principal work on devotion for the Gauḍīya Vaishṇavas and the Hare Krishna Movement. It was written by Rūpa Goswāmi, one of the six Goswāmis of Vṛindāvan responsible for the development of Chaitanya's philosophy. It was translated and interpreted by Swāmi Bhaktivedanta under the title, *Nectar of Devotion.*

Bhakti Siddhānta Sarasvatī Goswāmi

The spiritual master of Swāmi Bhaktivedanta, the former head of the Gauḍīya Vaishṇavas, who ostensibly requested that his disciple, Bhaktivedanta, spread the teachings of Chaitanya to the West.

Bhaktivedanta Swāmi Prabhupada, A. C.

The founder of the International Society for Krishna Consciousness who has brought to the West the teachings and practice of *bhakti-yoga* of Chaitanya, which is represented best in India by the Gauḍīya Vaishṇavas.

Bhakti Vilas Tirtha Goswāmi Mahārāj, Śri Śrīmad

Regarded by most of the Gauḍīya Vaishṇavas as their spiritual master and successor to Bhakti Siddhānta.

Bhaktivinode Thākur, Śrīla

Founder of the Gauḍīya Vaishṇava Mission under the formal name of Śrī Viśva Vaishṇav Rāj Sabhā. This is an association of Vaishṇavas interested in propagating Chaitanya's philosophy.

Bhakti-yoga

See *bhakti.*

Bharati

Name of the order of *sannyāsis* or holy men in which Chaitanya was said to have been initiated.

Bhedābheda

Inconceivable dualism and nondualism. The philosophical belief of several Hindu philosophers including those belonging to the tradition of Chaitanya, such as the Gauḍīya Vaishṇavas and those belonging to the International Society for Krishna Consciousness. A belief in which the ultimate reality is characterized as being both monistic and dualistic at the same time, or different and nondifferent from the component parts. In Chaitanya's thought the various forms of Krishna's energy are considered to be both part of him and yet entirely different and separate from him at one and the same time.

Bhūmi

The predominating deity of the earth who requested Brahmā, the creator deity, to intercede with Kshīrodakāśāyī Vishṇu, the source of all *avatārs,* to have Krishna sent down to settle the strife among evil kings.

Bon Mahārāj, Swāmi B. H.

A philosopher of the Gauḍīya Vaishṇavas who preceded Swāmi Bhaktivedanta in bringing Chaitanya's message to America in the 1930s. His lectures were delivered to university audiences; no movement was established until Swāmi Bhaktivedanta came to America in 1965.

Brahmā

Here, a manifestation of Garbhodakāśāyī Vishṇu as a personal creator deity. Predominating deity of each universe and regarded as one of Krishna's (Vishṇu's) *guṇa avatārs.*

Brahmachārī (*brahmacārī*)

The student stage, or first of the traditional four stages (*aśrāmas*) in the life of a Brahmin.

Brahmachāriṇī

The student and unmarried stage for women of the Hare Krishna Movement. It represents an American adaptation of the *brahmachārī* stage and gives a type of spiritual status to the women.

Brahmajyoti

In Bhaktivedanta's interpretation, this is the effulgence or halo of Krishna which includes all that exists, and emanates from his abode, or Krishnaloka.

Brahmaloka

Here, the planet on which the creator deity Brahmā resides. Bhaktivedanta says that it is lower than Goloka-Vṛindāvan, the highest spiritual world of Krishna, where he sports with the *gopīs,* and the ultimate place for Krishna Conscious people. Brahmaloka, however, is an impermanent heaven world where good people go after death to enjoy happiness.

Brahman

The Brahman or Krishna's personal effulgence or halo is one phase of Absolute Reality according to the Hare Krishna Movement. It is, however, only part of the complete whole, is the origin of everything, according to the *Bhāgavata Purāṇa,* and yet as spirit is the opposite of matter, according to this belief.

Brāhmaṇas

The sacrificial commentaries to the four *Vedas,* which give instructions concerning the rituals and often the reasons for doing so.

Brāhmaṇda

One of the *Purāṇas* which adds material to the Vaishṇava tradition and which was composed in its present form after the fourth century A.D.

Brāhma Purāṇa

One of the *Purāṇas* which has been judged as perhaps containing the oldest version of the story of Krishna.

Brāhma Samāj

A Hindu reform movement founded in the latter part of the nineteenth century by Ram Mohan Roy.

Brahma Saṁhitā

A work that has been proclaimed by the Gauḍīya Vaishṇavas as a *Pañcharātrā* work, and one of the few works highly praised by Chaitanya. It contains the doctrine of the *vyūhas,* or Krishna's (Vishṇu's) emanations for purposes of creation.

Brahma Sūtras

Short, terse, philosophical aphorisms depending on the *Upanishads* and concerned largely with the nature of Brahman. Their systematization has been ascribed to Bādarāyaṇa in the early centuries of the Christian era.

Brahmavaivarta Purāṇa

One of the *Purāṇas,* which has been regarded as the first one to depict in sensuous imagery Rādhā, the consort of Krishna.

Brahmin

Traditionally the priestly and highest caste in Hindu society. Bhaktivedanta places Krishna Conscious people in a higher status, and as the true Brahmins whose status depends upon their spirituality rather than upon birth. In interpreting the *Bhagavad-gītā* he classes them as "the intelligent class belonging to the material mode of goodness."

Burfly

A coconut and powdered milk confection.

Caitanya Bhāgavata

A sixteenth-century source of Chaitanya's life written by Vṛindāvan Dāsa. Regarded by S. K. De as the earliest biographer of Chaitanya.

Caitanya Caritāmṛita, Śrī Śrī

The sixteenth-century biography of Chaitanya, and most highly regarded as being authentic by the Gauḍīya Vaishṇavas and the Hare Krishna Movement. It was composed by Krishnadāsa Kavirāja Goswāmi.

Caitanya Maṅgala

A sixteenth-century biography of Chaitanya written by Jayānanda independently of Vaishṇava orthodoxy, according to S. K. De, and is therefore not canonical.

Chaitanya Mahāprabhu, Śrī Krishna

The founder of the school of *bhakti-yoga,* best represented today by the Gauḍīya Vaishṇavas and the devotees of the Hare Krishna Movement.

Chaṇḍīdās (Caṇḍīdās)

A Bengali poet who lived about the end of the fourteenth century and whose songs formed one source of the philosophy of Vaishṇavism.

Chandogya Upanishad

One of the earliest and most important of the *Upanishads.* According to S. Radhakrishna it may have been composed as early as the eighth or seventh century B.C.

Chapatis

A type of thin flat wheat tortilla.

Charaṇāmṛita (*caraṇāmṛita*)

Water used in bathing the deities and offered in spoonfuls at a temple, to be drunk by devotees.

Chit (*cit*)

Here, one of the three paramount attributes of Krishna representing knowledge.

Chit-śakti (*cit*)

Here represents Krishna's energy or spiritual power corresponding to the knowledge aspect of his personal nature.

Dahl

A lentil soup.

Dās or *dāsa*

Literally, servant. Word added often to names of Hare Krishna male devotees. Signifies their recognition of themselves as servants of Krishna.

Dāsya

Service, servitude. The second stage in Krishna Consciousness, in which one feels like a servant to Krishna.

Devakī

The mother of Krishna in his Vṛindāvan *līlā,* or manifestation.

Dharma-śāstras

The law books, or books of righteousness (*dharma*), governing traditionally the actions of people in society. They contain material on religion, politics, and social customs for the divisions of Hindu society. They were composed in the Epic period, 500 B.C. to A.D. 200.

Dhoti

The flowing cloth garment often worn by Hindu males.

Durgā

Traditionally the daughter of Himavat and the wife or consort of Śiva, the destroyer. She is also known as Umā, Pārvati, etc. In the philosophy of Chaitanya she represents the eight-armed younger sister of Vishṇu and a form of Yogamāyā, Krishna's internal power.

Dvaitādvaita

Literally, dualistic-nondualism. A philosophy that, like the *bhedābheda* system of Chaitanya, held that God was both one with and separate from each soul. It is best represented by Nimbārka, a Vaishṇava philosopher, who lived in the thirteenth century.

Dvārakā

The city that Krishna, the divine charioteer of Arjuna, built for his kinsmen, the Yādavas, and to which he returned after the battle of Kurukshetra.

Ekādāśī

Fasting day on the eleventh day after the full moon, and the eleventh day after the new moon. At these times the Hare Krishna devotees eat only moderate amounts of vegetables and milk, but no grains, cereals, or beans.

Ekāntins

Name of an early sect that worshipped Nārāyaṇa-Vishṇu Vāsudeva, according to the *Nārāyaṇīya* section of the *Mahābhārata*.

Gadādhara

One of Chaitanya's closest disciples. According to the Gauḍīya Vaishṇavas and the Hare Krishna Movement he was a representative of Krishna's internal energy as a pure devotee and as part of Krishna's *avatār*.

Garbhodakāśāyī Vishṇu

The second Purusha in the process of creation, according to the Chaitanya philosophy. He is a manifestation of Vishṇu lying in the middle cosmic ocean and from whose navel a lotus springs from which Brahmā, the creator god emerges.

Gauḍīya Vaishṇavas

The best Hindu representatives of the Chaitanya school of philosophy. Bhakti Siddhānta Goswāmi, the spiritual master of Swāmi Bhaktivedanta, was the leader of this group until his death.

Ghee

Melted clarified butter.

Gīta-govinda

Work by Jāyadeva toward the end of the twelfth century A.D. It was revered highly by Chaitanya for its erotic poetry describing the love of Krishna for Rādhā, his consort.

Gokula

Literally, a herd of cows. Alternative name for Krishna's highest heaven as well as the temple sanctuary where the devotees worship him.

Goloka-Vṛindāvan

Name of Krishna's highest heaven world which is associated with the pastimes of Krishna as the cowherd deity. Goloka, literally, cow-world, like Vṛindāvan is also used alone to designate this heaven where Krishna sports with the *gopīs* and Rādhā in loving pastimes.

Gopāla

Literally, cow protector, a name applied to Krishna as the cowherd deity of Vṛindāvan, and then also applied to Vaishṇavas as a name.

Gopāl Bhaṭṭa

Name of one of the six Goswāmis of Vṛindāvan whom Chaitanya commissioned to systemize his philosophy.

Gopāls

These were twelve later devotees who helped Nityānanda spread the *bhakti-yoga* of Chaitanya in Bengal during the sixteenth century A.D.

Gopīnātha

Literally, protector or lord of the cowherdesses, which refers to Krishna. Here the name of the Vaishṇavite temple in Purī. Into the images of its deities Chaitanya is believed by the Hare Krishna devotees to have disappeared.

Gopīs

Here, cowherdesses or milkmaids with whom Krishna sported erotically during his Vṛindāvan pastimes, and with whom he sports eternally in the heavenly Vṛindāvan.

Goswāmi

Religious title, now synonymous with "Swāmi," which is given to some Krishna devotees who have become saṅnyāsis.

Govardhana Hill

Here the name of the hill near Vṛindāvan which Krishna raised and held over his head like an umbrella with his little finger. This was to protect the people from the devastating rain that the demigod Indra had sent because of their refusal to worship him.

Govinda

Name given to Krishna in his sportive capacity as one who gives pleasure to the senses.

Gṛihastha

Literally, staying in (anyone's) house. A householder, or traditionally, a Brahmin in the second period of his religious life, when after having finished his student stage, he marries and raises a family.

Guṇa avatārs

These refer here to the manifestations of Krishna as Brahmā, the creator; Vishṇu, the preserver; and Śiva, the destroyer, according to the three *guṇas* (qualities): *rājas, sattva,* and *tamas,* respectively, of which they are presiding deities. These operate in the process of creation, preservation, and destruction during any one cosmic cycle.

Guṇas

Qualities or modes of matter of which there are three: Goodness (*sattva*), passions (*rājas*), and ignorance (*tamas*).

Guru

Spiritual master or religious teacher.

Gurukula

Name of the Hare Krishna parochial school in Dallas, Texas, where children of devotees may be sent to receive complete elementary and eventually high-school education.

Halvah

A type of Hindu food made of cereal grains.

Haṁsa sect

Founded by the Vaishṇava, Nimbārka, a Telugu Brahmin, whose life is still of uncertain date, but was certainly later than Rāmānuja upon whom he evidently depended. The philosophy is a type of *bhedābheda* or dualistic monism.

Hari

Here, another name for Krishna.

Hari-vaṁśa

A later supplement to the *Mahābhārata.* Contains important material for the development of Vaishṇavism.

Haridās

Name of one of Chaitanya's favorite disciples.

Haridās (Junior)

Name of a disciple banished by Chaitanya for associating with a woman.

Harsha-carita

The biography of the emperor Harsha, by Bāṇa.

Haṭha-yoga

The practice of *yoga* that is primarily concerned with postures and exercises for the promotion of bodily health.

Hlādinī

The name of the ecstatic principle or power (*śakti*) of Krishna which allows him to have enjoyment, and to cause others to have enjoyment, and which is separated by him from himself as Rādhā, his consort.

Indra

A *Vedic* deity of the storm. In the early *Vedic* period Indra was preeminently the leader and most powerful of the gods with his great thunderbolt. He was the deity to whom more sacrificial hymns were addressed than to any other deity.

Iśa Upanishad

One of the *Upanishads*. As it concerns itself with a personal rather than an impersonal god, it receives more attention among devotees of Krishna than some of the others. It has been translated and interpreted by Swāmi Bhaktivedanta for the Hare Krishna Movement.

ISKCON

Acronym for International Society for Krishna Consciousness, the official name for the Hare Krishna Movement.

Īśvara Purī

The *guru* or spiritual master of Chaitanya who initiated him into the spiritual life.

Jagannātha

Literally, lord of the world. Here refers to one of the *archā* incarnations of Krishna, and one popular form in which Krishna is worshiped in Hare Krishna temples. His image is like the image in the famous temple at Purī where Chaitanya worshiped in all of his later life.

Jagannātha Festival

See Ratha-yātrā.

Jagannāth Miśra

Name of Chaitanya's father, who was a Brahmin.

Japa

Here refers to the private chanting of the names of Krishna by the Hare Krishna devotees, who are required to chant in private sixteen rounds a day on their 108 prayer beads.

Jāyadeva

Author of the *Gīta-govinda,* which was composed about the end of the twelfth century and was concerned with the love of Rādhā and Krishna. It was highly pleasing to Chaitanya.

Jīva

The spiritual part of the Oversoul, as the soul of a living entity, which is both one and yet separate from Krishna (Vishṇu), the Supersoul.

Jīva Goswāmi

One of the six Goswāmis of Vṛindāvan. Commissioned by Chaitanya to formulate in written form his philosophy. Jīva Goswāmi's works are one of the most important sources of the Gauḍīya Vaishṇava philosophy and indirectly that of the Hare Krishna Movement.

Jīva-śakti

Name for Krishna's marginal energy and the source of man's soul as part of Krishna's energy, which is qualitatively one with Krishna, but much smaller.

Jñāna-yoga

The *yoga* of knowledge in which one strives to become one with the impersonal absolute Brahman. This path, which is recognized by the Hare Krishna Movement as the path of those following

Śaṅkara's type of Vedānta, is regarded as more difficult and inferior to *bhakti-yoga* according to the devotees of Krishna.

Kāliya

A demon in the form of a great water snake who was polluting the Jumna River with his poison, but was subdued by Krishna.

Kali Yuga

The last and worst of the four ages or *yugas,* at the end of which the world will be destroyed. An age of strife and vice.

Kalki *avatār*

In traditional Hinduism, the future and last *avatār* who will appear in this last age, but whom the followers of Chaitanya's philosophy have identified with Chaitanya.

Kāma

Physical love or sex. Distinguished here from *prema,* spiritual love for Krishna, which transcends the material kind, a perversion due to *māyā.*

Kaṁsa

Name of king ruling country in vicinity of Mathurā where he lived; was grandfather of Krishna and father of Devakī, Krishna's mother, and was slain by Krishna.

Karaṇodakāśāyī Vishṇu

The first Purusha *avatār* of Krishna and a manifestation of Māhā Vishṇu for purposes of creation. He is the primary cause of all universes and lies in the ocean of cause (*karaṇa*); the creator of Mahat, the principle of the eleven senses, five elements, etc.

Karma

Literally, one's deeds; the effects of one's deeds good or bad which determine the place and condition in which one is born, and one's rewards or punishments after death. According to the Krishna devotees, chanting the *mahāmantra* is purifying of one's evil deeds and lessens the hold of *māyā* so one may become Krishna Conscious.

Karma yoga

Salvation through the merit gained by one's good works. Reinterpreted by the *Bhagavad-gītā* as salvation by performing works with no thought of reward. For the Hare Krishna devotee this entails performing all action for Krishna's pleasure.

Karmi

Name of one who is attached to the fruits of his actions, instead of performing all action for Krishna's pleasure with no thought of his own reward.

Kartāla

Name of the small metal hand cymbals that the Hare Krishna devotees use to accompany their chanting.

Kaṭha Upanishad

One of the early *Upanishads,* which some authorities feel anticipates the doctrine of grace that the Vaishṇavas later developed. One of the more frequently cited *Upanishads* by Swāmi Bhaktivedanta.

Kātyāyanī

The name of the goddess who as the answer to the *gopīs'* prayers had promised them to have Krishna as their husband, and which led to the later *rāsa* dance. It is this vow of Kātyāyanī supported by the *Bhāgavata Purāṇa* that led later to severe disputes concerning whether Krishna was actually married to the *gopīs.* While the earliest theologians, such as Jīva Goswāmi and Rūpa Goswāmi, argue for the state of marriage, the later theologians finally established the consort relationship as being the valid interpretation.

Kauravas

The cousins of the Pāṇḍavas, with whom they fought and by whom they were exterminated in the battle of Kurukshetra. The events leading to this battle form the main story of the *Mahābhārata.*

Kavirāja dāsa (Krishnadāsa Goswāmi)

Author of the *Caitanya Caritāmṛita.*

Keshup Chandra Sen

A nineteenth-century member of the Brāhma Samāj, a Hindu reform movement, who introduced many features of Chaitanya's *bhakti-yoga* into its practice.

Khole

A Hindu type of drum used by the Hare Krishna devotees to accompany their chanting. It is the same as the *mṛdanga* drum except that its shell is made of clay.

Kīrtan

See *saṅkīrtan.*

Ko-ans

Illogical or paradoxical sentences or phrases, such as "the sound of one hand clapping," used by some Zen Buddhists to exhaust the mental reasoning processes and lead one to the state of illumination (*satori*).

Krishna Chaitanya Mahāprabhu, Śrī

See Chaitanya Mahāprabhu, Śrī Krishna.

Krishna Consciousness

A state of consciousness that is purely centered on Krishna by one who has surrendered to him completely, and whose every action is only for the pleasure of Krishna. It is believed by the Hare Krishna devotees to be a return to the original consciousness which the soul had before love for Krishna (*prema*) gave way to lust (*kāma*). Then it is believed that one forgot his original nature as an eternal servitor of Krishna, who is the Absolute Controller and the Supreme Personality of Godhead.

Krishna-karṇāmṛita

A devotional work by Līlāśūka much admired by Chaitanya, which added inspiration to the devotion of Chaitanya and his early followers.

Krishna Vāsudeva

The identification of Krishna with Vāsudeva who according to epigraphic evidence was worshiped in the third or fourth century B.C. Swāmi Bhaktivedanta notes that Krishna is sometimes known as Vāsudeva because he appeared as the son of Vāsudeva in his Vṛindāvan pastime. The identification of Krishna with others is likewise explained as designating various functions with which Krishna is involved.

Kriyā-yoga

A practical form of *yoga* through performance of one's duties. Here the type of *yoga* practiced by Yogānanda's Self-Realization Fellowship.

Kshatriya

One of the four traditional *varnas* or castes. Refers to the warrior or administrative class and is regarded here as born into the mode of passion.

Kshīrodakāśāyī Vishṇu

A form of Vishṇu as the third Purusha or fourth *vyūha* for the purpose of creation. He is also the source of all *avatārs* of Krishna, according to the Gauḍīya Vaishṇavas and the Hare Krishna Movement, and the Supersoul in each living person.

Kuṇḍalinī-yoga

A form of *yoga,* which involves special practices to stimulate the *kuṇḍalinī,* an occult power or *śakti* lying at the base of the spine. By proper stimulation and control it is believed that it can stimulate various *chakras* or force centers, giving occult powers, but most of all can stimulate the *sahasrāra chakra* at the top of the head which leads to ecstatic liberation or *samādhi.*

Kurukshetra

The site of the famous battle between the Pāṇḍavas and their cousins the Kauravas, as depicted in the *Mahābhārata.*

Kushāna

Name of a branch of the Yueh-Chi, a Central Asian tribe of nomads, which swept over Northern India in the second century B.C. and was most powerful about A.D. 78 under Kanishka. The dynasty in India ended in A.D. 176 with King Vāsudeva, a devotee of Śiva.

Laddu

A pastry made of flour and cardamom.

Lakshmī

Name of the *śakti* of Vishṇu, as his consort. Often also cited as Śrī, or Śrī Lakshmī. Lakshmī was also the name of Chaitanya's wife.

Līlā

Literally, sport. Refers to the sports or pastimes of Krishna, his actions that have occurred at various times in history. They occurred during his various manifestations as *avatārs,* but are also regarded as eternal events. For example, Nara Siṅha, the manifestation of Krishna as the man-lion, is believed to have occurred in history, but still exists eternally, today and forever.

Līlā avatārs

The twenty-four manifestations or descents (*avatārs*) of Krishna as listed by Rūpa Goswāmi in his work *Samkṣepa-bhāgavatāmṛta.* This particular list contains the ten more traditionally Hindu *avatārs* but includes Balarāma and omits Rāma (Chakravarti, 1969:151). The *Bhāgavata Purāṇa* has one list of the same *avatārs* in the same arrangement. The *Gīta-govinda* lists only nine *avatārs* including both Rāma and Balarāma as seventh and eighth respectively, and followed by the Buddha and the Kalki *avatār* (Majumdar, 1969:70).

Līlāśūka (Bilvamangala)

Author of *Krishna-karṇāmṛita.*

Mādhurya

Fifth stage of devotional feeling toward Krishna, which is the conjugal relationship of a lover. All higher stages contain the qualities of those preceding them.

Madhva

Founder of a dualistic Vaishṇava sect in South India in the thirteenth century A.D.

Mahābhārata

Hindu epic, and one basis for much of the popular religion of India, past and present.

Mahā-Lakshmī

Name of an expansion of Rādhā through her internal power that is the same as Rukminī, one of Krishna's wives.

Mahāmantra

The most important *mantra* of the Hare Krishna Movement. Represents the "holy names of Krishna." It is the *mantra* recited in the daily private recitation of the devotees of Krishna as well as the concluding *mantra* during every public worship service. Its words are: Hare Krishna, Hare Krishna, Hare Hare/ Hare Rāma, Hare Rāma, Rāma Rāma, Hare Hare.

Mahāṛishi Mahesh Yogi

The founder of a popular Hindu self-realization movement and form of *yoga* known as Transcendental Meditation.

Mahā-Saṅkarshaṇa

Here, a form of Balarāma, Krishna's older brother. Also Nityānanda, Chaitanya's disciple and part of his *avatār* in Krishna's later *līlā*.

Mahat

Cosmic or universal intelligence that is the principle of intelligence, the eleven senses and the five elements, etc. It is created by Karaṇodakāśāyī Vishṇu, the first Purusha through the agency of *karma* which transforms the three *guṇas* or modes of matter into Mahat. Mahat is then changed into *manas,* mind; *buddhi,* the sense organs, and finally five subtle elements, the *tanmātras,* and so forth.

Mahā-Vishṇu

Mahā-Vishṇu represents Vishṇu, the plenary expansion of Krishna as unexpanded into his three Purusha forms. From his pores the universes emanate. He is also later identified with Advaitāchārya, Chaitanya's disciple, and part of Krishna's descent as Chaitanya.

Maṅgala ārati

Name of the early morning devotional service to Krishna conducted daily at about 4:30 A.M. in the Hare Krishna temples.

Mañjarī

The form that expresses man's highest relationship to Krishna in his heaven world. This applies only to those attaining the conjugal state with Krishna, according to the Gauḍīya Vaishṇavas.

Mantra

A prayer, song of praise, or a sacred formula addressed to a deity. Here, one of the many chants in praise of Krishna, Chaitanya, and Swāmi Bhaktivedanta, in addition to one's own spiritual master and to others. The most famous and most used is the *mahāmantra* or "great *mantra*" devoted to Krishna.

Manvantara avatārs

These are *avatārs* as *manus,* each of whom appears to preside over one of the fourteen *manvantaras,* or periods of the *manu.* The period of a *manu* is equal to 4,320,000 years or one-fourteenth of a day of Brahmā.

Matsya *avatār*

Literally, fish. Here refers to an *avatār* in which Krishna descends in the form of a fish to save Manu, the Hindu Noah, from the flood.

Māyā

Here, the lower and inferior energy (*śakti*) of Krishna, which is one with him as his energy and at the same time is entirely separate from him.

Māyā

The hypostatization of Krishna's inferior *śakti* as the conceiving power and through whose intercourse with Śambhu (Śiva), the symbol of Vishṇu, the world and the faculty of mankind's perverted cognition were created.

Māyā-śakti

See *māyā.*

Māyāvāda

Doctrine affirming that the world is an illusion. Applied to the *advaita* Vedānta of Śaṅkara in particular by the Hare Krishna Movement.

Mṛidañga

A Hindu type of drum used as an accompaniment in *saṅkīrtans* or group chanting ceremonies.

Musalin

An epithet meaning "one who wields a pestle." Applied to the deity Saṅkarshaṇa in the early period of his worship.

Nagara-saṅkīrtan

A term not often used today, referring to a *saṅkīrtan* conducted publicly in the city (*nagara*) streets. Today *saṅkīrtan* is generally used to denote a number of devotees chanting together in a devotional service to Krishna, whether publicly or in the temple. The term *kīrtan,* which etymologically does not give the idea of a number performing the devotion together, is also used in the same sense.

Nal-ayir-divya-prabandham

A collection of 4000 hymns of the Alvars that was made by a disciple of Rāmānuja.

Nanda

Name of the foster father of Krishna who raised and cared for him when he was brought as a newborn by Vāsudeva, his father, to Yaśodhā, his foster mother.

Nārada

One of Krishna's greatest devotees according to Swāmi Bhaktivedanta. He appears in the *Bhāgavata Purāṇa* as one of the great teachers who passed down its secret knowledge from Nārāyaṇa to Prahlāda. He is also included among the *āveśa avatārs* and among the *līlā avatārs* in the lists of the *Bhāgavata Purāṇa* and of Jīva Goswāmi.

Nara Siṁha

Literally, man-lion, name of an *avatār* of Krishna who came down in the form that was half lion and half man to kill a powerful and wicked demon who could be killed by neither man nor beast.

Nārāyaṇa

A deity who appears first in the *Śatapatha Brāhmaṇa*. Regarded here as an expansion of Krishna representing his aspect of majestic power.

Nārāyaṇa Vishṇu Vāsudeva

The later syncretistic deity, regarded by the Gauḍīya Vaishṇavas as an expansion of Krishna.

Nārāyaṇīya

A part of the *Mahābhārata* that identifies Nārāyaṇa with Krishna and adds material for the development of Vaishṇavism.

Narottama Datta

A Vaishṇava who helped in the revival of Chaitanyaism in the seventeenth century.

Nera-Neris

Remnants of an outcaste decadent Buddhist order who were admitted to the ranks of the Chaitanya Vaishṇavas in the seventeenth century.

Nimāi

Name of Chaitanya given to him when he was a boy.

Nimbārka

Founder of a Vaishṇava sect in the thirteenth century, which had a dualistic monistic philosophy. Nimbārka was devoted to Krishna, and regarded Rādhā as his consort.

Nityānanda

A disciple of Chaitanya, who was charged by him to spread his philosophy in Bengal. He is also considered an expansion of Krishna and part of his descent as Chaitanya.

Nyāya

One of the six orthodox schools of philosophy. Represents a school of logic.

Padma Purāṇa

One of the *Puraṇas* that has contributed to the development of Vaishṇavism.

Pañcharātrā (Pañcarātrā)

A type of literature developed perhaps between the fifth and eighth centuries A.D. Contributed material to the development of Vaishṇavism.

Pañcharātrins (Pañcarātrins)

Name of a sect responsible for the Pañcharātrā literature.

Pañchatattva (*Pañcatattva*)

The five parts comprising the *avatār* of Krishna as Chaitanya: Chaitanya, Advaitāchārya, Nityānanda, Gadādhara, and Śrivāsa.

Pāṇḍavas

The hero brothers of the *Mahābhārata* who fought against their cousins the Kauravas in the battle of Kurukshetra.

Parā-brahman

Name of Krishna as the Supreme Spirit, which represents the personal side of the Absolute Reality of which Brahman is the impersonal side.

Parakīya-rasa

The relation of Krishna to the *gopīs* as that of a paramour's love. The love of Krishna for the *gopīs* as his consorts.

Parama bhāgavata

Literally, highest or chief *bhāgavata.* A title taken by some of the Gupta kings indicating their patronage of one of the Vaishṇava deities.

Paramātman

Here, Krishna (Kshīradakāśāyī Vishṇu) as the highest self of Supersoul dwelling in each living person as the inner controller.

Parā śakti

Literally, the highest power. The power of Krishna's own highest nature in the view of Chaitanyaism.

Pariṇāmavāda

Philosophical doctrine of some Vaishṇava schools in which Brahman is believed to have substantial modification during creation.

Pradyumna

Name of son of Krishna. Also name of one of his *vyūhas.*

Prajñāpāramitā

The Perfection of Wisdom, a Mahāyana Buddhist text.

Prakṛiti

Name of that which comprises man's soul as higher *prakṛiti* and which forms his material body as lower *prakṛiti,* according to the Hare Krishna Movement.

Prapatti

The Vaishṇavite doctrine of *bhakti-yoga* that enjoins mankind to seek liberation by complete surrender to Krishna (Vishṇu).

Prasādam

Food presented to people after having been offered first to the deities.

Prema

Spiritual love for Krishna, as opposed to lust (*kāma*).

Pūjari

One who officiates in the *ārati* ceremonies at the Hare Krishna temples.

Purāṇas

A type of popular Hindu religious literature dealing theoretically with five subjects: creation, destruction and recreation, the genealogy of the gods, the reigns of the different *manus,* and the history of the solar and lunar kings.

Purusha

Name of a primeval cosmic deity of the *Ṛig Veda* through whose sacrifice of himself creation occurred. Later identified with Nārāyaṇa and also with three of the four *vyūhas* or expansions of Krishna for the purpose of creation. Also as Krishna, the enjoyer.

Purusha *avatārs*

The three manifestations of Krishna as Karaṇodakāśāyī Vishṇu, Garbhodakāśāyī Vishṇu, and Kshīrodakāśāyī Vishṇu for purposes of creation.

Purusha-sūkta

The hymn of the *Ṛig Veda,* X, 90, in which is found the heavenly sacrifice of Purusha for creation.

Purushottama

Literally, the highest Purusha, which in the Hare Krishna philosophy is identified with Krishna.

Pūrva Mīmāṁsā

One of the six orthodox schools of Hindu philosophy, a system of *Vedic* interpretation traditionally ascribed to Jaimini. It concerns the ceremonial duties of man in reference to the *Vedic* sacrifices.

Pūtanā

A female demon sent by Kaṁsa to kill the infant Krishna. When she offered him her poisoned breast, he sucked out her life.

Rādhā

The name of Krishna's favorite consort among the *gopīs* or cowherdesses, according to the Hare Krishna Movement. She represents his Hlādinī energy or ecstatic principle, which he separated from himself for his own enjoyment.

Rāgānugā

Name for the spontaneous development of Krishna Consciousness, which may grow out of the regular process of following sixty-four rules.

Raghunātha Bhaṭṭa

One of the six Goswāmis selected by Chaitanya to develop his philosophy.

Raghunātha Dās

One of the six Goswāmis commissioned by Chaitanya to systematize his philosophy at Vṛindāvan.

Rājas

The mode of passion, one of the three modes of matter.

Rakshasa

An ancient style of marriage by kidnapping one's wife.

Rāma

Here one of the *avatārs* of Krishna, and hero of the Hindu epic, the *Rāmāyaṇa.*

Rāmānanda

Name of a close friend to Chaitanya who like him had a deep love for Rādhā-Krishna, as recorded in the *Caitanya Caritāmṛita* by Krishnadāsa Kavirāja.

Rāmānuja

An eleventh-century Vaishṇavite philosopher who formulated a qualified monistic form of Vedānta known as Viśishtādvaita Vedānta.

Rāmāyaṇa

One of the two great Hindu epics. It concerns the deeds of Rāma.

Rasa

Relish or the principle denoting a person's intrinsic relationship to Krishna in one's original consciousness.

Rāsa dance

The erotic dance that Krishna performs with the *gopīs.*

Rasikā Murarī

A wealthy *rāja* of the seventeenth century who used his money to help expand the Chaitanya Movement.

Ratha-yātrā

The Car Festival occurring in July each year in Purī, when the Jagannātha deities are paraded down the streets. The festival has its counterpart among the Hare Krishna devotees each year in several places, including San Francisco and London.

Ṛig Veda

The oldest of the four *Vedas,* which represent the most ancient Indo-European literature. These are hymns to various deities to be chanted during the sacrifices.

Rohiṇī

One of the wives of Krishna who became the mother of Balarāma, Krishna's eldest brother, when the embryo was transferred from Devakīs' womb to hers through the power of Yogamāyā, Krishna's energy.

Romā

Name of one of the consorts of Vishṇu, the regulatrix of all sentient beings, and the one who carried Vishṇu's glance in the process of creation.

Rukminī

One of the wives of Krishna whom he married by kidnapping her first. The *Caitanya Caritāmṛita* considers her to be the supreme goddess of fortune.

Rūpa Goswāmi

One of the most important of the six Goswāmis of Vṛindāvan, who did much in the systematization of Chaitanya's philosophy during the sixteenth century A.D.

Śabda

Literally, sound. Here "revelation" or "authority" as the only authentic independent source of knowledge.

Sachī Devī

The name of Chaitanya's mother.

Sakhī

Literally, friend. Refers to one class of those with whom Krishna sports erotically in his heaven world in "loving friendliness."

Sakhya

Friendship, the third stage in Krishna Consciousness, in which one feels toward Krishna as a friend.

Śakta

One who worships the active power (*śakti*) of a deity.

Śakti

The active power or energy of a deity, which may be personified as his consort or wife. Here, refers to one of the innumerable powers or energies of Krishna that may be personified, for example, as Rādhā.

Śaktism

Name of the *tantric* philosophy that worships the female energy of a deity.

Śambhu

Here, a representation of Śiva as the masculine symbol of Vishṇu, through whose intercourse with Māyā the material world, and so forth, is created.

Saṁvit

The power or energy of Krishna's original nature, which represents an attribute of his "spiritual power" (*chit-śakti*). It is the potency that governs all spiritual relations and affections.

Sanātana

One of the six Goswāmis of Vṛindāvan commissioned by Chaitanya to systematize his philosophy.

Sandhinī

The power or energy of Krishna's original nature, which represents an attribute of his "spiritual power" (*chit-śakti*). This potency represents his power to produce all existence associated with the action of his ecstatic principle, according to the Gauḍīya Vaishṇavas.

Śaṅkara

The leading exponent of the *advaita* or nondualistic form of Vedānta, who lived from A.D. 788 to 820 according to some authorities.

Saṅkarshaṇa

Here, one of the four *vyūhas* who represents the first Purusha or expansions of Krishna for creation. He is also identified with Balarāma (Baladeva), Krishna's older brother as well as Krishna's *avatār* as Chaitanya. In the development of Vaishṇavism, he earlier had his own cult as an agricultural deity.

Saṅkarshaṇa-Baladeva

The syncretistic deity who plays a role in creation. See Saṅkarshaṇa.

Sāṅkhya

A philosophical dualism. One of the six Hindu orthodox philosophies, which has been traditionally ascribed to a semimythical sage, Kapila.

Saṅkīrtan

Here, the ceremonial chanting together of "Krishna's holy names," as well as praise to him and to others worthy of it, by his devotees. It may occur either in the temple or on public streets.

Saṅnyāsa

Order or general name for the order of *saṅnyāsis,* or holy men, or the state of world renouncement for the search of salvation. This represents the traditional fourth stage (*āśrama*) in the life of a Brahmin.

Saṅnyāsi

Name for one who has entered into the fourth stage of life as a holy man. See *saṅnyāsa.*

Śānta

First stage of devotional feeling toward Krishna in which one can fix his mind steadfastly upon Krishna with faith and with no material desires.

Sāri

Name of a type of common wearing apparel for Hindu women.

Sarvabhauma

A famous Vedāntist living at the time of Chaitanya who was converted to the worship of Krishna by Chaitanya, and thereby aided in getting royal support of the movement in Orissa.

Sat

Literally, being. Here represents one of Krishna's paramount attributes as "being."

Śatapatha Brāhmaṇa

One of the most famous and early *Brāhmaṇas.* Supplied important material for the development of the philosophy later known as Vaishṇavism.

Śaṭhakopa

Name of one of the Alvars who as a group lived probably between the middle of the seventh and the middle of the eighth centuries A.D., and who made important contributions to the philosophy now known as Vaishṇavism.

Sattva

One of the three modes of nature according to the Hare Krishna Movement. This mode expresses goodness.

Sātvatas

Name of the clan in which Krishna was traditionally born. Also named in the *Nārāyaṇīya* section of the *Mahābhārata* as among those worshiping Nārāyaṇa-Vishṇu Vāsudeva.

Śesha (Śeshanāga)

See Ananta Śeshanāga.

Shree Brahma Saṁhitā

See *Brahma Saṁhitā.*

Shree Gauḍīya Maths

Name of the sixty-four centers for the teaching and practice of Chaitanya's philosophy of *bhakti-yoga* established by Bhakti Siddhānta Sarasvatī Goswāmi, Swāmi Bhaktivedanta's spiritual master.

Śikhā

The tuft of hair remaining on the heads of the Hare Krishna devotees after they have been shaved.

Śiva

Here, Krishna's *guṇa avatār* in his capacity as the destroyer of creation at the end of the last age of the cycle, the Kali Yuga.

Śrī

Denotes Krishna's aspect of beauty. See also Lakshmī.

Śrīnivāsa Āchārya

Name of one of the disciples of Jīva Goswāmi, one of the six Goswāmis of Vṛindāvan, who aided in a new revival of Chaitanya's faith in the seventeenth century.

Śrīvāsa

Name of one of Chaitanya's close disciples, who formed part of Krishna's *avatār* as Chaitanya. He is regarded as Krishna's marginal energy as a confidential devotee.

Śruti

Name for the sacred literature that was considered by the orthodox Brahmins as revealed in contrast to the *smṛitis,* the law books or traditional texts. It applies to the literature of the *Vedic* period, which was considered as ending with the composition of the *Upanishads.*

Subhadrā

Name of Krishna's sister who appears often with Krishna in the form of Jagaṅnātha, and with his older brother, Balarāma, in the Hare Krishna temples.

Sudras

The lowest of the four traditional *varnas* or castes representing the laborer class, which according to Swāmi Bhaktivedanta are those who are in the "ignorant mode of material nature."

Surabhi

The cows of plenty, the wish-granting cows of Krishna's heavenly Vṛindāvan, which give all the milk one wishes to drink.

Sūtra

A text of short, terse philosophical aphorisms that present the doctrines of various philosophical schools developing in the early centuries of the Christian era.

Svāṁsā

A division of Krishna's *tadekātma* form "which is identical in essence" with Krishna's *svayam-rūpa,* which is his independent form, but at the same time is lesser in power than his self-existent form.

Sva-rūpa

Krishna's own essential selfhood, as distinguished from his various expansions as *avatārs.*

Sva-rūpa-śakti

The power or energy of Krishna's own original nature.

Svayam-rūpa

Here, a division of Krishna's *sva-rūpa,* referring to his self-existent form as distinguished from his *tadekātma-rūpa,* which is essentially the same but different in appearance.

Śvetadvīpa

Literally, white island. Name of an abode of the blessed according to the *Mahābhārata.* Here, specifically a spiritual planet lying in the ocean of milk where Kshīrodakāśāyī Vishṇu resides.

Śvetasvatara Upahishad

One of the theistic *Upanishads* that was a source of the developing Vaishṇavism.

Śyāmānanda Dās

Name of a seventeenth-century Vaishṇava of the Chaitanya school of philosophy who helped contribute to its revival at the time.

Tadekātma-rūpa

One of the three forms of Krishna's essential selfhood. This form is identical with Krishna's self-existent form (*svayam-rūpa*) in essence, but differs in appearance.

Tamas

Ignorance, as one of the three *guṇas* or modes of material existence.

Tantras

Texts concerned especially with the feminine power or energy of the deities.

Tantric Buddhism

A late form of Buddhism in India that paralleled the *tantric* Hindu development, in which the personalized female energy of the Buddhas received devotion.

Tatāsthā-śakti

Krishna's marginal power, or *jīva-śakti,* which is manifested through his *sva-rūpa-śakti* or essential power. It represents his power of dividing himself into numerous finite selves.

Tilaka

Name of the mixture of white clay and water that the Vaishṇava devotee marks on his body in twelve different places each day. These marks identify the devotee as being a Vaishṇava.

Tirtha Goswāmi Mahārāj

Name of the one who is regarded by probably the majority of Gauḍīya Vaishṇavas as being their spiritual master and successor to Bhakti Siddhānta Goswāmi.

Tṛiṇāvarta

A demon sent by Kaṁsa to kill but instead killed by the child Krishna.

Tulasī

An Indian plant sacred to Krishna.

Ujjvala-nīlamaṇi

Title of a treatise written by Rūpa Goswāmi, one of the six Goswāmis, one of Vṛindāvan.

Upanishads

The philosophical treatises that are loosely attached to the individual *Vedas,* and that mark the end of the *Vedas* (Vedānta). They are the most important Hindu philosophical works, on which the different Hindu philosophies and religions depend in varying degrees.

Vaibhavaprakāśa

A form of Krishna that represents his expansion of power which is less than that of his intrinsic nature. While essentially the same, it appears in a slightly differing form, Krishna's brother, Balarāma, who is "whitish" instead of "blackish," is an example.

Vaidhī

The regular process of following sixty-four rules in developing Krishna Consciousness.

Vaikuṇtha

Here, the name of the spiritual planetary system over which millions of Krishna's four-armed expansions govern. It is a manifestation of Krishna's internal energy. Goloka-Vṛindāvan is Krishna's highest heavenly abode in this system, where he lives and sports erotically in his original form.

Vaiśeshika

One of the six orthodox schools of Hindu philosophy; it postulates a type of atomic philosophy and is of uncertain date. According to tradition, it was founded by Kanāda.

Vaiśyas

The third of the traditional *varnas* or castes, representing the merchants who according to Swāmi Bhaktivedanta are mixed between modes of passion and ignorance.

Vallabhāchāryas

A sixteenth-century Vaishṇava sect, now almost absorbed by the Vaishṇuswāmin group.

Vāmāchāri

Name of the left-hand school of Śaktism, which worshiped the female energy of the deity and whose practices were accompanied by sexual license.

Vānaprastha

Traditionally, the third stage in an orthodox Brahmin's life, in which the recommended pattern was for him to go into the forest after his family was raised to meditate on the ultimate reality. For the Hare Krishna Movement it is defined as the "retired" stage.

Vāsudeva

Here, the name of Krishna's father and also the name of one of the first of his *vyūhas.* Earlier, the name of a deity to whom devotion was given according to epigraphic evidence and who has been successively identified with the deity Nārāyaṇa and with Krishna, as in the *Nārāyaṇīya* section of the *Mahābhārata.*

Vāsudeva Krishna Movement

A formative movement in Vaishṇavism in which Vāsudeva was syncretistically identified with Krishna. It existed probably either shortly before or after the beginning of the Christian era.

Vātsalya

Fourth stage of devotional feeling toward Krishna, expressing the fondness of a parent for him. In this stage "instead of the Lord being worshiped, the living entity as a parent of the Supreme Person becomes the object of worship for the Supreme Person." (Bhaktivedanta, 1968a:33)

Vāyu Purāṇa

One of the *Purāṇas.* Added material toward the development of Vaishṇavism.

Vedānta

Originally the *Upanishads,* which marked the end of the *Vedas* (*Veda* plus *ānta*). Then applied to the orthodox philosophy of the same name, which is best exemplified in the West by Śaṅkara's *advaita* school. Also applies to later theistic systems opposing Śaṅkara's philosophy, such as Rāmānuja's qualified monism or Viśishtādvaita Vedānta.

Vedānta Sūtras

See *Brahma Sūtras.*

Vedas

The earliest Indo-European religious literature. Applies to the four *Vedas* whose hymns are addressed to the various deities of the early Hindu pantheon. Applies also to the *Brāhmaṇas, Āraṇyakas,* and to the *Upanishads,* which end the class of literature belonging to the *Vedas,* and to the *śruti* or revealed literature in the traditional and orthodox meaning of the term, although later sectarians have enlarged greatly the meaning of the term.

Vidyāpati

Fifteenth-century poet whose poems are thought to have influenced the thought of Chaitanya, who admired them.

Vilāsa

Name of a manifestation of Krishna, which is essentially the same as his own original nature, is equal in power, but differs in appearance—for example, the four-handed figure of Nārāyaṇa.

Vīrabhadra

Son of Nityānanda, who continued his father's work of spreading Chaitanyaism particularly among those who were either low caste or outcaste.

Vīra Hamvīra

A wealthy *rāja* of the sixteenth century who used his money to help spread Chaitanya's message.

Virāṭa-rūpa

Name of the form of Krishna as he appeared at the battle of Kurukshetra. Although he seemed to be of material nature having a material body, this was only an appearance since actually Krishna never really incarnates, that is, takes on a physical body, but always remains spiritual and separate from matter.

Vishṇu

The plenary expansion of Krishna according to the Gauḍīya Vaishṇavas and the Hare Krishna Movement. Exists in one of his manifestations also as the *paramātman* or Supersoul.

Vishṇupriyā

Chaitanya's second wife, whom he left shortly after marriage when he became a *sannyāsi,* or holy man.

Vishṇu Purāṇa

One of the principal sources of Vaishṇavism for the story of Krishna's life when he descended as an *avatār.*

Vishṇuswāmi

Founder of a mediaeval sect of Vaishṇavism known as the Rudra Sampradāya. This is represented today almost entirely by the Vallabhāchāryas.

Viśishtādvaita Vedānta

The qualified monistic philosophy of Rāmānuja of the eleventh century A.D. The philosophy declared that although man was part of Brahman, he never lost his individuality by merging into the Brahman.

Viśuddhādvaita

The pure nondualism of Vishṇuswāmi.

Viśvambhara

The given name of Chaitanya.

Viśva Vaishṇav Rāj Sabhā, Śri

Official name of the Gauḍīya Vaishṇava organization founded in the latter half of the nineteenth century by Bhaktivinode Thākur, the father of Bhakti Siddhānta Goswāmi, who was Swāmi Bhaktivedanta's spiritual master.

Vivartavāda

The doctrine usually associated with the *advaita* form of Vedānta, such as was exemplified by Śaṅkara, that the world is an illusory form covered by ignorance.

Vivekananda

The disciple of Rāmakrishna who was sent to America to spread the Vedānta philosophy during the last decade of the nineteenth century. His work here was responsible for the establishment of the Vedānta Society in various cities.

Vṛindāvan

"Rādhā's forest," a town in the district of Mathurā celebrated as the place where Krishna passed his youth, associating with his consort, Rādhā, and other *gopīs* or cowherdesses. Also the heavenly counterpart, the highest of the spiritual planets of the Vaikuṇtha or spiritual planetary system. Often known also as Goloka or Gokula or together as Goloka-Vṛindāvan.

Vṛindāvan Dāsa

Author of the *Caitanya Bhāgavata,* the earliest Bengali biography of Chaitanya written shortly after Chaitanya's passing, perhaps at the request of Nityānanda, Chaitanya's close disciple.

Vyāsa

An *āveśa avatār* of Krishna through whom sacred scriptures have been given to mankind, according to Swāmi Bhaktivedanta.

vyūhas

Expansions of Krishna in four different forms for purposes of creation. These are Vāsudeva, Saṅkarshaṇa, Pradyumna, and Aniruddha. Originally perhaps a Pañcharātrā doctrine, it has been combined with a doctrine in which three expansions of Krishna as three Purushas correspond to three forms of Mahā Vishṇu: Karaṇodakāśāyī, Garbhodakāśāyī, and Kshīrodakāśāyī. These take precedence over the four *vyūhas* in the Gauḍīya Vaishṇava system.

Yādavas

The associates of Krishna in the city of Dvārakā and Mathurā, which are not only earthly cities associated with his pastimes here but are among the highest planets where Krishna dwells. The companions are to be distinguished from the *gopīs* (cowherdesses) and *gopas* (shepherds) with whom he associates in Goloka-Vṛindāvan.

Yajña

Literally, sacrifice, which in the Hare Krishna Movement is performed by chanting the "holy names of Krishna" and by giving up everything that is not conducive to serving Krishna for Krishna's own pleasure.

Yamuna

Ancient name of a river in India that flows through Mathurā and the country associated with Krishna's pastimes. Now known as the Jumna River. Also name of eleventh century Hindu teacher.

Yaśodā

Name of Krishna's foster mother who raised him after Vāsudeva brought him secretly to her and exchanged him for the baby born to Yaśodā.

Yaśovanta

One of the six Dāsas, poets of the seventeenth century A.D. whose poems and songs helped popularize Chaitanyaism in the state of Orissa.

Yātrā

A type of dramatization of one of Krishna's pastimes.

Yoga

Name for any one of a number of the many systems of practices by means of which salvation or liberation is aided or obtained.

Yoga

One of the six orthodox Hindu philosophies that is a dualistic system attributed traditionally to Patañjali.

Yogamāyā

Name for Krishna's highest energy of his own original form. It is completely separate from his inferior energy, *māyā śakti.*

Yogānanda

Hindu philosopher who lived in the twentieth century and founded the Self Realization Fellowship in the United States.

Yuga avatārs

Avatārs as manifestations of Krishna, as presiders over the four ages (*yugas*) into which the day of Brahmā is divided, during which the world is created, preserved, and finally destroyed.

Yugas

The four ages into which the day of Brahmā is divided.

APPENDIX

KṚṢṆA THE RESERVOIR OF PLEASURE

His Divine Grace A. C. Bhaktivedanta Swami Prabhupāda is the present *ācārya* or teacher by example in the unbroken chain of disciplic succession begun five thousand years ago by Lord Śrī Kṛṣṇa, the Supreme Personality of Godhead. He is the founder and spiritual master of the International Society for Krishna Consciousness, which now has thousands of members and over ninety centers around the world. Śrīla Prabhupāda came to the United States seven years ago under the instruction of his spiritual master, who requested that the ancient knowledge of the Vedic literatures be given to the English speaking world. Thus Śrīla Prabhupāda is now freely distributing this pure transcendental knowledge, which is the real wealth of India, the eternal teaching of man's relationship to the Supreme.

Kṛṣṇa—this sound is transcendental. Kṛṣṇa means the highest pleasure. Each of us, every living being, seeks pleasure. But we do not know how to seek pleasure perfectly. With a materialistic concept of life, we are frustrated at every step in satisfying our pleasure because we have no information regarding the real level on which to have real pleasure. To enjoy real pleasure, one must first understand that he is not the body but consciousness. Not exactly consciousness, for consciousness is actually the symptom of our real identity: we are pure soul, now merged within this material body. Modern material science lays no stress on this; therefore the scientists are sometimes misled in their understanding of spirit soul. But spirit soul is a fact, which anyone can understand by the presence of consciousness. Any child can understand that consciousness is the symptom of the spirit soul.

Now the whole process we are trying to learn from the *Bhagavad-gītā* (The Song of God) is how to bring ourselves to this level of consciousness. And if we act from that level of consciousness; then we may not be pushed again into the level of this bodily consciousness, then, at the end of this body we shall be free from material contamination, our spiritual life will be revived, and the ultimate result will be that in our next life, after leaving this body, we shall have our full, eternal spiritual life. Spirit, as we have already discussed, is described as eternal.

Even after the destruction of this body, consciousness is not destroyed. Rather, consciousness is transferred to another type of body and again makes us aware of the material conception of life. That is also described in the *Bhagavad-gītā.* At the time of death, if our consciousness is pure, we can be sure that our next life will not be material—our next life will be spiritual. If our consciousness is not pure at the point of death, then, after leaving this body, we shall have to take another material body. That is the process which is going on. That is nature's law.

We have now a finite body. The body which we see is the gross body. It is just like a shirt and coat: within the coat there is a shirt, and within the shirt there is a body. Similarly, the pure soul is covered by a shirt and coat. The garments are the mind, intelligence and false ego. False ego means the misconception that I am matter, that I am a product of this material world. This misconception makes me localized. For example, because I have taken my birth in India, I think myself Indian. Because I have taken my birth in America, I think myself American. But as pure soul, I am neither Indian nor American. I am pure soul. These others are designations. American, or Indian, or German, or Englishman; cat or dog, or bee or bat, man or wife: all these are designations. In spiritual consciousness we become free from all such designations. That freedom is achieved when we are constantly in touch with the supreme spirit, Kṛṣṇa.

The International Society for Krishna Consciousness is simply intended to keep us in constant touch with Kṛṣṇa. Kṛṣṇa can be in constant companionship with us because He is omnipotent. Therefore, He can be fully in touch with us by His words. His words and He are not different. That is omnipotence. Omnipotence means that everything relating to Him has the same potency. For example, here in this material world, if we are thirsty and we want water, simply repeating "water, water, water, water," will not satisfy our thirst, because this word has not the same potency as water itself. We require the water in substance. Then our thirst will be satisfied. But in the transcendental, absolute world, there is no such difference—Kṛṣṇa's name, Kṛṣṇa's quality, Kṛṣṇa's word—everything is Kṛṣṇa and provides the same satisfaction.

Some people argue that Arjuna was talking with Kṛṣṇa because Kṛṣṇa was present before him, whereas in my case, Kṛṣṇa is not present. So how can I get directions? But Kṛṣṇa is present by His words—the *Bhagavad-gītā*. In India, when we speak on the *Bhagavad-gītā* or *Śrīmad-Bhāgavatam,* we regularly perform worship with flowers, or with other paraphernalia, as is required for worshiping. In the Sikh religion also, although they have no form of the Deity, they worship the book *Granthasahib.* Perhaps some of you are acquainted with this Sikh community. They worship this *Grantha.* Similarly, the Moslems worship the *Koran.* Similarly, in the Christian world, the *Bible* is worshiped. It is a fact that the Lord Jesus Christ is present by his words. Kṛṣṇa is also present by His words.

These personalities, either God or the son of God, who come from the transcendental world, keep their transcendental identities without being contaminated by the material world. That is their omnipotence. We are in the habit of saying that God is omnipotent. Omnipotence means that He is not different from His name, from His quality, from His pastimes, from His instruction. Therefore, the discussion of *Bhagavad-gīta* is as good as discussion with Kṛṣṇa Himself.

Kṛṣṇa is seated in your heart, and in my heart too. *Īśvaraḥ sarva-bhūtānāṁ hṛd-deśe 'rjuna tiṣṭhati.* God is situated in everyone's heart. God is not away from us. He is present. He is so friendly that He remains with us in our repeated change of births. He is waiting to see when we shall turn to Him. He is so kind that though we may forget Him, He never forgets us. Although a son may forget his father, a father never forgets his son. Similarly, God, the original father of everything, everybody, all living entities, will never forsake us. We may have different bodies, but they are our shirt-coats. That has nothing to do with our real identity. Our real identity is pure soul, and that soul is part and parcel of the Supreme Lord. There are 8,400,000 species of life. Even the biologist and the anthropologist cannot calculate this accurately, but from authoritative, revealed scripture we get this information. Human beings represent 400,000 species, and there are 8,000,000 other species. But Kṛṣṇa, the Supreme Lord, claims that all of them, whether beast, man, snake, god, semi-god, demi-god—anything whatever—all of them are, in reality, His sons.

The father gives the seed, and the mother receives the seed. The body is formed, according to the mother's body. And when the body is completely formed, it comes out—either from cats, from dogs, or from man. That is the process of generation. The father gives the seed, and it is emulsified with two kinds of secretion in the womb of the mother, and on the first night the body is formed just like a pea. Then, gradually, it develops. There are nine holes that develop: two ears, two eyes, nostrils, a mouth, a navel, a penis, and an anus.

According to his past *karma,* or action, one gets this body to enjoy or to suffer. That is the process of birth and death. And after finishing this life, again one dies, and again one enters into the womb of some mother. Another type of body then comes out. This is the process of reincarnation.

We should be very diligent as to how we can discontinue this process of repeated birth and death and change of body. That is the prerogative of the human form of life. We can stop this process of repeated change through birth and death. We can get our actual spiritual form again and be blissful, full of knowledge and have eternal life. That is the purpose of evolution. We should not miss this. The entire process of liberation begins just as we have now begun this chanting and hearing. I wish to point out that this chanting of the holy name of God (HARE KṚṢṆA, HARE KṚṢṆA, KṚṢṆA KṚṢṆA, HARE HARE/ HARE RĀMA, HARE RĀMA, RĀMA RĀMA, HARE HARE) and hearing the truths of the *Gītā* is as good as bodily association with Kṛṣṇa. That is stated in the *Gītā.* This process is called *kīrtana.* Even if one does not understand the language, still, just by hearing, he acquires some piety. His assets lead him to a pious life, even if he does not understand—it has such power.

There are two topics concerning Kṛṣṇa. Two kinds of topics, actually. One topic is this *Bhagavad-gītā.* It is spoken by Kṛṣṇa. And the other topic concerning Kṛṣṇa is *Śrīmad-Bhāgavatam.* That is spoken about Kṛṣṇa. So there are two types of Kṛṣṇa *kathā* (topics), and both of them are equally potent because they are connected with Kṛṣṇa.

Because the *Bhagavad-gītā* is spoken on the Battlefield of Kurukṣetra, some people have asked what we have to do with the battlefield. We have nothing to do with any battlefield. We are after knowledge of the spiritual sphere. Then, why should we bother about this battlefield? Because Kṛṣṇa is on the battlefield, and therefore the whole battlefield has become Kṛṣṇaized. Just as when an electric current is passed into some metal, the whole metal becomes surcharged with electricity; so too, when Kṛṣṇa is interested in some matter, that matter becomes Kṛṣṇa-ized. Otherwise, there would be no need of discussing the Battlefield of Kurukṣetra. That is His omnipotence.

This omnipotence is also described in *Śrīmad-Bhāgavatam.* There are many Kṛṣṇa *kathās.* The Vedic literature is full of them. *Vedas* means that they are Kṛṣṇa *kathās.* Scripture, including the *Vedas,* may appear to be different, but they are all meant for Kṛṣṇa *kathā.* If we simply hear these topics on Kṛṣṇa, then what will be the result? It is pure transcendental vibration, and the result will be spiritual consciousness.

We have accumulated many inauspicious things within our hearts due to our material contamination during the course of many, many births. Many, many births—not only this birth, but past births as well. So, when we search into our hearts with the Kṛṣṇa *kathā,* then the contamination we have accumulated will be washed off. Our hearts will be cleansed of all rubbish. And, as soon as all the rubbish is cleared off, then we are situated in pure consciousness.

It is very difficult to eradicate all the false designations from oneself. For example, I am Indian. It is not very easy to immediately think that I am not Indian, but pure soul. Similarly, it is not a very easy task for anyone to end his identification with these bodily designations. But still, if we continue hearing the Kṛṣṇa *kathā,* it will be very easy. Make an experiment. Make an experiment to see how easily you'll be able to free yourself from all these designations. Of course, it is not possible to clear out the rubbish from the mind all of a sudden, but we are immediately aware that the influence of the material nature has become slackened.

The material nature is working in three modes—goodness, passion and ignorance. Ignorance is hopeless life. Passion is materialistic. One who is influenced by the modes of passion wants this false enjoyment of material existence. Because he does not know the truth, he wants to squeeze out the energy of the body just to enjoy this matter. That is called the mode of passion. As for those in the mode of ignorance, they have neither passion nor goodness. They are in the deepest darkness of life. Situated in the mode of goodness, we can understand, at least theoretically, what I am, what this world is, what God is, and what our interrelationship is. This is the mode of goodness.

By hearing Kṛṣṇa *kathā,* we will be freed from the stages of ignorance and passion. We will be situated in the mode of goodness. At least we'll have the real knowledge—knowledge of what we are. Ignorance is like the animal existence. The animal's life is full of suffering, but the animal does not know that he is suffering. Take the case of a hog. Of course, here in New York, no hog is seen. But in villages in India one sees the hog. Oh, how miserable his life is, living in a filthy place, eating stools and always unclean. Yet the hog is very happy by eating stools, and having constant sexual intercourse with the she-hog and just getting fat. The hog gets very fat, because of the spirit of enjoyment which is there, although, for him, it is sensual enjoyment.

We should not be like the hog, falsely thinking that we are very happy. Working hard all day and night, then having some sex life—we think that in this way we are very happy. But this is not happiness. This has been described in the *Bhāgavatam* as a hog's happiness. Man's happiness is when he is situated in the mode of goodness. Then he can understand what true happiness is.

In our daily routine, if we hear this Kṛṣṇa *kathā,* the result will be that all the dirty things in the heart, accumulated life after life, will be cleared out. As a matter of fact, we will see that we are no longer in ignorance or in passion, but are situated in the mode of goodness. What is that position?

We will find ourselves joyful in every circumstance of life. We will never feel morose. In the *Bhagavad-gīta* we find that this is our *brahma-bhūta* (highest stage of goodness) situation. The *Vedas* teach us that we are not this matter. We are Brahman. *Ahaṁ brahmāsmi.* Lord Śaṅkarācārya preached this gospel to the world. We are not this matter; we are Brahman, spirit. When spiritual realization is actually accomplished, then our symptoms will change. What are those symptoms? When one is situated in his own spiritual consciousness, then he will have no hankering and no lamentation. Lamentation is for loss, and hankering is for gain. Two diseases characterize this material world: what we do not possess, we hanker after, "If I get these things I'll be happy. I have no money, but if I get a million dollars, then I'll be happy." And when we have a million dollars, somehow it will be lost. So we'll cry, "Oh, I have lost it!" When we hanker for earning, that is a kind of distress. And when we suffer loss, that is also distress. But if we are situated in *brahma-bhūta,* we will neither be distressed nor will we hanker. We will view equally everyone and everything. Even if we are situated in the midst of fiery turbulence, we will not be disturbed. That is the mode of goodness.

Bhāgavatam means the science of God. If one perseveres in the science of God, he will be situated in the *brahma-bhūta* status. From that *brahma-bhūta* status, we have to work, for work is recommended here. So long as we have this material body, we have to work. We cannot stop working; it is not possible. But we have to adopt the tactics of *yoga,* and in this way, even by doing some ordinary work, which, by destiny or circumstances we are put into, there is no harm. Suppose that, in one's own occupation, one must speak a lie or his business can't go on. Lying is not a very good thing, so one concludes that the business is not based on very moral principles and one should therefore give it up. In the *Bhagavad-gītā,* however, we find instruction not to give it up. Even if we are put in such circumstances that our livelihood cannot go on without some unfair practice, we should not give it up. But we should try to make it purified. How is it purified? We should not take the fruitive result of our work. That is meant for God.

Sukṛta means pious activities. And *duṣkṛta* means impious activities. On the material level we can be pious or impious. Either we are performing some pious activities, or we are performing some impious activities—or we have a mixture, pious and impious. Lord Kṛṣṇa advises that we should act with knowledge of, or devotion to the Supreme. What does that knowledge mean? It means that I am the part and parcel of the supreme consciousness, or that I am not this body. If I identify myself as an American, as an Indian, or this or that, then I am on the material plane. We should identify ourselves as neither Americans nor Indians, but as pure consciousness. I am a subordinate consciousness of the supreme consciousness; in other words, I am the servant of God. God is the supreme consciousness, and I am His servant. So, for our present understanding, subordinate means servant.

We don't ordinarily carry out the work of a servant in relationship to God. Nobody wants to be a servant, but everyone wants to be the master, because to become a servant is not a very palatable thing. But to become the servant of God is not exactly like this. Sometimes the servant of God becomes the master of God. The real position of the living entity is to be the servant of God, but in the *Bhagavad-gīta* we can see that the master, Kṛṣṇa, became the servant of Arjuna. Arjuna is sitting in the chariot, and Kṛṣṇa is his driver. Arjuna is not the owner of the chariot, but in the spiritual relationship we should not cling to the concept of the material relationship. Although the whole relationship, just as we have experience of it in this world, is there in the spiritual world, that relationship is not contaminated by matter. Therefore it is pure and transcendental. It is of a different nature. As we become advanced in the spiritual conception of life, we can understand what the actual position in the spiritual, transcendental world is.

Here the Lord instructs us in *buddhi-yoga. Buddhi-yoga* means that we have full consciousness that we are not this body; and if I act with this understanding, then I am not body—I am consciousness. That is a fact. Now, if we act on the level of consciousness, then we can overcome the fruitive result of good work or bad work. It is a transcendental stage.

It means that we are acting on another's account—on the Supreme's account. We are not liable to loss or gain. When there is gain, we should not be puffed up. We should think, "This gain is for the Lord." And when there is loss, we should know that this is not our responsibility. It is God's work—His. Then we will be happy. This we have to practice: everything on account of the Supreme. This transcendental nature we have to develop. This is the trick of doing work under these present circumstances. As soon as we work on the level of bodily consciousness, we become bound by the reaction of our work. But when we work through spiritual consciousness, we are not bound either by pious activities or by vicious activities. That is the technique.

Manīṣiṇaḥ—this word is very significant. *Manīṣī* means thoughtful. Unless one is thoughtful, he cannot understand that he is not this body. But if one is a little thoughtful he can understand, "Oh, I am not this body. I am consciousness." Sometimes, in our leisure time, we can see, "Oh, this is my finger, and this is my hand. This is my ear, and this is my nose. Everything is mine, but what am I, what am I?" I am feeling this is mine, and that I am. Simply a little thought is required. Everything is mine—my eyes, my finger, my hand. My, my, my, and what is the I? The I is that consciousness, in which I am thinking, "This is mine."

Now, if I am not this body, then why should I act for this body? I should act for myself. Then, how can I work for myself? What is my position? I am consciousness. But what kind of consciousness? Subordinate consciousness—I am part of the supreme consciousness. Then, what will my activities be? My activities will be under the guidance of the supreme consciousness, just as in the office, the managing director is the supreme consciousness. For example, in the office everyone is working under the direction of the manager; therefore they have no responsibility. They have only to discharge their duties. Either pious or impious duties—never mind. In the military line, too, the order of the captain or commander is there. The soldier has to execute it. He does not consider whether it is pious or impious. That does not matter. He simply has to act; then he is a real soldier. He acts in that way and he gets his reward. He gets title and honor. He doesn't care. The commander says, "Just go and kill the enemy," and he is rewarded. Do you think that by killing one gets reward? No—it is for the duty discharged.

Similarly, here the situation is that Kṛṣṇa is instructing Arjuna. Kṛṣṇa is the supreme consciousness. I am consciousness, the part and parcel of the supreme consciousness. So my duty is to act according to that supreme consciousness. For example, I consider my hand as a part of my body. Now, it is moving in its own way. "As I want, let my hand be moved. Let my legs be moved. Let my eyes be opened and see." So, I am dictating, and these parts are working. Similarly, we are all parts and parcels of the Supreme. When we train ourselves to move and act in accordance with supreme consciousness, then we become transcendental to all these pious or impious activities. That is the technique. What will the result of this technique be? We become free from the bondage of birth and death. No more birth and death.

Modern scientists and philosophers do not think about these four things: birth, death, disease and old age. They set them aside. "Oh, let us be happy. Let us enjoy this life." But human life is meant for finding a solution to this bondage of birth, death, disease and old age. If any civilization has not found a solution to these four problems, then that is not a human civilization. Human civilization is meant for finding a complete solution to these things.

So here in the *Bhagavad-gītā,* the Lord says, *karma-jaṁ buddhi-yuktāh. Karma-jaṁ* means whenever there is action there will be some reaction. If one acts in badness, there will be a bad reaction. But reaction, either good or bad, is, in the higher sense, all suffering. Suppose that by good action I get a good birth, fine bodily features and a good education. All these good things I may have, but that does not mean that I am free from material pains. The material pains are birth, death, old age and disease. Even if I am a rich man, a beautiful man, an educated man, born in an aristocratic family, etc., I still cannot avoid death, old age and disease.

So, we must not be concerned with pious activities or impious activities. We must be concerned with transcendental activities only. That will save us from this bondage of birth, death, old age and disease. That should be our aim in life. We should not be hankering after good or bad things. For example, suppose one is suffering from some disease. He is lying in bed, eating, passing nature's call uncomfortably, taking bitter medicines. He always has to be kept clean by the nurses; otherwise there is an obnoxious smell. While he is lying in this condition some friends come to him and ask how he is feeling. "Yes, I am feeling well." What is this well? Lying in bed uncomfortably taking bitter medicine, and unable to move! Yet despite all these inconveniences he says, "I am well." Similarly, in our material conception of life, if we think, "I am happy," that is foolishness. There is no happiness in material life. It is impossible to have happiness here. In this condition, we do not know the meaning of happiness. That's why this very word is used—*manīṣiṇaḥ*—thoughtful.

We seek happiness by some extraneous, artificial means, but how long does it last? It will not endure. We again come back to sorrow. Suppose, by intoxication, we feel happy. That is not our actual happiness. Suppose I am made unconscious by chloroform, and I don't feel the pain of an operation. That does not mean that I am not having an operation. This is artificial. Real pleasure, real life exists.

As is commanded in the *Bhagavad-gītā* by Śrī Kṛṣṇa, the thoughtful give up the reaction of work, being situated on the level of pure consciousness. The result is that this bondage of birth and death, disease and old age comes to an end. This end is in union with the true identity, Kṛṣṇa, the reservoir of pleasure and eternal bliss. There, indeed, is the true happiness for which we are intended.

Kṛṣṇa the Supreme Lovable Object (from *The Nectar of Devotion*). *Bhakti* means devotional service. Every service has some attractive feature which drives the servitor progressively on and on. Everyone of us within this world is perpetually engaged in some sort of service, and the impetus for such service is the pleasure we derive from it. Driven by affection for his wife and children, a family man works day and night. A philanthropist works in the same way for love of the greater family, and a nationalist for the cause of his country and countrymen.

That force which drives the philanthropist, the householder and the nationalist is called *rasa,* or a kind of mellow (relationship) whose taste is very sweet. *Bhakti-rasa* is a mellow different from the ordinary *rasa* enjoyed by mundane workers. Mundane workers labor very hard day and night in order to relish a certain kind of *rasa* which is understood as sense gratification. The relish or taste of the mundane *rasa* does not endure, and therefore mundane workers are always apt to change their position of enjoyment. A businessman is not satisfied by working the whole week; therefore, wanting a change for the weekend, he goes to a place where he tries to forget his business activities. Then, after the weekend is spent in forgetfulness, he again changes his position and resumes his actual business activities. Material engagement means accepting a particular status for some time and then changing it. This position of changing back and forth is technically known as *bhoga-tyāga,* which means a position of alternating sense enjoyment and renunciation. A living entity cannot steadily remain either in sense enjoyment or in renunciation. A change is going on perpetually, and we cannot be happy in either state because of our eternal constitutional position of being eternal fragmental parts of the Supreme Lord.

Sense gratification does not endure for long, and it is therefore called *capala-sukha,* or flickering happiness. For example, an ordinary family man who works very hard day and night and is successful in giving comforts to the members of his family thereby relishes a kind of mellow, but his whole advancement of material happiness immediately terminates along with his body as soon as his life is over. Death is therefore taken as the representative of God for the atheistic class of man. The devotee realizes the presence of God by devotional service, whereas the atheist realizes the presence of God in the shape of death. At death everything is finished, and one has to begin a new chapter of life in a new situation, perhaps higher or lower than the last one. In any field of activity, political, social, national or international, the result of our actions will be finished with the end of life. That is sure.

Bhakti-rasa, however, the mellow relished in the transcendental loving service of the Lord, does not finish with the end of life. It continues perpetually and is therefore called *amṛta,* that which does not die but exists eternally. This is confirmed in all Vedic literatures. The *Bhagavad-gītā* says that a little advancement in *bhakti-rasa* can save the devotee from the greatest danger, that of missing the opportunity for human life. The *rasas* derived from our feelings in social life, in family life, or in the greater family life of altruism, philanthropism, nationalism, socialism, communism, etc., do not guarantee that one's next life will be as a human being. We prepare our next life by our actual activities in the present life. A living entity is offered a particular type of body as a result of his action in the present body.

The basic principle of the living condition is that we have a general propensity to love someone. No one can live without loving someone else. This propensity is present in every living being. Even an animal like a tiger has this loving propensity at least in a dormant stage, and it is certainly present in the human beings. The missing point, however, is where to repose our love so that everyone can become happy. At the present moment the human society teaches one to love his country or family or his personal self, but there is no information where to repose the loving propensity so that everyone can become happy. That missing point is Kṛṣṇa, and the process of devotional service teaches us how to stimulate our original love for Kṛṣṇa and how to be situated in that position where we can enjoy our blissful life.

In the primary stage a child loves his parents, then his brothers and sisters, and as he daily grows up he begins to love his family, society, community, country, nation, or even the whole human society. But the loving propensity is not satisfied even by loving all human society; that loving propensity remains imperfectly fulfilled until we know who is the supreme beloved. Our love can be fully satisfied only when it is reposed in Kṛṣṇa. This theme is the sum and substance of the science of Kṛṣṇa consciousness, which teaches us how to love Kṛṣṇa in five devotional transcendental mellows.

Our loving propensity expands just as a vibration of light or air expands, but we do not know where it ends. *Bhakti-yoga* teaches us the science of loving every one of the living entities perfectly by the easy method of loving Kṛṣṇa. We have failed to create peace and harmony in human society, even by such great attempts as the United Nations, because we do not know the right method. The method is very simple, but one has to understand it with a cool head. *The Nectar of Devotion* teaches all men how to perform the simple and natural method of loving Kṛṣṇa, the Supreme Personality of Godhead. If we learn how to love Kṛṣṇa, then it is very easy to immediately and simultaneously love every living being. It is like pouring water on the root of a tree or supplying food to one's stomach. The method of pouring water on the root of a tree or supplying foodstuffs to the stomach is universally scientific and practical, as every one of us has experienced. Everyone knows well that when we eat something, or in other words when we put foodstuffs in the stomach, the energy created by such action is immediately distributed throughout the whole body. Similarly, when we pour water on the root, the energy thus created is immediately distributed throughout the entirety of even the largest tree. It is not possible to water the tree part by part, nor is it possible to feed the different parts of the body separately. *The Nectar of Devotion* will teach us how to turn the one switch that will immediately brighten everything, everywhere. One who does not know this method is missing the point of life.

As far as material necessities are concerned, the human civilization at the present moment is very much advanced in living comfortably, but we are still not happy because we are missing the point. The material comforts of life alone are not sufficient to make us happy. The vivid example is America: The richest nation of the world, having all facilities for material comfort, is producing a class of men completely confused and frustrated in life. I am appealing herewith to such confused men to learn the art of devotional service, as directed explicitly in *The Nectar of Devotion,* and I am sure that the fire of material existence burning within their hearts will be immediately extinguished. The root cause of our dissatisfaction is that our dormant loving propensity has not been fulfilled despite our great advancement in the materialistic way of life. This transcendental science will give us practical hints as to how we can live in this material world perfectly engaged in devotional service and thus fulfill all our desires in this life and the next. This knowledge is not presented to condemn any way of materialistic life, but the attempt is to give information to religionists, philosophers and people in general how to love Kṛṣṇa. One may live without material discomfiture, but at the same time he should learn the art of loving Kṛṣṇa.

At the present moment we are inventing so many ways to utilize our propensity to love, but factually we are missing the real point, Kṛṣṇa. We are watering all parts of the tree but missing the tree's root. We are trying to keep our body fit by all means, but we are neglecting to supply foodstuffs to the stomach.

Missing Kṛṣṇa means missing one's self also. Real self-realization and realization of Kṛṣṇa go together simultaneously. For example, seeing oneself in the morning means seeing the sunrise also; without seeing the sunshine no one can see himself. Similarly, unless one has realized Kṛṣṇa there is no question of self-realization.

Lord Śrī Kṛṣṇa Caitanya Mahāprabhu, who was Kṛṣṇa Himself, appeared 485 years ago in Bengal and gave us the process for attaining pure love of God in this age. Simply by constantly chanting and hearing the transcendental sound vibration Hare Kṛṣṇa, Hare Kṛṣṇa, Kṛṣṇa Kṛṣṇa, Hare Hare/ Hare Rāma, Hare Rāma, Rāma Rāma, Hare Hare, one can achieve the desired goal of life.

We invite all people of all colors, of all creeds and of all walks of life to come and join us in chanting this Hare Kṛṣṇa *mahāmantra* and experience its transcendental potency. Anyone of any religion who takes up this process of God realization, Kṛṣṇa consciousness, will develop his love of God and thereby perfect his life.

The Perfect Person. Kṛṣṇa consciousness is a very important movement meant to bring all living entities back to their original consciousness. Just as there are many mental hospitals like Bellevue, established for the purpose of bringing a crazy man back to his original consciousness, similarly the purpose of this Kṛṣṇa consciousness movement is to bring all crazy men back to their original consciousness.

Anyone who is not Kṛṣṇa conscious may be understood to be more or less crazy. There was a murder case in India in which a murderer pleaded that he had become mad and therefore did not know what he did. So in order to test him to see whether he was actually a lunatic at that time, the expert civil psychiatrist was brought to examine him. The doctor gave his opinion saying that he had studied many cases, and all the patients with whom he had come in contact were more or less crazy, and the court could excuse him on those grounds if it desired. In a Bengali poem a great Vaiṣṇava poet has written, "When a man becomes haunted by ghosts, he speaks only nonsense. Similarly, anyone who is under the influence of material nature is haunted, and whatever he speaks is nonsense." Although one is a great philosopher or a great scientist, if he is haunted by the ghost of *māyā,* illusion, whatever he theorizes and whatever he speaks is more or less nonsense.

The intent of this movement is to bring such a man back to his original consciousness, which is Kṛṣṇa consciousness, clear consciousness. When water falls from the clouds, it is like distilled water—without contamination. But as soon as it touches the ground it becomes muddy and colored. Similarly, we are spirit soul, part and parcel of Kṛṣṇa, and therefore our original constitutional position is as pure as God's. In *Bhagavad-gītā* it is stated, *mamaivāṁśo jīva-loke:* the living entities are part and parcel of Kṛṣṇa (Bg. 15.7). As a fragment of gold is gold, so, similarly, we are minute particles of God's body and are therefore qualitatively as good as God. The chemical composition of God's body and our body (not the material body but our spiritual body) is the same, and thus ours is as good as God's, for the chemical composition is one. But as rain water falls down to the ground, so we come in contact with this material world, the material nature, which is manipulated by the material energy of Kṛṣṇa.

When we speak of nature, it must be inquired, "Whose nature?" God's nature. Nature is not active independently. Such a concept is foolish. In *Bhagavad-gītā* it is clearly said that material nature is not independent. A foolish man sees a machine and thinks that it is working automatically, but actually it is not—there is a driver, although we sometimes cannot see the driver behind the machine due to our defective vision. There are electronic machines working very wonderfully, but behind the electronics there must be a scientist who pushes the button. This is very simple to understand. Since a machine is matter, it cannot work on its own accord but must work under spiritual direction. A tape recorder works, but it works under the direction of a living entity, a human being. The machine is complete, but unless it is manipulated by a spirit soul it cannot work. Similarly, we should take it for granted that the cosmic manifestation of nature is a great machine; but behind this material nature there is God, Kṛṣṇa.

Kṛṣṇa says in *Bhagavad-gītā, mayādhyakṣeṇa prakṛtiḥ sūyate sacarācaram:* "All material nature is acting under My direction and superintendence." (Bg. 9.10) There are two kinds of entities—the moving (such as human beings, animals and ants) and non-moving (such as trees and mountains). Kṛṣṇa says that material nature, which controls both kinds of entities, is acting under His direction. There is a supreme control. Modern civilization does not understand this due to lack of knowledge, so our Kṛṣṇa consciousness movement is trying to enlighten people. People are all crazy because they are conducted by the influence of the three modes of material nature. They are not in their normal condition.

There are so many universities, especially in the United States, and so many departments of knowledge—why aren't they discussing these points? Where is the department for this knowledge? In 1968, when I went to Boston and was invited to speak at Massachusetts Institute of Technology, my first question was, "Where is the technological department which is investigating the difference between a dead man and a living man?" When a man dies, something is lost. Where is the technology to replace it? Why do the scientists not try for it? Because this is a very difficult subject, they set it aside. They are busily engaged in the technology of eating, sleeping, mating and defending. This is animal technology. Animals are also trying their best to eat nicely, to have nice sex life, to sleep, and to defend. What is the difference between man's knowledge and animal knowledge? Man's knowledge should be developed to explore the technology which deals with the difference between a living man and a dead man, a living body and a dead body. That spiritual knowledge was taught by Kṛṣṇa in the beginning of *Bhagavad-gītā*. Arjuna was talking to Kṛṣṇa as a friend. Of course, whatever he was saying was right, but it was right only to a certain point. Beyond that point there are other subject matters of knowledge, which are called *adhokṣaja* because our direct perception of material knowledge fails to approach them. We have many powerful microscopes to see what we cannot see with our limited vision, but there is no microscope that can show us the soul within the body. But nevertheless the soul is there.

Bhagavad-gītā informs us that within this body there is a proprietor. I am the proprietor of my body, and others are the proprietors of their bodies. I say "my hand." I don't say "I hand." Therefore, since it is "my hand," I am different from this hand. When I say "my book," this indicates that the book is different from me. Similarly, it is "my table," "my eye," "my leg," "my this," "my that"—but where am I? Searching out the answer to this question is meditation. One asks, "Where am I? What am I?" We cannot search out the answers to such questions by material effort. Therefore all the universities are setting this aside: "It is a very difficult subject." Engineers are very proud of creating the horseless carriage. Formerly horses were drawing carriages, but now there are cars, so the scientists are very proud. "We have invented horseless carriages and wingless birds," they say. They can invent imitation wings for the airplane, but when they invent a soulless body, then they will deserve credit. Such an invention cannot be, for no machine can work without a soul. Even computers need trained men to handle them. Similarly, we should understand that this great machine known as the cosmic manifestation or material nature is manipulated by a supreme spirit. That is Kṛṣṇa. Scientists are searching for the ultimate cause or the ultimate controller of this material nature and are putting forth different theories and propositions, but our means of knowledge is very easy and perfect because we are hearing from the perfect person, Kṛṣṇa. Because Kṛṣṇa says so, we immediately know that the cosmic machine, of which the earth is part, is working so nicely and wonderfully because behind this machine is a driver—Kṛṣṇa. Exactly as behind any machine there is a machine driver, similarly, behind this big machine of material nature there is Kṛṣṇa.

Our process of knowledge is very easy. Kṛṣṇa's book, *Bhagavad-gītā,* is the book of knowledge which is given by the perfect person. One may argue that although we have accepted Him as a perfect person, others do not; but He is the perfect person on the evidence of many authorities. It is not by our whims that we accept Kṛṣṇa as perfect. No—there are many Vedic authorities like Vyāsadeva, the author of all Vedic literature. The treasure house of knowledge is contained in the *Vedas,* and their author, Vyāsadeva, accepts Kṛṣṇa as the Supreme Personality of Godhead. His spiritual master, Nārada, accepts Kṛṣṇa as the Supreme Personality of Godhead and his spiritual master, Brahmā, accepts Kṛṣṇa as the Supreme Person. Brahmā says, *īśvaraḥ paramaḥ kṛṣṇaḥ:* "The supreme controller is Kṛṣṇa."

No one can say that he is without a controller. That is not possible. Everyone, no matter how big an officer he is, has a controller over his head. But Kṛṣṇa has no controller; therefore He is God. He is the controller of everyone, but He has no controller. There are many so-called gods nowadays. Gods have become very cheap. They are especially imported from India. People in other countries are fortunate that gods are not manufactured there, but in India gods are manufactured practically every day. One of my disciples recently told me that a god was coming to Los Angeles and that people were requested to receive him. Kṛṣṇa is not that kind of god. I mentioned in my introduction to *Kṛṣṇa Book* that Kṛṣṇa is not the type of god manufactured in a mystic factory. No. He is God. He was not made God, but He is God.

Behind the gigantic material nature, the cosmic manifestation, there is God—Kṛṣṇa—and He is accepted by all authorities. We must accept that knowledge which is accepted by authorities. For education we go to a teacher or to a school or learn from our father and mother. They are all authorities, and our nature is to learn from them. In our childhood, we asked, "Father, what is this?" Father would say, "This is a pen," "These are spectacles," or "This is a table." So a child learns from his father and mother—"This is a table, these are spectacles, this is a pen, this is my sister, this is my brother, etc." Similarly, if we get information from an authority and if the authority is not a cheater, then our knowledge is perfect. The father and mother never cheat when the son inquires from them, and they give exact and correct information. If we get the right information from the right person, that is perfect knowledge. If we want to reach the conclusion by speculation, that is imperfect. The inductive process will never become perfect. It will always remain imperfect.

Since we get information from the perfect person, Kṛṣṇa, whatever we speak is perfect. I don't say anything which is not spoken by Kṛṣṇa or by authorities who have accepted Kṛṣṇa. That is called disciplic succession. That is Kṛṣṇa consciousness. In *Bhagavad-gītā* Kṛṣṇa recommends this process of knowledge (*evaṁ paramparā-prāptam imaṁ rājarṣayo viduḥ*). (Bg. 4.2) Formerly knowledge was passed down by great saintly kings who were the authorities. Nowadays the government or president is the authority. Formerly, however, those authorities or kings were *ṛṣis*—great learned scholars and devotees, not ordinary men. That system of government was very nice. One talented and well trained person as the head of the government could very peacefully execute the governmental functions. There are many instances in Vedic civilization of the perfection of such kings. Dhruva Mahārāja is such an example. He went to the forest to search out God, and by practice of severe penance and austerities he found God within six months. How? He was a five-year-old boy, a king's son with a very delicate body, but according to the direction of his spiritual master, Nārada, he went alone to the forest. The first month there he simply ate some fruits and vegetables every three days. For the next three months he drank a little water every six days. For the next month, he would inhale some air every twelve days. For six whole months he stood on one leg and executed these austerities, and at the end of six months, God became manifest before him, eye to eye. If we practice austerities, it will be possible for us to also see God eye to eye. This is the perfection of life.

The Kṛṣṇa consciousness movement is based on austerity, but it is not very difficult. We recommend that our students not have illicit sex. We don't stop sex, but we regulate it. We don't stop eating, but we regulate it; we eat Kṛṣṇa *prasādam,* food first offered to Kṛṣṇa. We don't say, "no eating," but "no meat-eating." What is the difficulty? Kṛṣṇa *prasādam* is made of many varieties of nicely cooked fruits and vegetables, so there is no difficulty. "No illicit sex" means don't be like cats and dogs—be married and have one wife or one husband and be satisfied. We must regulate ourselves and must undergo austerities, although we cannot undergo such severe types of austerity as Dhruva Mahārāja. In these days it is impossible to imitate Dhruva Mahārāja, but the method we are prescribing is possible. If one takes to these principles, he will make advancement in spiritual consciousness, Kṛṣṇa consciousness. As one makes advancement in Kṛṣṇa consciousness, he becomes perfect in knowledge. What is the use of becoming a scientist or a philosopher who cannot say what his next life will be? These students of Kṛṣṇa consciousness can very easily say what their next life is, what God is, what we are and what our relationship with God is. Their knowledge is perfect because they are reading perfect books of knowledge such as *Bhagavad-gītā* and *Śrīmad-Bhāgavatam.*

This is our process. It is very easy, and anyone can adopt it and make his life perfect. If someone says, "I am not educated; I cannot read books," still there is the possibility that he can perfect his life. He can simply chant Hare Kṛṣṇa. Kṛṣṇa has given us a tongue and two ears, and we may be surprised to know that Kṛṣṇa is realized through the tongue, not through the eyes. After the tongue the other senses follow, but the tongue is the chief. We have to control the tongue. How does one control it? Simply chant Hare Kṛṣṇa and taste Kṛṣṇa *prasādam.*

One cannot understand Kṛṣṇa by sensual perception or by speculation. It is not possible, for Kṛṣṇa is so great that He is not within our sensual range. But He can be understood by surrender. Kṛṣṇa therefore recommends this process. *Sarva-dharmān parityajya mām ekaṁ śaraṇaṁ vraja:* "Give up all other processes of religion and simply surrender unto Me." (Bg. 18.66) Our disease is that we are rebellious. We don't want to accept authority. Yet although we say that we don't want authority, nature is so strong that it forces authority upon us. We are forced to accept the authority of nature by our senses. To say that we are independent is nonsense; it is our foolishness. We are under authority, but still we say that we don't want authority. This is called *māyā,* illusion. We do, however, have a certain independence—we can choose to be under the authority of our senses or the authority of Kṛṣṇa. The best and ultimate authority is Kṛṣṇa, for He is our eternal well-wisher, and He always speaks for our benefit. Since we have to accept some authority, why not accept His? Simply by hearing of His glories from *Bhagavad-gītā* and *Śrīmad-Bhāgavatam* and by chanting His names—Hare Kṛṣṇa—we can swiftly perfect our lives.

INDEX

Achintya bhedābheda, see Bhedābheda philosophy
Āchāryas, lines of, 39
Achyutānanda, 39
Activism, social, 75, 78, 145, 100
Activity,
for only Krishna's pleasure, 73, 176
without desire for fruits, 176
see also Engagement
Adler, Nathan, 127, 194
Advaita, see Vedānta (*advaita*)
Adler, Nathan, 127, 194
Advaitāchārya,
as Chaitanya's emissary, 36-37
as founder of line of Goswāmis, 39
as part of Chaitanya *avatār,* 48, 54, 94-95
as same as Mahā-Vishṇu, 55
Affiliation, religious, of devotees' parents, 147-148
Age, of devotees, 111
end of, 288-289
Piscean, 192
as factor,
in following discipline, 5-6, 13, 81-82
in religious experience, 5-7
Aghāsura, 63
Ahaṁ brahmāsmi, 76
Ahaṁkāra, false ego, 25, 70, 76
Ahirbudhnya Saṁhitā, 29
Alcott, Amos Bronson, 14
Alienation,
before conversion, 110, 151
due to Vietnam War, 115
removed by Krishna Consciousness, 153
as result of anomie, 152, 159-160
Alternative life style, *see* Hare Krishna Movement
Alvars, 22, 25, 31-32
American Baptist Convention,
report of church decline, 139
Amphetamines, use of, 129
Anahdāsī, 133-134
Ānanda, 48, 51, 59
Ananda Marga Yoga, 168
Ananta, one of six Dasas, 39
Ananta Śeshanāga, 62
Aniruddha, one of Krishna's *vyūhas,* 25, 48, 53
Anomie,
as cause of religious enthusiasm, 151-152
definition of, 152
examples of, 160-161
Antiochus, 26
Apocalypse, expectations of, 192
Aquarius, Age of, 192
Āraṇyakas, 20-21, 86
Ārati ceremony, 34, 89, 91, 93-96
Ārātrika ceremony, *see Ārati* ceremony
Archā descent of Krishna, 93-94
Arjuna, 27, 75, 164
Āśramas, four stages of life, 74, 85, 157
Atharva Veda, 20
Ātman (self)
attachment to, 76-77
distinguished from *ahaṁkāra* (ego), 76
not absorbed in Brahman (impersonal Absolute), 162

Authority,
of countercultural leaders, 136-137
protest against, 125-127, 134
in religious conversion, need of, 161, 170-172
of scriptures, 47
of spiritual master, 3-4, 6-7, 47, 73, 172
in times of crisis, need of, 126-127, 170-172
Avatārs of Krishna, 28, 47-48, 50-51, 53-54, 94, 194
Avikṛita-parināmavāda, 55
Avidya, see Ignorance

Back to Godhead, 42, 71, 93, 183
as factor in conversion, 173
Baladeva (Balarāma),
as *avatār* of Krishna, 54
as brother of Krishna, 28-29, 54, 62-64, 67, 94
identified with Mahā-Saṅkarshaṇa, 55
identified with Saṅkarshaṇa, 28
six century temples of, 29
Balarāma, one of six Dasas, 39
Bāna, 25
Barbituates, use of, 129
Barta, Russel, 196
Baxter, Richard,
Works of the Puritan Divines, 190
Bellah, Robert, 187, 191
Bengal,
social conditions before Chaitanya's time in, 33
Bhagavad-gītā, 14, 30, 51, 66, 73-74, 114, 118, 123
as Bhāgavata tradition, 25
date of, 21
as factor in conversion, 173
ideas of, concerning war, 117
interpreted by Brahmin orthodoxy, 47
as mediating influence, 47
as source of Vaishṇavism and *bhakti,* 22, 26-27, 46-47
Bhagavad-gītā As It Is, 42
Bhagavān as Krishna, 51
Bhāgavata Purāṇa, 75, 91, 123, 175
dating of, 9, 22, 30
favors Pañcharātrā sect, 25
as source for Gauḍīya Vaishṇavism, 30, 32-33, 47, 60
unaccepted as revelation by conservatives, 47
use of, in worship, 33
Bhāgavatas, 24-25
Bhāgavatism, 21, 25, 27
Bhajan, Yogi, 161
Bhakta, 34
Bhakti see Bhakti-yoga
Bhakti Siddhānta Sarasvatī Goswāmi, 22, 56, 59, 172, 182
as founder of Gauḍīya Maths, 10
life of, 40-41
as son of Bhaktivinode Thākur, 40, 45
as spiritual master of Swāmi Bhaktivedanta, 23, 40-41
Bhaktivedanta, A. C. Swāmi Prabhupāda, 1, 5, 9, 19-20, 23, 26, 38, 40, 49, 54-55, 57, 61, 65-66, 68-76, 86, 121, 123, 156, 163, 185, 193
as accepted authority, 123, 127, 171-172
brings his philosophy to United States, 1, 18
as charismatic authority, 81, 171-172
defines authoritative texts, 46-47
as disciple of Bhakti Siddhānta Saraswatī Goswāmi, 40-41
extends meaning of "Vedic," 46-47
founds International Society for Krishna Consciousness, 10, 18, 23, 40-42
as head of Hare Krishna Movement, 97
as initial attraction to Krishna, 171-172
interprets social activism, 75-76
life of, 40-42
meaning of surrender to, 94-95
as praised in worship, 94-95
as pure devotee, 173
speaks on education, 121-123
speaks on Jesus Christ, 149-150
speaks on politics, 118
speaks on social system, 118
speaks on war, 116
as translator and commentator, 38, 42
as true interpreter of Chaitanya, 10
voices countercultural protests, 112, 114
see also Spiritual master
Bhakti Vilas Tirtha Goswāmi Mahārāj, Sri Śrīmad, 41-42

Bhaktivinode Thākur, 23, 40-41, 45, 121
Bhakti-yoga,
  as action for Krishna's enjoyment, 175-176
  meaning and rules of, 87-97
  as represented by Chaitanya, 18, 38-40
  results of, 87-88
  sources to fifteenth century, 26-33
  as supreme way to salvation, 27, 50, 70
  as way to discover original consciousness, 50
  as way out of bondage, 71
Bharati (name of Order of Saṅnyāsis), 35
Bhedābheda philosophy, 32, 47-48, 50, 55
Bhūmi, deity, 61
Blavatsky, Helena P., 15, 192
B'nai B'rith, 153
Body, material, 69-70
Bon Mahārāj, Swāmi B. H., 19, 37-39, 60
Brahmā, 61
  as creator from Aniruddha's navel, 25
  as creator through Vishṇu, 53, 57
  as deity in Brahmaloka, 57
  as *guṇa avatār* of Krishna, 48, 50
Brāhma Purāṇa, 30
Brāhma Samāj, 40
Brahma Saṁhitā, Shree, 10, 22, 35, 123
Brahma sect, 22
Brahma (Vedānta) Sutras, 21, 47
Brahmachārī (student stage), 85, 125, 157
Brahmachāriṇis, 125
Brahmajyoti, 49
Brahmaloka, 57
Brahman,
  as bliss, 52
  as impersonal reality, 19, 26
  as not ultimate reality alone, 162
  personalized as Krishna, 49-50
  as Rāhdā and Krishna, 49-50
  as spirit, 49
  realization of, 132
  with and without qualities, 49, 51
  without qualities, 47
Brāhmaṇas, 20
  dating of, 23
  description of, 20
Brāhmaṇda Purāṇa, 29
Brahmavaivarta Purāṇa, 22, 29
Brahmins,
  interpretation of meaning of, 74
  orthodoxy of, 46-47
  "the intelligent class," 73
  true, 118
Buddha, Krishna's *avatār,* 54
Bunyan, John
  Pilgrim's Progress, 189, 191
Burfly, 89
Businesses of the Hare Krishna Movement, 42-43, 45
  as factors toward stability, 182

Caitanya Bhāgavata, 37-38
Caitanya Caritāmṛta, Śri Śri, see Kavirāja, Śrī Śrī Krishnadāsa Goswāmi
Caitanya Maṅgala, 36
Capitalism,
  moral basis of, in Calvinism, 188-189
  sacralized by Calvinism, 189
Car Festival, *see* Ratha-yātrā festival
Caranāmṛita, 91
Castes,
  birth rights of, 74
  importance of, 157
  nature of, 73, 86, 157
  reasons for, 73
Chaitanya, Śrī Krishna, 26, 28, 32-33, 46, 66, 75, 93-95, 160, 173, 190, 196
  attitude of, towards women, 36
  birthday festival of, 96
  concept of love for Krishna of, 75
  contribution of, 19
  as Krishna and Rādhā, 48, 54
  as Krishna's *avatār,* 48, 54
  life of, 33-37
  philosophy of, associated with Gauḍīya Maths, 18
  purpose of descent of, 54
  religious experience of, 9
  on social duties of caste, 15, 71
  theological inclusiveness of, 26
  valued *Gītā-govinda,* 32
Chaitanya, one of six Dāsas, 39
Chaitanyaism and Movement,
  development of, 37-45, 47
  as mediating synthesis, 28, 51
  parallels with Calvinism of, 188-190
  see also Bhedābheda philosophy
Chakravarti, Sudhindra Chandra, 72

Chandīdās, 23, 32
Chandogya Upanishad, 21
Chandragupta, 27
Chanting,
  in *ārati* ceremony, 93-96
  of Krishna's names, 8, 16, 19, 89, 91
  as means of religious experience, 170
  as means to conversion, 162-166
  significance of, 16, 92, 95
Chapatis, 89
Children,
  education of, 121-123
  purpose of having, 88
Children of God, 146
Chit, 48, 51
Chit-śakti, see Krishna, energies of
Christianity, conservative, growth of, 139, 142, 144
Christianity, liberal,
  attacks by Jesus People on, 193-194
  compared with Hare Krishna Movement, 75-78
  criticism of, 138-139, 193
  decline of, 138-144, 194-195
  factors in decline of, 78, 139, 144-146, 193, 197
  reasons for abandoning, 151, 171
  revitalization of, 196-197
  victim of cultural change, 149
Churches, American, decline of, 143, 197
  Episcopalian, decline of, 141
  Lutheran, decline of, 140
  Pentecostal, 107, 139
  Southern Baptist, growth of, 144
  and synagogues, youth abandonment of, 150
  underground, 146, 196-197
  United Methodist, decline of, 142
Church schools, decline of, 139-141
Commander, temple, 97
Commissioners, twelve, 97
Communal living, 13
Communes, countercultural, 109
Community,
  ages, similarity of, factor in, 7
  decline of, in America, 184
  feeling of, as reason for conversion, 153, 164-166, 169
    as reason to worship Krishna, 153
  among Jewish youth, 154
  lack of, in counterculture, 109
    in organized churches, 151, 164, 171, 193
  meaning of, 102, 109
  as necessary to stable society, 184
  need for, 7, 102, 161
Competition, life of,
  rejected by devotees, 103, 177, 184-185
  rejected by Swāmi Bhaktivedanta, 175
Conduct, rules of, 59, 88-92
  See also Ethics, principles of,
Conformity,
  in Hare Krishna Movement, 13
  as norm in society, 84, 152
Consciousness, man's conditioned, 70
  new, 12, 104-105, 114, 151, 160, 183, 197
Constas, Helen, 107
Control, choice of, 186
Conversion, religious, 168-169, 178
  age as factor in, 5
  definition of, 159
  degrees of, 166-170
  despair as factor in, 163-165
  distinguished from intellectual conversion, 168
  effects of, 129
  factors inhibiting, 166-168, 178
  as implying cultural change, 11
  as intensive interaction, 180
  as interpersonal emotional response, 178
  to Krishna, instrumental factors in, 165-178
  to Krishna, situational factor of, 163-165
  to Krishna, stages in, 159-181
  meaning of, 149-150, 154
  time required for, 163, 168-170
  as validation of way of life, 178
Convert,
  total, 166
  verbal, 166
Counterculture,
  antinomianism of, 126
  causes of, 102-106, 151, 159-160, 191-192
  charismatic stage of, 108-109, 125
  commune stage of, 108-110
  decline of, 98-99
  definition of, 98

failure of, 108-109
in India, 43-44
lack of common purpose in, 110
lack of common religious experience in, 109-110
lack of community in, 109
leaders of, 109, 136-137
protests of, 103-106, 159-160, 180-182
reasons for transformation of, 108-109
rejection of establishment by, 11, 112-129
as representing a new consciousness, 12, 104-105, 114, 160, 183, 197
revolution of, as revelation, 186-187
vanguard of new mythology, 188
Cowherdesses, *see Gopīs*
Cow veneration, 86
Cramer, Malinda, 15
Creation,
as function of, Brahmā, 55-56
Krishna's inferior energy, 55
the three Purushas, 55-56
Vishṇu's breath, 55-56
of man, Krishna's reason for, 71-72
of world, 54-56
reason for, 69
Crises,
cultural responses to, 133
personal responses to, 163-165
Culture,
change of, 102-106, 152
dependent upon meaning, 105-106
old and new, characteristics of, 103-106
sacralization of, 174-177
Curriculum, ISKCON educational, 123

Dahl, 89
Darwin, Charles, 107, 188-189
Dās (*dāsa*), definition and use of word, 14, 155
Dasgupta, Surendranath, 23
Dāsya, 59
Davis, Andrew Jackson, 15
De, Abhay Charan, *see* Bhaktivedanta, A. C. Swāmi, Prabhupāda
De, Sushil Kumar,
Early history of the Vaiṣṇava Faith and Movement in Bengal
Demigods, status of, 57-58
Demythologization, effects of, 193
Dependence,
as factor in stable society, 184-185
need for, 103
Deprivation, ethical, 106
Despair as factor in conversion, 163-165
Devakī, mother of Krishna, 61-62, 67-68
Devotees,
as actors for Krishna's pleasure, 176
ages of, 110
when abandoning parents' faith, 148-149
concern of, for parents and friends, 178-179
culture, alternative of, 84-87
dependence of, upon spiritual master, 6-7, 174
discipline of, 87-97
disinterested in dialogue, 146
economic status of parents of, 111
education of, 119-124
first encounter with Krishna Consciousness, 162-163
forbidden in Vaishṇava temples, 45
as former hippies, 11, 110-111
and the Kingdom of God, 191
and the law, 79
as missionaries of Krishna Consciousness, 3, 79
mobility of, 2, 111
necessity of obedience of, 145
original homes of, 1
political views of, 117-119
protests of, 112-158
relations of, to parents, 3, 77
to those outside the Society, 3, 179
retaining former faith, 150
rights as ministers, 17
as teachers, 3-4, 7
testimony of former, 193-194
transformation of, through conversion, 4, 11, 79
use of *nagara-saṅkīrtan* by, 36-37
witness, public of, 99, 177-178
Dharma-śāstras, 21
Diet, Hare Krishna,
effects of, 82
foods of, 89
as offering to Krishna, 88
preparation of, 89-90

Diet (*continued*)
  restrictions of, 88
Dimock, Edward, 18
Dionysos identified with Saṅkarshaṅa, 29
"Disciplic succession," 6-7, 18, 41
Discipline, religious,
  age as factor in maintaining, 5-6, 13
  importance of, 81
  rules of, 87-92
  schedule of, 92-96
  as way to spiritual freedom, 180
Distress as factor in conversion, 163-165
Divine Marriage, mysticism of, 195-196
"Divine Precepts," 159
Divine Science (philosophy), 15, 106
Drop outs, education, record of, 119-120
  from Hare Krishna Movement, 181, 193
Drug abuse
  correlation of, and spiritual discipline, 129-32, 135, 137, 160-161
  disenchantment with, 135-136
  as ego-gratification, 113
  extent of prior, 128-129
  as factor in religious conversion, 131
  prior, 128
  reasons for, 129-130, 133
  as search for meaning, 129
Drug legislation, attitude toward, 127
Drug release,
  through chanting, 83-84
  through Krishna Consciousness, 135
Durgā, 62
Duty and salvation, 73
Dvaitādvaita philosophy, 32
Dvārakā, 68

Eddy, Mary Baker, 15
Education,
  guru method of, 122-123
  philosophy of, 119-124
Ekādāśi, 91
Ekāntins, 24
Election, doctrine of, 190
Eliade, Mircea, 8
Emerson, Ralph Waldo, 14-15, 30
Energy, *see* Krishna, energies of,
Engagement as factor in stable society, 102-103
Enthusiasm, religious,
  comparison of, 37, 159
  need for, 193
  as result of anomie, 151-152, 194
Epic, Hindu, 20-21, 24, 27, 47
Establishment, culture of,
  abandonment of, 80, 106
  as *māyā,* 158
  protests against, 16, 84, 101-102
  rejected elements of, 16
  see also Culture
Ethics,
  compared with Judeo-Christian, 75-78
  principles of, 73-77
  see also Conduct, rules of,
Eucharist, demythologization of, 196
Evil, no effect of, on Krishna Consciousness, 73-74
Experience, religious,
  as aid, to, change of belief, 161
    to psychological wholeness, 197
  through drugs, 130-132, 161-162
  as factor, in conversion, 161, 165-166
    in internalizing cultural changes, 4, 151
  of Hare Krishna devotees, 9
  as illogical expression, 8-9
  importance of, to Hare Krishna devotees, 4
    to Jesus People, 196
  lack of, among Jewish youth in synagogues, 154
    as reason for leaving former religions, 151
  as means, of understanding Krishna's pastimes, 7-8, 170
    of validating new culture, 17, 83, 149, 161, 194-195
  as reason for becoming devotee of Krishna, 153
  as response, to Hare Krishna *mantra,* 153
    to needs, 5
  as way to new meaning, 17, 151
Fellowship, *see* Community
Festivals, 96-97
Fillmore, Charles and Myrtle, 15
Flowers, use of, 90, 94
Foster, A. Durwood, 170
"Fox sisters," 15
Free will, limited, 69, 71
Future life, 57-60

Gadādhara, as part of Krishna's descent, 48, 54, 94-95
Gambling, restrictions against, 88
Garbhodakāśāyī Vishṇu, 48, 53, 56
Garga Muni dāsa Adhikāri, 43
Gauḍīya Math, *see* Gauḍīya Vaishṇavas
Gauḍīya Math Institute, 40
Gauḍīya Vaishṇavas, 1, 9-10, 18, 28, 30, 50-51, 53-54, 60, 96, 182
  contrasted with Hare Krishna Movement, 36-37, 87
  history of, 23, 40-42
  literary sources of, 20-33, 46
Gayā, 34
Generation gap, 5-7
Gerlach, Luther, 168
Ghee, 89
Ginsberg, Allen, 164
Gīta-govinda of Jayadeva, 23, 32
Glock, Charles Y., 106
Glossolalia, 8
Gnosticism, 107
God, personal, love of,
  as factor in conversion, 134-135, 173-174
  through Krishna Consciousness, 135
  without attachment, 76-77, 92
  see also Kāma, Prema
Gokula (Vṛindāvan), 62-63
Goloka-Vṛindāvan,
  as goal of Krishna Conscious people, 8, 57, 60
  as heaven world, 64-65
  as Krishna's temple or sacred place, 8
Goodness, mode of, *see Sattva*
Gopāl Baṭṭa, 38
Gopāla, 25
Gopāls, twelve, 38
Gopīnātha temple, 36
Gopīs, 18
  and *rasa* dance, 64-66
  associated with Krishna in *Bhāgavata Purāṇa,* 22, 30
  associated with Krishna in *Hari-vaṃśa,* 29
  associated with Krishna in his sport (*līlā*), 36, 59
  Krishna's pranks with, 63
  represented by *japa* beads, 88
Govardhana, Mount, 19, 63-66
Government (United States), protest against, 117-118
Govinda, 52
Grace (at meals), 89
Grace, spiritual master's, 172
Grace (theological doctrine), 26, 71-72, 88, 190-191
Grades, educational, of devotees, 120
Gṛihastha (householder), 85-86, 88-89, 157
Grimm, Richard, 136, 180
Guṇa avatārs, 48, 53, 56
Guṇas, see Matter, modes of
Gupta period, Vaishṇava inscriptions in, 31
Guru Basar, 170
Guru, see Spiritual master
Gurukula, 121-123

Halvah, 89
Haṁsa sect, 23
"Hang loose ethic," 128
Hanuman, 156
Happiness, attainment of, 73
Hare, meaning of, 96
Hare Krishna Movement, 12, 50, 52, 54, 60, 71-72, 87, 97, 102, 161, 188
  as alternative life style, 80-96, 109-111, 146, 158, 161-162, 174-178
  appeal to youth of, 80, 153-154
  attacks by Jesus People on, 193-194
  autocracy of, 145
  benefits of, to youth recognized, 79
  compared to Jesus People, 106
  contrasted with metaphysical sects, 106-107
  decline of, 183
  and decline of counterculture, 182-183
  development of,
    in India, 43-45
    in other countries, 42-43
    in the United States, 42-43
    see also Chaitanyaism and Movement; Gauḍīya Vaishṇavas
  as escape from material existence, 156
  ethical principles of, 73-77
  expansion of, 42
  future prospects of, 182-184
  growth limitations of, 13-14, 43-44, 82-84, 166-168
  independent of Gauḍīya Maths, 10, 42

Hare Krishna Movement (*continued*)
  industries of, 43, 45, 83
  influence of, 42-43
  introductory materials to, 1
  literalism of interpretation of, 146
  literary sources of, 10, 19-33
  as ministry to individuals, 184
  non pacifism of, 116-117
  opinion of, concerning drugs, 127-128
  as part of sub-culture, 16-17, 109
  political aspirations of, 118-119
  relates to individuals, 145
  as religious response to establishment, 16, 106-108
  rules of conduct of, 59, 88-92
  as sanctification of life style, 174-178
  as stable society, 182, 184-186
  uncooperative with other religions, 145
Haridās, 45
Hari-vaṃśa, 21, 29
Hashish, use of, 129, 164, 173
Heaven as a goal, effect of loss of, 191
Heliodorus, 27
Herakles, identified with Krishna Vāsudeva, 28
Heroin, use of, 129
Hinduism,
  as all embrasive, 167
  in American religious thought, 14-16
  dating religious literature of, 20-32
  and Hare Krishna Movement, 84-87
Hine, Virginia M., 168
Hippiedom,
  characteristics of, 11, 100
  classes of, 99-100
  decline of, 98-99, 182-183
  stages of, 108-110
Hlādinī,
  as Krishna's ecstatic principle, 52
  mankind partakes of, 59
  as Rādhā personified, 48, 52, 59
Holmes, Ernest, 15
Home of Truth (sect), 106
Homosexuality, 84
Hopkins, Emma Curtis, 15
Householders, rules for, 86, 88-89, 157
Hoyt, David, 193
Humility
  as loss of individualism, 14
  as a virtue, 9
Hypocrisy and organized religions, 151, 164

Ignorance,
  as cause of bondage, 70-71
  effects of, 71
  as origin of sin, 72
Images,
  meaning of, 94
  worshiped, names of, 93-94
Incense,
  business of making, 43
  use of, 91, 94
Individualism, American, 103, 184-185, 192
Individuality, loss of, 13-14
Indra, 26, 58, 64
Inferior energy, *see* Krishna, energies of
Influence, *tantric,* upon Vaishṇavism, 30-31
Initiation, 85
Intelligence, mankind's, 70
Interaction, intensive, as stage in conversion, 180
International Society for Krishna Consciousness, *see* Hare Krishna Movement
Intoxicants, prohibition of, 88
Iśa Upanishad, 21, 26, 123
ISKCON, *see* Hare Krishna Movement
Īśvara Purī, 34, 74

Jagaṅnāth Misra, 33
Jagaṅnātha
  as *avatār* of Krishna, 51
  bathing of, 96-97
  festival of, *see* Ratha-yātrā festival
  temple of, 35, 40, 45, 93
  worship of, 93, 95
Jagaṅnātha, one of six Dāsas, 39
Jaiswal, Suvira, 26
Japa
  characteristics of, 88, 90
  definition of, 88
  as discipline, 88, 93
Japa beads, use and symbolism of, 88
Jayadeva, 23, 32
Jayānanda, *Caitanya Maṅgala,* 36
Jehovah's Witnesses, 93, 148, 177
Jesus Christ, 9, 167, 193-194

as the bridegroom, myth of, 195-196
as God, 149-150
as Krishna Conscious, 145
second coming of, 192
as son of God, 150
Jesus People, 12, 99, 106-108, 125, 139, 146, 149-150, 152-153, 192-194
Jewish youth, *see* Youth, Jewish
Jīva Goswāmi, 10, 22-23, 38-40, 47
Jīva-śakti, see Krishna, energies of
Jīvas, the souls, 25, 56, 57, 69, 73
Jñāna-yoga, 27
Johnson, Gregory, 109, 129, 136, 169
Jung, Karl, 195-196

Kali Yuga, 87, 129
Kāliya, 63
Kalki *avatār,* 54
Kāma (material love or lust), 59, 71-72, 125
Kaṁsa, 61-63, 67
Karandhar dāsa Adhikāri, 145-146, 177, 183
Karaṇodakāśāyī Vishṇu, 48, 53, 55
Karma, 162
caused by modes of nature, 70
causes forgetfulness, 71
determines one's rebirth, 72, 86
ways to impede, 74-75
Kartālas, 34, 42, 173
Kaṭha Upanishad, 21, 26
Kātyāyanī, 66
Kauravas, 20
Kavirāja, Śrī Srī Krishnadāsa, Goswāmi, 10, 23, 45, 55, 58, 64, 68, 74-75
Kelley, Dean M., 138, 144
Kellom, Gar, 2, 12, 185
Kennedy, Melville T., 14, 45
Keshup Chandra Sen, 40
Kholes,
manufacture of, 45
use of, 34
Kingdom of God, search for, 191
Kīrtan, see Saṅkīrtan
Knowledge,
necessary for free will, 71
way of, 26-27, 51, 132
Ko-ans, 8
Krishna, 2, 47, 67, 71, 77, 162
as absolute beauty, 60
as answer to competetive life, 175-176, 184
as *avatār,* 54
as Bhagavan, 51
as Brahman with qualities, 49
Chaitanya's love for, 34
as charioteer to Arjuna, 27
as controller, 50, 171, 176, 186, 190
as cosmic deity, 50
as cowherd deity of Vṛindāvan, 25, 50-52, 60-67, 162
as creator, 54-56, 69
dating of biographical literature concerning, 9
dating of descent of, 9
descent of, as Chaitanya, 54
disappearance of, 68
as ecstatic principle, 51-52
energies of, 19, 22, 30-31, 48, 50, 52, 54-55, 64, 69-70
as epitome of meaning, 154, 158
evidence of worship of, 27-28
expansions of, 48, 50, 52-53
as fulfillment of beauty, 51
in Gītā-govinda, 32
in Goloka-Vṛindāvan, 57
and *gopīs,* love of, 60-61
as highest personality of Godhead, 1, 49
historicity of, 9
identical with his name, 96
identified with Vāsudeva, 31
as Infinite Self (Vishṇu), 50
and Jesus Christ, 9, 63
all love and action for pleasure of, 73, 176
love for, 173-174
love sport of, with Rādhā and friends, 58
as Nārāyaṇa, 51
as only enjoyer, 65, 70
as one's security, 174
as Original Personality of Godhead, 53
as *paramātman,* 51
pastimes of,
as eternal and transcendental, 61, 66
as medium of experience, 8, 170
as tenets of faith, 60
definition of, 7
dramatic presentation of, 34
literal acceptance of, 7-8, 170

Krishna (*continued*)
restoration of sites of, 38
reward of hearing, 61
as personal deity, *see* Krishna, as cowherd deity of Vṛindāvan
popularity of, in India, 18-19
as prototype for man's personalism, 13-14
as Purushottama, 55
and Rādhā, love of, 58
as realization of bliss, 51
and *sakhīs,* 58
salvation through, 146
in Śankara's interpretation, 47
as sole possessor of everything, 176, 190
son of Vasūdeva, 61-63, 67-68
speaks about war, 117
as supersoul (Vishṇu), 50
as supreme and original form of Godhead, 19, 26
as Supreme Personality of Godhead, 166
as supreme spirit, (*para-brahman*), 50
as symbol of regeneration, 12
as transcendent to his material energy, 56
wants devotees as consorts, 59
worship, early, 27-28
worship by Hare Krishna devotees of, 87-97
worshiped as supreme by Chaitanya Movement, 19
worshiped by Vishṇuswāmins, 32
Krishna Consciousness, 3, 8, 177, 190, 192
as action for Krishna, 117
attained through spiritual master, 6-7, 72-73
attractions to, 156-158
defined briefly, 5
as devotee's sole concern, 189
as devotion to Krishna, 73
dissemination of, as aim, 3, 177
as epitome of countercultural search, 11-12, 17, 156-158
as escape from material life, 65, 156, 158, 174-175
as ethical goal, 73-74, 77
ethical goal of, 75
first encounter of, 162, 169
frees from material nature, 57
frees from misdeeds, 123
as liberation, 72
as man's original consciousness, 72-73
as neither attachment nor detachment, 76-77
only for serious minded, 83-84
as only way to self-realization, 146
as personal shelter, 174
as real welfare work, 75-76, 116-145
reasons for seeking, 155, 163-178
as result of discipline, 6, 87
as return to original love, 73
rules for attaining, 87-93
as service to Krishna and mankind, 157
significance of life changes through, 12
as source of community, 13
as spiritual engagement, 154, 156
spiritual nature of, 133
sought largely by youth, 13
stages of, 59-60
superiority of those with, 118-119
as surrender to Krishna, 87
testimonies of life changes in, 6, 133-135, 150, 152-156, 169
transcends caste system, 73-74, 118
transcends good and evil, 73-74
as way to meaning, 154-157
as way to security, 155
Krishna Kanti, 185-186, 197
Krishna Karṇāmṛita, 35
Krishna Vāsudeva,
as an incarnation of Nārāyaṇa-Vishṇu, 27
as deity of Sātvatas, 25
early evidence of worship of, 21, 27-28, 31
as Nārāyaṇa, 25
Krishna Vilasinī, 150
Krishna *yātrā,* definition of, 34
Kshīrodakāśāyī Vishṇu, 48, 53, 61
Kushāna period, 30

Laddu, definition of, 89
Lakshmī
as *śakti* of Vishṇu, 30-31
as wife of Chaitanya, 34
Langer, Susanne, 187
Latikā, 3
Latter Day Saints, 98, 139, 148, 177-178
Leaders, countercultural, failure of, 136-137
Leary, Timothy, 109, 136
Liberation,

through Krishna Consciousness, 57
through Krishna's grace, 72
meaning of, 72
ways of, 27
Life, material fruitlessness of, 156
Life style,
sanctification of, 174-178
supported by scriptures, 146
Līlā, 31-32
Līlā avatārs, 48, 53-55
Līlāśūka Bilvamaṅgala, 35
Lochan, 180, 197
Lofland, John, 159, 163, 166, 178, 180
Love,
conjugal, *see Mādhurya*
dance of, 57, 64-66
for Krishna, meaning of, 52, 59, 75-76, 92-93, 125
meanings of, contrasted, 77-78
LSD, *see* Lysergic acid diethylamide
Lysergic acid diethylamide, use of, 110, 129, 131-132, 135-136, 164, 173

Mādhurya, relation of, 59-60
Madhva, 22, 32, 46
Mahābharata, 28, 46
authority of, 46
date of, 20-21, 24, 26-27
historical setting and purpose, 27
Mahā-Lakshmī, 68
Mahāmantra, 81, 88
as attraction to Hare Krishna Movement, 153, 164
recitation of, 50, 90, 95-96, 193
results of recitation of, 12, 96, 153
words of, 96, 169
Mahā-Saṅkarshaṇa, 48, 55-56
see also Saṅkarshaṇa
Mahā-Vishṇu, 48, 55
see also Vishṇu
Mahat, 48, 55
Majumdar, A. K., 24-26
Man
body of, composed of *prakṛiti,* 70
component parts of, 69-70
as conditioned by, *karma,* 71, 73
matter, 70-71
Supersoul, 73
as eternal servitor of Krishna, 72
fall of, 71-73
as forgetful of his nature, 71-72
inclination of, to sin, 72-73
as measure of all things, a myth, 187, 192
original state of, 71
perverted consciousness of, 70
propensity of, for good and evil, 72
relation of, to Krishna, 70
as spirit, 69
Maṅgala ārati, 123
Mañjarī, 60
Mantra, 4, 34, 42, 60, 95, 166, 177
see also Mahāmantra
Manvantara avatārs, 53
Maoism, position concerning, 117
Marginal energy, *see* Krishna, energies of
Marriage,
characteristics of, 85-86
rakshasa style of, 68
significance and purpose of, 85
Marty, Martin, 139
Marxism, position concerning, 117
Material energy, *see* Krishna, energies of
Matsya (*avatār*), 48
Matter, 69-70
modes of, 57, 70-71
Māyā, as creator, 55-56
Māyā,
equated with world of establishment, 16, 135
as illusion, 49, 52, 56, 69, 96
as reason for leaving the Society, 181, 184
Māyāpur, temple at, 44
Māyā-śakti, see Krishna, energies of
Mazzini, Giuseppe, 101
Meaning,
lack of, among Jewish youth, 153-154
in former religion, 151, 171
need for, 14, 110, 129, 152, 195
search for, 152-153, 160-161
Megasthenes,
identifies Saṅkarshaṇa, 29
Merton, Robert, 152
Thomas, 4
refers to worship of Krishna Vāsudeva, 27-28
Messer, Mark, 187
Metaphysical sects, *see* Sects, metaphysical
Mind, man's, 70

Moti Chandra, 26
Morality, sexual, protests against, 124-125
Mormons, *see* Latter Day Saints
Mouledoux, Joseph, 132
Mukunda, 118, 169, 173
Myth,
  as expression of psychological traits, 189
  as form of symbolic system, 187
  Jungian interpretation of, 195-196
  need for new, 197
  need for revitalization of, 196
  as subjective reality, 189, 196
  use of, by Jesus People, 195-196

Nadia, India, 18
Nagara-saṅkīrtan
  lack of Hindu emphasis, 37
  revival of, 40
  uses of, compared, 36-37
Nakayama, Don, 79
Nal-ayir-divya-prabhandham, 31
Nanda, foster father of Krishna, 62-63
Nara Siṅha (Avatār), 48
Nārada, 66
Nārāyaṇa,
  as author of *Pañcharātrā* literature, 25
  as expansion of Krishna, 25, 48-50, 55
  as expression of Krishna's majesty, 51
  as Krishna's four-handed form, 53
  identified with Purusha, 28, 55
  as Vāsudeva, 25
  worshiped in *Mahābharata,* 21
Nārāyaṇa-Vishṇu Vāsudeva, syncretistic deity, 28
Nārāyaṇīya (section of *Mahābharata*), 21, 24-25, 28
Narottama Datta, 39
Nature,
  acquisitive, of mankind, 188-189, 192
  sharing, of man, 188-189
Nature, as eternal reality, 56
  modes of, *see* Matter, modes of
Navadvīp, India, 18
Needs, humanity's basic, 102
Nera-Neris, 39
New Thought (philosophy), 15, 106
Nimai, 33
Nimbārka, 23, 32
Nityānanda Goswāmi,
  as Chaitanya's emissary, 36-38
  establishes line of Goswāmis, 39
  identified with Mahā-Saṅkarshaṇa, 55
  as part of Krishna's descent, 38, 54, 94-95
Nonviolence, interpretation of, 117
Norms, cultural, disintegration of, 152
Nyāya, 22

Occultism, 106, 152, 192
Occupations, prior, of devotees, 128
O'Dea, Thomas, 186
Offerings to Krishna, 88-91
Olcott, Henry Steel, 15

Pacifism, uncharacteristic of Movement, 116-117
Padma Purāṇa, 22
Pahlavis, 26
Pañcharātrā literature, 22, 24-25, 29, 53
Pañcharātrā sacrifice, 28
Pañcharātrā sect,
  as source of Vaishṇavism, 24, 29, 46
  distinguished from Bhāgavatas, 25
  praised and reviled by Purāṇas, 25
  reviled by conservative Brahmins, 29
Pañcharātrins, *see* Pañcharātrā sect
Pañchatattva, 94
Pāṇḍavas, 20
Para-brahman, 50
Parakīya-rasa, 64
Parama bhāgavata, 31
Paramātman, 51, 69, 73
Parents of devotees, religious affiliation of, 147-148
Para-śakti, 50
Pariṇāmavāda, 55
Participation, religious, value of, 4-5, 7-8
Passion, mode of, *see Rājas*
Pastimes of Krishna, *see* Krishna, pastimes of
Pathans, 36
Poll, Gallup, on religious needs, 139
Possessions, protest against accumulation of, 112-115, 185
Pradyumna, Krishna's *vyūha,* 25, 48, 53
Prajñāpāramitā, 8
Prakṛiti, 48, 56, 70
Prapatti, doctrine of, 31
Prasādam,

as attraction to Hare Krishna Movement, 153, 166
definition of, 88
eating, as discipline, 88, 91-94, 96, 186
as means to community, 82
value of eating, 89
Prasutī, 135-136
Pratt, James Bissett, 78
Prema (love), *see* Love for Krishna, meaning of
Presidents, temple, 97
Principles, ethical, *see* Ethics, principles of
Problem, attempts to solve, 160
Problems, world, reason for, 115-116
Property, theory of, 176, 190
Protest, nineteenth century, 106-107
twentieth century, of devotees,
against a surfeit of possessions, 112-115, 185
against all war, 116-117
against authority in general, 125-127, 133-134
against being cog in a machine, 105, 185
against competitive life, 103, 177, 184-185
against established codes of sexual morality, 124-125
against established laws concerning drugs, 127-128
against institutional religion, 138-139, 150
against lack of freedom, 184-186
against meaningless secularization, 187
against methods of education, 119-124
against parental authority, 125-127
against the Vietnam War, 100-102, 115-116
against United States form of government, 117-119
as element of different consciousness, 12
Pūjari, 87, 93-94, 97
Purāṇas, 49-50
authoritative for Hare Krishna Movement, 46-47, 51
dating of, 24
as source of Vaishṇavism, 22, 27, 29, 46-47
Purī, Chaitanya moves to, 35
Puritanism, parallels of, with Chaitanyaism, 189-190
Purpose, discovery of, 80
Purusha,
as cosmic deity in *Ṛig Veda,* 28, 55
Purusha *avatārs,* 48, 53
Purusha-*sūkta,* 28, 55
as Vishṇu, the Supersoul, 55
Purushottama, the Supreme Person, 55
Pūrva Mīmāmśa, 22
Pūtana, 63

Questionnaires, as method of research, 1-3

Racism, protest against, 151
Rādhā,
in *Brahmavaivarta Purāṇa,* 29
Chaitanya's love of, 34
consummation of love of, 58
cult of, 19, 32
friends of, 58
in *Gītā-govinda,* 23, 32
and Krishna as Chaitanya, 54
as Krishna's consort, 29, 32
as Krishna's ecstatic energy personified, 48, 51-52, 96
as Krishna's favorite *gopī,* 18
as Krishna's highest love, 58
as Krishna's projection in beauty, 60
as Krishna's wife, 22
worshiped by Vishṇuswāmins, 32
Rādhā-Krishna mysticism compared with Christian, 196
Radhakrishnan, Sarvepalli, 23-24
Rāgānugā, 59
Raghunātha Bhaṭṭa, 38
Raghunātha Dās, 38
Rājas, (passion), 48, 70-71
Rakshasa, 68
Rāma,
as *avatār* of Krishna, 19, 51
in the *mahāmantra,* 96
Rama Charaka, née William Walker Atkinson, 15
Rāmānanda, 75
Rāmānuja, 22, 25, 31-32
Rāmāyana
authority of, 46
dating of, 20-21, 26

Rāmāyana (*continued*)
as literary source of Vaishṇavism, 20, 24, 26
Rasa, 51
Rāsa dance, 57, 64-66
expansions of Krishna during, 53
Rasikā Murāri, 39
Ratha-yātrā festival, 35, 79, 97, 177
at Purī, 97
Reich, Charles, 12
Reincarnation, 56-58, 71, 162
necessary for those not Krishna Conscious, 57
Religion of parents, abandonment of,
ages of devotees, 148-149
reasons for, 151
Religious Science, 15, 106
Research methods and problems, 3-12
Response, interpersonal, factor in conversion, 178
Revelation, as independent source of knowledge, 47
Revivalism, 27
Revolution, countercultural, as revelation, 186
Ṛig Veda,
dating of, 20-21
as earliest literary source of Vishṇu, 26
as earliest source of *bhakti-yoga,* 20-21, 26
Ṛishava dās Adhikāri, 180
Ritual, Christian, loss of efficacy of, 195
Rohiṇī, wife of Vāsudeva, 29, 62
Romā, consort of Vishṇu in creation, 56
Romakas, 26
Roszak, Theodore,
Making of a Counterculture, 98
Rudra sect, 22
Rukminī, 68
Rūpa Goswāmi, 23, 35, 38, 92
Bhakti-rasāmṛita-sindhu, 23, 38

Śabda, 47
Sachī Devī, 33
Sakhīs, (friends)
attain Krishna's love, 58, 60
projected into *mañjarīs,* 60
relation of, to Rādhā, 60
Sakhya, relation of, 59
Śakti, see Krishna, energies of
Śaktism, 30, 33
Salvation, *see* Liberation
Śambhu (Śiva) as masculine progenitor of world, 48, 56
Saṁvit, 48, 51
Sanātana Goswāmi, 23, 35, 38
Sandhinī, 48, 52
Śaṅkara, 19, 32, 47, 51, 55, 76, 132
Saṅkarshaṇa,
cult of, 29
as one of Krishna's *vyūhas,* 25, 48, 53
Saṅkarshaṇa-Baladeva, 28-29
Sāṅkhya (philosophy), 22, 50
Saṅkīrtan, 12, 39, 44, 83, 93, 96, 169
Chaitanya's use of, 34, 36
definition of, 4
importance of, 5, 162-163, 177
leader of, 97
parties, 177
use of, by Brāhma Samāj, 40
by Gauḍīya Vaishṇavas, 37, 87
see also, Nagara-saṅkīrtan
Saṅnyāsa, 85, 125
definition of, 41
Saṅnyāsi, 85, 173, 177, 179
Chaitanya becomes, 35
duties of, 4, 157
Śanta, relation of, 59
Sarvabhauma, 74
Sat, chit, ānanda, Krishna's attributes, 48, 51
Śaṭhakopa, 31
Śatapatha Brāhmaṇa, 21, 28
Sātvatas, 24
Sattva, 48, 70-71
Scholasticism, period of Hindu, 22-23
School (Hare Krishna Movement), 121-123
Science, effects of, on religion, 78
Scriptures,
authority of, 47
literal interpretation of, 146
reading of, as means of conversion, 172-173
use of, in cultural change, 146
Second International Seminar on Youth Policy, 100
Sects, metaphysical,
as cultural responses, 106-107
as influenced by Hindu philosophy, 14-15
Sects, Pentecostal, 107

Security,
of Krishna Consciousness, 156-157
lack of, in former religions, 151, 154-155
through worship of personal God, 174
Seekership as step to conversion, 160-161
Seleucus Nicator, 27
Self, *see ātman, jīvas*
Self Realization Fellowship, 161, 193
Senses, man's, 70
Service to Krishna, importance of, 157
Śesha identified with Saṅkarshaṇa, 25
Seventh Day Adventist churches, 139
Sex, restrictions of, 88, 124-125
Sharing, as innate trait, 188
Shree Brahma Saṁhitā, see Brahma Saṁhitā
Śikhā, 84, 169
Sin,
doctines of, compared, 72
original, 72
Śiva, 19
as *guṇa avatār,* 48, 51, 53
as Śambhu, creator through Vishṇu, 56
"Six Dāsas," 39-40
"Six Goswāmis," 28, 38
Slater, Philip E., 102-103, 137, 182, 184
Souls, mankind's, *see Jīvas*
Southern Baptists, 144, 148
Sovereignty of God, 188
Spiritual master,
dependence upon, 184-185
necessity of, 91
as *only* authorized guide to Krishna Consciousness, 3-4, 6-7, 47, 73, 172
as representative of Krishna, 73, 172
Spiritualism, 15, 106
Śrī Vaishṇava sect, 22, 31-32
Śrī Viśva Vaishṇav Rāj Sabhā, 40
Śrīnivāsa Āchārya, 39
Śrīvāsa, part of Krishna's descent, 54, 94-95
Stark, Rodney, 159, 163, 166, 178, 180
Status, material, 177
Subhadrā, 94
Śudras, 73-74
Suffering, cause of, 76
Superior energy, *see* Krishna, energy of
Supersoul, *see Paramātman*
Surabhi cows, 57
Sūtras, period of, 21
Sva-rūpa, 48, 50, 52
Sva-rūpa-śakti, see Krishna, energies of
Svāmśa (forms of Krishna), *see* Krishna
Svayam-rūpa, 48, 52-53
Śvetadvīpa, 61
Śvetasvatara Upanishad, 21, 26
Śyāmānanda Dās, 39

Tadekātma-rūpa forms of Krishna, 48, 52
Tamas, 48
as cause of bondage, 70-71
effects of, 71
Tantras, 22, 24, 50
Tatastha-śakti, see Krishna, energies of
Teaching, religious, of former faith, 151
Technology and cultural change, 102-105, 114, 152, 185, 187-188
Temple,
Berkeley, 1-2, 136
Los Angeles, 1
Māyāpur, 44-45
New York, 18, 42
San Francisco, 2, 42
Temples,
composition of, 2
number of, 42
Vaishṇava, in India, 45
Tension, a step toward conversion, 159-160
Theism in India, 102
Theosophical Society, 15
Theosophists, 192
Theosophy, 15, 106
Thoreau, Henry David, 14
Tilaka, 84, 92, 118
Time,
eternal, as element of mankind, 69-70
liturgical or sacred, 8
Tingley, Alice, 192
Trai dās, 115, 156, 174
Transcendental Meditation, 193
Transcendentalism, American, 14, 107
Trees, worship of, 91
Tṛiṇavarta, 63
Tulasī (plant), offerings to, 94

Union, mystical,
with Jesus Christ, 195
with reality, 149, 162
Unification Church, 159
Unified Family, 99, 159, 178

Unity School of Christianity, 15, 106
Upanishads, 14, 20-21, 23, 25-26, 46, 49-51, 76

Vaidhī, see rules of conduct
Vaikuṇṭha, 57, 134
Vaiśeshika, 22
Vaishṇava sects, 31-32
Vaishṇavism,
  of Chaitanya, *see* Chaitanyaism and Movement
  contrasted with conservative Brahmin orthodoxy, 46-47
  dating of, 21-27, 29-32
  sources of, to the twelfth century A.D., 26-31
    from the twelth to fifteenth century A.D., 31-33
  as syncretistic development, 28-33
Vaishṇavism, Bengal, 18, 33, 35, 39
Vallabhacharyas, 32
Vāmāchāri, 33, 36
Vānaprastha, 86, 157
Vāsudeva,
  as father of Baladeva (Balarāma), 29, 62, 67
  as father of Krishna, 62-63, 67-68
  as identified with Nārāyaṇa, 25
  as a *vyūha* of Krishna, 25, 48, 53
Vātsalya, relation of, 59
Vayu Purāṇa, 29
Vedānta (*advaita*) philosophy, 22, 32
  in America, 15, 19, 107, 193
  criticism of, 162, 174
Vedānta, meaning of word, 46
Vedānta Society, 15
Vedānta (Brahma) Sūtras, 21, 47
Vedas,
  authority of, 46
  as sources of Vaishṇavism, 20-21, 46-47, 74
Vices to be avoided, 75
Vidyāpati, 23, 32
Vietnam War, protest against, 100-102, 115-116
Vilāsa (forms of Krishna), 48
Violence, causes of, 175, 193, 197
Vīra Hamvīra, 39
Vīrabhadra, 39
Virāṭa-rūpa, 68
Virtues enjoined by ISKCON, 74-75
Vishṇu, 51, 92
  as Ananta Śeshanāga, 62
  as creator and destroyer, 30-31
  as four armed deity, 62
  as Garbhodakāśāyī, Vishṇu, 48, 53, 56
  as *guṇa avatār,* 48
  as infinite self, 50
  as inner controller, 69
  as Karaṇodakāśāyī Vishṇu, 48, 53, 55
  literary sources of, 21, 26-31
  as Mahā-Vishṇu, 48, 55
  as *paramātman* or Supersoul, 69, 71, 189
  as plenary expansion of Krishna, 19, 50, 53
  as preserver of world, 53
  as *Vedic* deity, 26
  worship of, 26-27
  worshiped by Brahmin advaitins, 47
  worshiped by Vaishṇavas of Gauḍīya Maths, 1, 19
Vishṇupriyā, 34
Vishṇu Purāṇa, 22, 29-30
Vishṇuswāmi, 22
Vishṇuswāmins, 32, 35
Viśishtādvaita Vedānta, 32
Viśvambhara, 33
Vivartavāda, 55
Vivekananda, 15, 193
Vṛindāvan,
  associated with Krishna's *līlā,* 32, 34, 38, 60, 62-65
  attained through discipline, 59
  Chaitanya's intended visit to, 35-36
  as literary center for Chaitanya Movement, 35, 38-39
  meanings of, materially and transcendentally, 8
Vṛindāvan Dasa, *Chaitanya Bhāgavata,* 37-38
Vṛindāvan-Goloka, *see* Goloka-Vṛindāvan
Vyāsa, 47-49
Vyūhas, 22, 25, 28, 29, 48, 53

War, protest against, 116
Warriors, duty of, 117
Wealth, acquisition of (theological doctrine), 190-191
  changing attitudes concerning, 191-192

Weber, Max, 108, 188-189
Welfare work, interpretation of, 75-76
Wesley, John, 190-191
Westhues, Kenneth, 108, 126
Widener, Warren, 79
Witness, public, to faith, 93, 177-178
Women, position of, in the Society, 86-87
Woods, Richard, 152
World,
  creation of, 54-56
  end of, 57
  nature of, 54-56, 77
  reason for creation of, 69
Worlds, spiritual, 57-58
Worship ceremony, *see Ārati* ceremony

Yajñas, 69
Yanuna, 24-25
Yaśovanta, 39
Yādavas, 68
Yaśoda, foster mother of Krishna, 62
Yati Mahārāj, Tridandiswāmi Bhakti Prajnan, 37, 41
Yātrā, Krishna, 34
Yavanas, 26
Yin and Yang, 188
Yoga, as philosophy, 22, 50
Yoga, as practice,
  haṭha, 161
  kriyā, 161
  kuṇḍalinī, 161
  see also Bhakti-yoga
Yogamāyā, Krishna's inconceivable energy, 54, 62, 64
Yogananda, Paramhansa, 161
Youth, alienation and stress of, 5
Youth, Jewish,
  in counterculture, reasons for, 153-154, 173
  percentage of, in Hare Krishna Movement, 153
Youth, world rebellion of, 100-102
Yuga avatārs, 53